SECRETS OF THE WORLD'S BEST-SELLING WRITER

The Storytelling Techniques of Erle Stanley Gardner

Jean Bethell and Gardner. Gardner wrote, "Once you take a secretary into the business and let her feel she has an interest in that business, she develops a loyalty for it that is far more than can be purchased with money."

SECRETS OF THE WORLD'S BEST-SELLING WRITER

The Storytelling Techniques of Erle Stanley Gardner

by
Francis L. and
Roberta B. Fugate

WILLIAM MORROW AND COMPANY, INC.
New York   1980

Library of Congress Catalog Card Number 80-82544

ISBN 0-688-03701-1

Printed in the United States of America

First Edition
1 2 3 4 5 6 7 8 9 10

BOOK DESIGN BY MICHAEL MAUCERI

For
TOMMY, JIMMY, and DAVID TREECE
who made our weekends sparkle

FOREWORD

The idea for this chronicling of the development of Erle Stanley Gardner as a writer evolved from what started out to be a cursory examination of the Gardner Papers in the Humanities Research Center at The University of Texas. It soon became evident that this is the most remarkable collection of literary archival material in existence in that it reveals the intimate workings of a creative writer's mind throughout his career.

We are indebted for the privilege of writing this book to the cooperation and faith of Lawrence Hughes and John C. Willey of William Morrow and Company. Grateful acknowledgment is made to Jean Bethell Gardner and Natalie Grace Naso, executrices of the estate of Erle Stanley Gardner, for permission to quote from the Gardner Papers. Careful reading of our first draft by Mrs. Gardner and Ruth "Honey" Moore produced many helpful suggestions. Sage advice from Dorothy B. Hughes, Gardner's biographer (*The Case of the Real Perry Mason:* Morrow, 1978) kept us from going astray during early stages of the work.

For the most part, quotations in this book are from material never intended for publication: correspondence, personal notes, and hurriedly written preliminary drafts. Stenographic and obviously inadvertent errors in spelling, capitalization, punctuation, and dating have been corrected to facilitate reading. Where ambiguity exists, the original text has been preserved for the reader's interpretation.

We would be remiss if we did not mention the attentive cooperation of staff members at the Humanities Research Center, particularly the reading-room librarians, cataloguers, and pages who service patrons of the many literary collections which they tend. Inevitably an attempt at names will result in omission; however, our special thanks go to Charlotte Carl-Mitchell, Ellen S. Dunlap, Lois Garcia, Carolyn Harris, John Kirkpatrick, Sally S. Leach, Mary Ellen MacNamara, and Erika Wilson.

Without the help of Eugene Faucheux, who so zealously mounts guard over the "Gardner study" in the Academic Center, our research chores there would have been much more tedious.

—Francis L. and Roberta B. Fugate

El Paso, Texas
August, 1980

CONTENTS

SECRETS OF THE WORLD'S BEST-SELLING WRITER

The Storytelling Techniques of Erle Stanley Gardner

1
INSIDE A WRITER'S MIND

In 1947 Erle Stanley Gardner was proclaimed "the most popular whoduniter of his times" by Frank Luther Mott in *Golden Multitudes: The Story of Best Sellers in the United States*. He went on to attain the distinction of being the "top-selling author" in the world, an estimated 310,910,603 copies as of January 1, 1979, with translations into twenty-three languages including such exotic tongues as Tamil and Urdu, a record which still stands in the *Guinness Book of World Records*. During the mid-1960s his paperback publisher was selling 2,000 of his books an hour, eight hours a day, 365 days a year.

All of this was due largely to the appeal of Gardner's fictional alter ego, the lawyer-detective Perry Mason. Erle Stanley Gardner did not conjure up Perry Mason either by accident or from whole cloth. Perry Mason was quite deliberately conceived from an amalgam of ten years' experience as a trial lawyer, a full decade and millions of words of intensive study and writing, a grim determination to escape the tedium of legal office work, a hyperactive physical makeup which fostered insomnia, and an incredibly agile imagination.

Neither is it by accident that the majority of Gardner's working notes, manuscripts, and correspondence—recording both the joys and the heartaches of his long literary career—have been preserved.

In 1960 Harry Huntt Ransom, Chancellor of The University of Texas and a confirmed mystery fan, had an eye out for literary collections to swell the holdings of the university's Humanities Research Center. He had already garnered a Poe collection, papers from the Ellery Queen collaborators, Sir Arthur Conan Doyle manuscripts, and other valuable literary archival materials. He asked Dr. Merton Minter, a university regent and friend of Gardner, to contact the creator of Perry Mason.

It was as simple as that: Gardner immediately approved the idea of making his papers available to interested writers and scholars, perhaps unaware of their potential value. Dr. Minter noted, "It is my sincere opinion that he never fully realized that he was the greatest writer of mystery fiction who ever lived, as demonstrated by the fact that his books have sold more copies worldwide than any book except the Bible."

Not until the collection began to arrive did anyone at the university realize what they had: It was an incredible array of notebooks, manuscripts, correspondence, photographs, galley proofs, voice re- cordings, artwork, office equipment, travel souvenirs, scrapbooks, and personal memorabilia. As it turned out, the entire contents of Gardner's study, including his desk "possibly measurable in rods instead of inches," was included. Newspaper columnist Robert de Roos wryly maintained the desk should be preserved as a national monument, and so it was. The entire study from Gardner's Rancho del Paisano near Temecula, California, was reassembled as an exhibit on the fourth floor of the university's Academic Center, where visitors can look through its windows, press a button, and hear Erle Stanley Gardner, via a recording, tell them about the contents of the room.

As shipping crates continued to arrive, the collection piled up to more than 36 million items—everything from schoolboy caricatures penciled on restaurant napkins to fan letters from Presidents. The initial reaction of the researcher is shock at the overwhelming profusion of source material. Two letters in the collection explain its vast scope. Gardner's copy editor at William Morrow and Company wrote asking what disposition to make of the original manuscript of *The Case of the Velvet Claws*, the first Perry Mason book. Gardner replied:

> I don't suppose that any sagacious manuscript collector is ever going to pay over a hundred thousand for the manuscript. The probabilities are I'll carry it around with me somewhere and lose it, but when it comes to being cold-blooded enough to say, "put the damn thing in the wastebasket" I just haven't got what it takes.

The value of the manuscript has not yet reached $100,000. However, in 1966, when logged into the Humanities Research

Center, that original typescript of *The Case of the Velvet Claws* with its markings to guide the printer, a carbon copy, the previous working copy under a different title out of which Perry Mason grew, and five assorted editions of the published work, including a first edition Gardner inscribed to his parents, were valued as a lot at $2,260.

Undoubtedly much credit for the completeness of the collection must go to his secretarial staff, who labored from the early 1930s onward to bring order out of the chaos that was Erle Stanley Gardner's unconventional life. And even the trivia were not saved in vain.

On the back of a receipt from a Hong Kong hotel we found the initial plot notes for one of his Lester Leith stories. Also, we discovered the mechanical plotting device which he had made, a series of cardboard discs lettered with basic plot elements; but we had not the foggiest notion of how or when he used it . . . until we came across a revealing doodle on a page ripped from a small pocket notebook, irrelevantly loose in a cluttered file folder, obviously random contents from a desk drawer. In another file we found a small notebook containing nothing but legal citations with no apparent bearing on anything. However, the stub of a torn page in the notebook matched the scrap containing the sketch of the "plot wheels," and a stationer's price label on the notebook told when he had stocked the item: We then knew not only how but when Gardner had experimented with his mechanical plotting device.

Had Gardner been like most other writers, there would be only a scattering of notebooks in which he recorded potential raw material and ideas. But lawyer-writer Erle Stanley Gardner came from a different mold: He kept a running account of his mind in action, with the result that the Humanities Research Center contains what is undoubtedly the best existing record of a creative mind in-process, a record that spans more than half a century.

Both the notebook habit and the determination to write surfaced initially in March, 1909, when a self-conscious, rebellious adolescent sat down with a thin, gray-backed notebook in front of him. He was starting a diary.

Erle Stanley Gardner had not been an exemplary high-school student and his brief bout with college at Valparaiso University in Indiana had been abortive; he departed under pressure after a fistfight with a professor. However, he was convinced that he wanted to be a lawyer. He had already started working in law offices, cleaning cuspidors, scrubbing windows, and running errands—"all for the privilege of having the right books to study and some one to answer my questions." Friends advised that he must go to college, and Gardner, in his rebellion against tradition, desperately needed to convince himself that he could do it without.

Gardner was "determined to qualify myself to enter the bar by an office education." The "Preface" to that diary was obviously written on the same day as the first entry, Sunday, March 21, 1909. In the introduction he argued the pros and cons of his decision and gave himself a pep talk:

> I believe however that by taking nine hours' sleep six nights a week and studying constantly that I can follow the course mapped out and be admitted to the bar in another year. At any rate I know that I am forcibly anxious to try it and to get out in the world on such a status that I will be treated as a man and a gentleman and not as a pupil, or perhaps in society as a "student."
>
> To follow this plan of action with any degree of success, however, it will be necessary for me to always keep in mind the fact that I must not let my English be neglected and to do this I have decided to follow the three steps herein designated:—
>
> (1) To practice elocution at the office nights after the force has retired and to study the dictionary.
>
> (2) To write a story occasionally for some magazine, as my experiences prompt me.
>
> (3) To keep a diary, which shall show my thoughts and my experiences together with my conclusions therefrom, which will register my progress either upwards or downwards and will at the same time afford me much amusement. . . .
>
> I may be wrong, in fact I realize that the odds are against me but it is better to fail and do it independently than to succeed after being fitted to the conventional mould by others who have been shaped by the same process.

The diary petered out as its ever-more-occasional entries focused on holiday interludes, trips, and associations with friends. As events developed, reading for the bar examination; doing legal chores, typing, and janitor work for lawyers; and legal practice after being admitted to the California bar in 1910, at the age of twenty-one, kept him too busy for the next ten years or so either to keep up his diary or to write any stories. However, the typing provided him with a facility which would soon come in handy. More important, his legal studies and experience taught him the importance of keeping a record of what was going on in his mind.

When Gardner discovered that the confining demands of a legal career would make serious inroads upon time to pursue his love affair with Nature, he had second thoughts. He turned to other things. At first it was a three-year business venture as president of a sales company for automobile accessories. Manufacturers could not meet orders during the 1921 depression, and the company went out of business. As a result of this experience, Gardner would look upon his future literary output as "merchandise" to be sold to readers. After the sales company folded, he went back to law and turned to authorship on the side, at first fitfully in 1921 and in dead earnest two years later.

One of his first writing texts from the Home Correspondence School in Springfield, Massachusetts, *Writing the Photoplay* by J. Berg Esenwein and Arthur Leeds, contained a passage which Gardner carefully marked:

> To have the plot instinct is a great blessing for the writer. Lacking this, however, the most valuable asset he can possess is the note-book habit. Carry one with you *constantly*. Jot down everything that may be of help in framing and developing a plot, as well as in creating a dramatic scene for a story. . . .
>
> The rule of jotting down your thought on the instant does not apply merely to ideas that come as inspirations, or thoughts suggested by what you read or see, but it applies especially to the ideas that come to you at the time you give yourself up to concentrated thinking on play-production.

From that time, Gardner's life and writing activities are increasingly documented by notes and notebooks: plotting notebooks, field books, diaries, assorted logbooks, notes on police seminars he attended, lists of people he met, documentation of photographs he took . . . He recorded daily comings and goings; trip notes, including gas mileage and speedometer readings; weather data; health and weight memoranda; information on guns and vehicles he owned; gin rummy and archery golf scores. The Gardner Collection contains titles such as "Formulae for Writing a Mystery," "Notes on 'Animal Communications'," "Problems with Archery," "Plot Notes and Valuable Plotting Methods," "Series Characters/Germ Plots in Process of Being Adapted into Complete Plots/Movie Ideas/General Wrinkles for Exploitation,"

"Legal Decisions Notebook," and "Synopses and Character Lists of Various Perry Mason and Bertha Cool–Donald Lam Books."

During the 1920s, his accumulation was chaotic as he vacillated between using notebooks, index cards, and whatever happened to be in his pocket. During the 1930s, coincidentally with the employment of regular secretarial help—in particular Jean Bethell, who "made Gardner's work her life"—his records became more orderly.

Gardner was not recording for posterity, as is the case with so many writers who grandiosely chronicle philosophical pontifications and self-consciously edit their notes. Learning to write or engaged in the even more serious business of writing, he did not know that future scholars would be pawing through his papers, and he cared less. About 1940 he wrote out a list of admonitions to keep himself on track, "Notes and Rules on Work":

1. To write good stories I have to have my mind exclusively on these stories. The minute I start thinking of other things the less effective my story work becomes.
2. Do the bulk of my plotting on paper—other kind makes for aimless thinking.
3. Sleeping is a habit. By napping during the day and only going to bed when tired I soon become highly irregular in my sleeping. This can't be avoided in the city at times, but on the ranch I should make it a rule not to sleep during daytime—if possible to stay awake and be in bed by 9.30 at night.

   Does no good to go to bed if not sleepy, therefore plan to do something, revising or [studying] Chinese which will make me sleepy an hour or so before bedtime.
4. My greatest trouble is aimless thinking. Cut it out. When in the study I should either be dictating, writing plots—or reading—not on a time-switching basis, but on a work-all-done relaxation program, or a period of study of what's being done— Naturally a man likes to procrastinate work—and this becomes a habit. The mind is a horse. It would rather have you chase it around the pasture than go to work. Therefore tie it up—make it work while it is supposed to be working until it gets the habit.

Gardner's various notebooks permit one to go back and literally enter his mind as he worked, for example, to see him make notes of writing technique as they came to mind—usually printed or underlined, sometimes with a marginal arrow or drawing of a pointing hand to highlight their importance. The following thought interrupted a plot-in-the-making and was accompanied by a marginal notation reminding him to transfer it to his notebook of techniques:

> In constructing a story block out the highlights—the emotional chords one wishes to touch—the rough outline of the color backgrounds of emotion—then fill in the details of the plot, make a skeleton and write. Just as an artist works out the color tones and highlights of pictures.

Often, as a prelude to launching into the plot of a new story, Gardner would remind himself of basic requirements for the particular type. In May, 1953, he had just been notified of the sale of *The Case of the Fugitive Nurse* to *The Saturday Evening Post*. He sat down to start another Mason story—"the basic Mason," he noted in the margin of his notebook:

> *Tuesday, May 19, 1953—Paradise Trailer Camp:*
> New Perry Mason due to sale Wide Awake Widow or Fugitive Nurse
>> 1st Must have pace
>> 2nd A situation story where both Mason and the characters are put in situations which fill the readers with suspense.
>> 3rd No thimblerigging
>> 4th Founded on something which appeals to the reader as real and which he can understand.
> Start with someone using power in an oppressive way and Mason calls for a showdown. This leads to the first situation which culminates in murder. The secret is to have this first situation a natural one which will grip the attention of the reader audience.
> The woman who calls on Mason should be mature, sophisticated and know all the answers. . . .

He used his diary as a bare-bones record of the progress of his work:

> *Sat. Feb. 22, 1930:*
> Experimented with book plot. . . .
>
> *Mon. Aug. 18, 1930:*
> Decide start book in earnest—wrestle with plot.
>
> *Fri. Aug. 22, 1930:*
> Go to Mammoth after writing 10 p. on book in camp wagon.
>
> *Tues. Aug. 26, 1930:*
> Start Paul Pry yarn "Wiker gets the works" and do 25 p. Also about 6

on book. ["Wiker Gets the Works" was published in the January, 1931, issue of *Gang World*.]

Gardner became increasingly sensitive to his physical condition, particularly as it affected his literary production. In his notebooks and diaries he monitored his sleeping habits, use of medication, diets, and general activities—always in relation to work-in-progress:

Sat. Apr. 23, 1938:
. . . . Now I'm damned if I can figure this mechanism of mine. I've been taking work as something of a chore and getting so sleepy when I dictate the words wouldn't seem to fit in after nine or nine-thirty. Sat. night was as usual, but I started to read a law journal, of all things, and suddenly became mentally alert and excited. To bed late after waiting in vain to get sleepy. Doze off, wake with a start and apparently some ductless gland or the other squirts its stuff into the brain and combine mental stimulus with fatigue poisons and toss and fret all night.

Sun. Apr. 24, 1938—Temecula Camp:
Feel wretched. . . . Sleep some during morning. . . . My brain burns as with poisons—and I seem to get the best plot work out of my system—although I feel my nerves are due to crack—get the scheme of The Case of the Bigamous Wife—or it may be some other title later. Go to ranch, climb all over hell to the upper spring above everything and even get tired—back and read. Time to bed late and am all whipped up. Take aspirin and Ipral, the first dose in over two months and repeat at two a.m. Can't seem to get relaxed from it.

Mon. Apr. 25—Temecula Camp:
. . . walk with Rip, don't feel as relaxed as usual after Ipral, feel perhaps I lived the simple country life too long—overtrained as the saying is— but I'm sure hitting on plots—figured bringing a profane parrot into the yesterday's plot and am all set to dictate.

Tues. Apr. 26, 1938 to } Temecula Camp—Building slowly near
Mon. May 9, 1938: completion *

Have been dictating The Case of the Profane Parrot. Finish dictation Thurs. (May 5) about nine days after starting. *Find I improve Plot by taking an hour a day to think of it as a whole after apparently having it all lined up.* Have been working early in morning and thinking in bed. Had some great ideas but the hour kept getting earlier and earlier— think I should try this say before bedtime.

* Gardner had recently purchased the land which would become Rancho del Paisano, and its buildings were under construction.

While reading, Gardner kept a notebook handy to take down passages which seemed important:

> "The whole difference between a tale and a story is made by the presence or absence of relation between events and personality." p. 15 T of F.W. [From Robert Saunders Dowst, *The Technique of Fiction Writing* (Franklin, Ohio: J. K. Reeve, 1921)]
>
> • • •
>
> "By a good murder I mean one that involves in the order named, sex, wealth, mystery, romance, celebrities, beauty and youth." Sidney Sutherland, *Liberty*, January 19, 1929.

Like most writers, Gardner recorded what seemed like particularly felicitous expressions, metaphors, and similes as they strayed through his mind; and, like most writers, he rarely found occasion to use them:

> Expression: "Nickle plated gold fish"
> Kicking up as much rumpus as a cat in a bath tub
> Man who complains he sold his mess of pottage for a heritage
> Poor as a snake
> Don't weigh no more than a gutted quail
> All the aimless activity of a moth wheeling about an arc light in a series of fluttering circles

When a story plot was going awry, Gardner would frequently chide himself, as at Palm Springs on Saturday, November 24, 1956, when he interrupted the plotting of a Perry Mason book to note: "The murder should be an integral part of the story development, not just something dragged in for a story. In doing that the childhood sweetheart idea may have become outmoded. However, let's play along with it for a while . . ." The plot simply was not jelling. After trying various alternatives, Gardner gave up the whole thing by printing across the page in a firm hand:

> *Entirely New Plot*
> This whole thing is highly mediocre and lacks the zing and suspense which will carry the reader through the opening. I want to start a story with a potential client of Mason in a very real jam where we have colorful characters and a real suspense. The tense opening in the Gilded Lily while it didn't suit Thayer's idea will I believe suit those of the reader. [Thayer Hobson was president of William Morrow and Company, Gardner's publisher.] I have used a guy picking up a hitchhiker, one giving a lift to a stalled motorist. How about one where the man perhaps tries to help out his secretary who is in some sort of a jam? *In*

any event keep these openings either a court scene or some highly dramatic battle for power.

Sometimes frustrations from the outside world intruded upon his thinking. In August, 1959, Carroll & Company of Beverly Hills, "Wardrobe for Gentlemen," announced a sale. Gardner's notebook reflected his reaction to the event:

> *August 13, 1959:*
> . . . Bought two suits at Carroll's in Beverly Hills, bought a fiber glass suitcase. . . .

And then a problem developed, as he ruefully recorded:

> *August 15, 1959:*
> . . . Find I have two pairs of stand-up pants in the new suits I bought at Carroll's. . . .

The Gardner notebooks are crammed with plot germs and character sketches. These entries had the effect of planting ideas in his subconscious from whence they would crop up in future stories, sometimes years later. The majority, of course, never made it into print. Following is a brief sampling:

> Try a series of historical novels in which the time is the future instead of the past—not the future of another generation, but the ten years future into which the reader can expect to live. Don't emphasize the backgrounds too much, but make it a novel of Human emotions—things which are good anywhere, anytime. Use inflation—new peace insurance—over-crowding, unexpected coalitions etc.

Shades of *1984* and *Brave New World!* It is a shame Gardner did not pursue this idea. Considering that it was written in the early 1930s, it displayed remarkable foresight.

> A man is always garbling proverbs, yet in the garbling they become more pungent. "Shucks," he said excitedly, "let him who is without stones among you throw the first sin." "People who live in glass houses shouldn't throw the first sin." "Let him who has no glass house throw the first sin." "You can't cast your bread on waters and eat it too." "As the branch is bent so the twig is broken." "The hand that rocks the cradle is mightier than the sword." "The fool and his money is only skin deep." "It's a long lane that has no slip twixt cup and lip." "Don't cast pearls before oysters." "A stitch in time is worth a pound of cure."

The character never materialized, but more than a decade later symptoms of his malady surfaced in Bertha Cool's fractured English.

> Lawyer who always places his hat on bust of Blackstone and angle determines lawyer's mental state.

Perry Mason eventually turned up with the habit of tossing his hat at the bust of Blackstone, without which no fictional attorney's office is completely furnished.

> Detective yarn—man who arranges room in exact duplication of room where murder was committed then invites the prospects to another room for dinner—rushes 'em into the other room on pretext of escaping from revenue officers then watches to see who leaves the same way murderer did. (for *Clues*)
>
> • • •
>
> Author whose characters come and sit on desk and ask him what t' hell. Girl who has been pale reflection of virtue, powders, paints, rolls stockings and as she shows shapely limb asks writer why he doesn't have her do thus and so and get in Cosmo or do this and that and make a true confession.

That last one is almost universal with beginning writers. Characters-who-come-to-life are still so prevalent that editors hardly change expression as they slip rejection notices into the return envelopes. Apparently Gardner had sufficiently good judgment not to waste any more time on it.

Gardner was meticulous in the use of facts in his fiction, particularly in the Perry Mason novels, which had to stand the scrutiny of thousands of lawyers. At his principal writing headquarters, Rancho del Paisano, he had an extensive library in the fields of law, medicine, and criminology. His correspondence and notes reveal many discussions with medico-legal friends on sticky medical points, and his brother, Dr. Kenneth Drake Gardner, was always handy in San Francisco for consultation. When away from his study, Gardner would make notebook entries of matters he needed to research upon his return, as at Camp Wickenburg on Saturday, January 24, 1953, when he reminded himself:

> Investigate what would happen if someone substituted sterile water for insulin shot and a diabetic patient not knowing went to sleep in a coma and died—particularly if there was a suspicion that there had been a

barbiturate used. Then the treatment for the barbiturate poison would delay that for diabetic coma.

Gardner accumulated an extensive collection of reference material with original sources elaborately cross-indexed from various notebooks containing commentaries. His "Reference Drawer" index contained sixty-eight headings for areas in which he maintained continuing professional or personal interest: Acambaro Figurines, Airplanes, Animals, Anthropology, Archeology, Article Material, Artificial Limbs, Astronomy, Ballistics, Bertillon, Birds, Blood, Burglaries, Calendars, Court Reporting, Crime and Crime Detection, . . . In one notebook, carefully indexed under G, is an analysis calculated to alleviate his problems on the golf course, as carefully prepared as any set of notes he ever carried into court:

1. Open stance or square
2. On heels for wooden, on toes for irons
3. Weight equally balanced
4. Right wrist does the work, especially in putting
5. Head still
6. Eyes on ball
7. Left knee bends in
8. Club head knocks the ball. Don't use more power than you can feel in the head.
9. Follow through

Some of Gardner's most spirited and entertaining writing was confined to his voluminous reference notebooks. For example, there is the "Oesterreichs Case." His notebook entry gives details of the Los Angeles murder: Without her husband's knowledge, one Walburga Oesterreich persuaded a 17-year-old boy to live in her attic. She supplied him with food, clothing, and reading matter and allowed him to come down and raid the icebox when she and her husband were away. This went on for nineteen years. One night Oesterreich came home unexpectedly and caught them together. The outraged husband tried to choke the interloper, who had supplied himself with a revolver against just such an eventuality. He killed Oesterreich. Neither the lover nor Mrs. Oesterreich was ever convicted. Gardner never found occasion to use the case, but he did write a commentary:

> This is the case where a nymphomaniac kept a lover in her attic for many years, keeping him as a sort of a captive stud horse to supplement

her husband's attentions which were woefully lacking. The interesting thing is that the guy was called on to perform three or four times a day and, in between times, having nothing else to do in the attic, wrote adventure stories of the South Seas and built up a pretty fair market in the woodpulp magazines. This shows that only two things are necessary to become a good writer. One of them is leisure.

The Gardner Collection will easily fulfill Erle Stanley Gardner's hope: The energies of that one man provided enough raw material to keep a continuing stream of writers and scholars busy in the Humanities Research Center at Austin, Texas, for decades to come. Gardner's papers have been augmented by friends and literary associates such as Ben Hibbs, editor of *The Country Gentleman* and *The Saturday Evening Post,* and Thayer Hobson, who made their files concerning Gardner available.

Here are the makings for many fat volumes on the history of the woodpulps, the 47-year chronicles of an author's relations with his publishers and agents, the story of the Court of Last Resort, the history of a television production company, personalities of the legal and literary worlds, the activities of criminals and lawmen. . . . The list is bounded only by the aspirations and patience of the researchers.

This book is a skimming of information relating to the man's work, how he learned to write and what it was he learned that made his work so successful.

2
"SLOWLY LEARN, THEN YOU WILL KNOW"

Erle Stanley Gardner became a student of both the Chinese people and the Chinese language as a young lawyer who defended Chinese clients in Oxnard, California. From the Chinese he learned a proverb which would serve as a guide for the rest of his life: "*Mahn mahn hohk, nay jow sik lok*—Slowly learn, then you will know."

The doctrine appealed to him. That was the way he had learned law, and he was proud of his self-sufficiency. So when he set out to learn to write, he determined to follow the same lonely process. "I started in the writing business with no talent and no knowledge." Since it had taken him five years to become a lawyer, he allowed himself five years to master the basics and become a writer.

His initial foray into authorship was in 1921. He had just completed three years with the ill-fated Consolidated Sales Company of San Francisco. He returned to Ventura, where his wife, daughter, and the law firm he left in favor of the sales venture were waiting. He decided to take a flyer at writing.

Like many another beginning writer, he started with short subjects, "fillers" in the publishing lingo—jokes or "skits," as Gardner called them. He had a plentiful supply from his recent three years in the sales business. He sold a couple which he managed to launder sufficiently to stand the light of print—"The Police of the House" to *Breezy Stories* and another to the *Chicago Herald-Examiner*. The going rate was $2 or $3 each, $10 at the most, and riches did not seem to be just around the corner.

NELLIE'S NAUGHTY NIGHTY

By Erle S. Gardner

NELLIE'S nightie was naughty. You know; sort of filmy and frivolous, clinging pink silk, low in the neck and tantalizingly transparent, smooth to the touch, and very, very thin.

O-o-o-o-o la-la!

Nellie, herself, was not a bit hard to look at. She was the type that attracts attention. When Nellie passed Mr. and Mrs. Middleaged Henpeck Smith on the street, Mrs. Smith would watch her spouse to make sure he didn't turn his head; and Mr. Smith, gently sniffing the elusive perfume, would be torn between desire and prudence. Desire telling him to give at least one backward glance at the short skirt, shapely ankles, voluptuous figure and baby stare; and prudence telling him he couldn't get away with it.

Nellie had upper six, in car nine, and she would have been very much pleased indeed had Mr. Joseph Merwin, who occupied lower six, car nine, offered to exchange with her. Merwin, however, had ideas of his own upon this subject. As it happened, he couldn't sleep in an upper berth, and had waited over in Salt Lake City for the sole purpose of getting a lower. Having settled himself comfortably in his seat, he started to read a magazine.

When Merwin first saw Nellie tripping down the aisle of the Pullman, taking steps about ten inches long, and wearing a skirt that didn't look much longer, he experienced a pleasant thrill. Some little traveling companion, and he was glad she was in the same car. When the porter escorted her to upper six and commenced arranging her baggage on the seat facing Mr. Merwin,

however, it was a different story. Merwin telepathically sensed that the young lady had her eye on that lower. Maybe she did, and again, maybe she didn't, but Merwin had worked hard to get that berth, and he was inclined to shy at anything which looked like an attempt to deprive him of it. Pulling his cap over his eyes, he became absorbed in his magazine.

The train started. So did Merwin. The train started because of a signal from the conductor. Merwin started because a dainty foot had rubbed against his shin.

"I beg your pardon," cooed a soft voice.

"Not at all," grunted Merwin to his magazine. This was going to be worse than he had expected.

The train swayed sharply to one side. So did Merwin. So did the girl. A soft hand brushed lightly across Merwin's knee.

"Oh, I do beg your pardon," purred the voice.

"Not at all," Merwin repeated to his magazine.

Five minutes of silence. Merwin stole a glance over the top of his periodical. Perched on the edge of the seat opposite, he saw a wonderful complexion surmounting a thin, silk blouse cut very low; a short length of skirt, and a longer length of silk hose. The skirt had evidently been pulled slightly up, and the stocking had unquestionably been rolled down. The smoking car was forward, and Joe Merwin made for it. The train by this time was going full speed ahead, and so was Joe. It was with a sigh of relief he flung himself into a leather

Gardner's first fiction sale was "Nellie's Naughty Nightie," a short story published in *Breezy Stories*, August, 1921.

"This convinced me that the money lay in writing stories rather than skits," he explained later.

He set out to contrive what he believed was a plot. Actually, his source of material was the same. He was merely elongating an old have-you-heard-the-one-about story: It seems there was this guy who was in an upper berth, and there was this good-looking babe in the lower. Well, she gets off the train first and forgets her nightgown—see. And the porter finds it and thinks it belongs to this guy—see. So he puts it in his suitcase. Well, when this guy gets home, his wife finds it—see. But—

Again *Breezy Stories* was the market. For something the editor thought long enough to classify as a short story, the rate was $15. The new author was proud of his check, but his mother—of *Mayflower* heritage and strict New England upbringing—was not enchanted. "Nellie's Naughty Nightie" was published in the August, 1921, issue under the name Erle S. Gardner. For the record, here are the opening paragraphs of Erle Stanley Gardner's first published short story:

> Nellie's nightie was naughty. You know; sort of filmy and frivolous, clinging pink silk, low in the neck and tantalizingly transparent, smooth to the touch, and very, very thin.
>
> O-o-o-o-o la-la!
>
> Nellie herself was not a bit hard to look at. She was the type that attracts attention. When Nellie passed Mr. and Mrs. Middleaged Henpeck Smith on the street, Mrs. Smith would watch her spouse to make sure he didn't turn his head; and Mr. Smith, gently sniffing the elusive perfume, would be torn between desire and prudence. Desire telling him to give at least one backward glance at the short skirt, shapely ankles, voluptuous figure and baby stare; and prudence telling him he couldn't get away with it.

Oh, yes, the rest of that old traveling salesman story: But his wife, her name was Helen, she didn't say a thing—see. It was driving this guy crazy. Then, just when he was getting ready to leave on another trip, she— Gardner had the ending, much as he had heard it in the jiggling smokers of a dozen trains:

> "Yes," crooned Helen, with that slow, provoking smile, which always set him on fire, "when I realized you liked to associate with women who wore those things, I decided to give you all the comforts of traveling right here at home."

Though Gardner wanted "a second economic string to my bow," writing did not seem to hold much promise. He had also thought about a mail-order business as something which would require a minimum of personal attention. As he settled into his law practice in Ventura, he and a partner in San Francisco cooked up a sideline, a mail-order course in salesmanship for lawyers. The idea proved too successful: A trial sales letter brought a flood of orders, and Gardner had to spend his lunch periods and nights batting out lessons for the as yet unwritten correspondence course. Shortly it became evident that he was going to have to quit practicing law in Ventura and go to San Francisco to manage the office end of the thriving business. This was precisely what he was trying to get away from; he abandoned the correspondence school.

In 1923 he turned back to writing as the only occupation in which one could be free of an office routine. This time, Gardner let himself be guided by the old Chinese proverb. He was going to give it a five-year try.

In those days there was comparatively little help for the aspiring writer. At first all he had was the magazines to which he hoped to sell. He studied the works of published writers such as H. Bedford-Jones and tried to emulate their stories. He subscribed to the *Writer's Digest* under a pseudonym, as he was submitting his manuscripts to magazines. He bought correspondence courses from the Home Correspondence School out of Springfield, Massachusetts, and from the *Writer's Digest*. He "scanned" the books and lessons he received, rather than take time to participate in the prescribed regimens, and turned back to his typewriter to pound out a continuing stream of stories.

He gleaned only four sales in 1923 for half a year's labor, but he was jubilant. He attributed his success to the "Ideal Course in Short Story Writing" and wrote the editor of *Writer's Digest* to tell him so:

> Just a word in regard to that Ideal course. I can't begin to tell you what it has done for me. I have purchased several courses in story writing, some of them running into real money, but have secured more practical assistance from your course than all the rest put together.

In October, 1923, he wrote Harry North of *Black Mask* explaining how he wrote:

> As I get to writing I can actually feel the emotion of my characters, and I tear along on the typewriter oblivious of time, grammar or

punctuation, trying to keep pace with the action. I then take the story and go over it correcting errors and occasionally changing a word or two and re-copy. Nearly all of my characters are real in at least some features. In fact I usually combine features of two persons in one character. That is, I will sketch some character I know and frequently give him an additional characteristic or two from some other person.

The woodpulp editors were friendly. From them he began to absorb criticism. He also found a book by H. Bedford-Jones, *The Fiction Business.* Bedford-Jones quoted Walter B. Pitkin's definition of plot: "Plot is a climactic series of events, each of which both determines and is determined by the characters involved." Gardner began to figure out that his ninety-percent rejection rate was caused by faulty plotting. "So I decided to analyze plots and find out just what they were and where they came from." He also established a "fault book" in which he entered editorial criticism as well as conclusions regarding his own work as a result of his study:

> My stories are too much inclined to be a shuffling of characters for 13,000 words in order to get them in a predetermined position for a finish in two thousand words which would be ingenious if the reader hadn't become tired by that time.

> • • •

> My problem [is] getting into my complications quickly enough to hold the reader's interest—try just leading them into the yarn as incidental facts and going on from there rather than building them up a step at a time.

> • • •

> I am inclined to make my heroes get into difficulties thru outside circumstances and to eavesdrop, climb trees etc and work out by ingenuity. Let 'em smash their way into the trouble more and two fist their way out.

> • • •

> Always I have tried to think up a trick situation—give it characters and setting and make a story.
> Wrong.
> What the reader wants is a strong man fighting against great odds for some principle—revenge—justice—liberty—and making the fight in a convincing manner.

By late 1925 Gardner had sold something over half a million words to the woodpulps, about fifty-five assorted stories and novelettes.

McCall's, The Saturday Evening Post, Delineator, People's Popular Monthly, Red Book, and *Blue Book* had "loosened up" with an occasional letter, but that was all he had gotten from the "big time" markets to which he really wanted to sell. During his first fiscal year of writing he made only $974. The second year showed a dramatic increase, $3,436, but that wouldn't go far toward replacing the $12,000-a-year income of a partner in a prosperous law firm, and he had his wife and daughter to think about.

His percentage of sales had increased to about two-thirds of his output, but some manuscripts took as many as twenty-five trips to market. He was so busy getting rejections back into the mail that he didn't have time either to polish his stories or to study the slick markets to which he aspired. It was time for a pep talk. He went back to Chinese lore, a quotation from Lao-tze with which he had recently been sprinkling his notebook: "The journey of a thousand miles must begin with a single step." He made an entry in his notebook laying out the steps:

> The Journey of a Thousand Miles:
> *Plan* each day's work to get results
> *Start* working
> Think on the typewriter
> Get it on paper

He jacked up his quota. He would aim for 60,000 words a month.

In October, 1925, Phil Cody, a pulp editor, sent him a brochure on a literary agent, Robert Thomas Hardy, "Playbroker and Author's Agent," and Hardy wrote to him. This seemed like the answer to a writer's prayer—if Hardy would just go along with his ideas:

> Some of my stories sell very well, but about one third of them don't make the grade, and I have a hunch that some of the others barely get by. It's this thing I want to remedy. I want some one to weed out the bum ones in advance, and to get tough with me and tell me when my work is sloppy and careless, when my plots are trite and when my stories don't get across, BUT I want this some one to know the game and know what he's talking about.
>
> Confidentially, I've been sending out my first draft, which I think is a mistake. However, I'm fighting always for time, and I have been trying to keep my production up. As a result I sit down at the machine and bang 'em off at about fifteen hundred words an hour, revise 'em for

typos and send 'em to the editors. I've come to the conclusion this is a poor practice. . . .

What I am working for is to get myself sufficiently established in the literary game so I can quit law entirely. I like the trial of cases, but I DO NOT LIKE OFFICE LAW, and I can not stand the continued confinement of an office. I took up writing, not because I felt any interior urge, but because I wanted some way to make a living where I could be out of doors a large portion of the day time, and be master of my own time. . . .

For the present I want to get away from sloppy work. I want to work out a first draft on the machine, correct it in pen and make such alterations as will improve the mss. then send it on to an agent who will have it typed by a real, honest to goodness expert, then give it careful study. I want this agent to fire anything back that doesn't come up to standard, take the stuff that is right, and sell that. I want us both to work together with the idea always in mind of continued and rapid betterment, both as to markets and as to stories. I've got unlimited confidence in my ability to make the better markets after I get on to the ropes, and this confidence arises from the fact that I know how to work. I can work like the devil when necessary, and I know it takes work to get anywhere in this game.

I want an agent who has more education than I have. (I know law pretty well, but I'm careless in English, and I forgot all of the grammar I ever knew.) . . .

I want an agent to give me a pen and ink picture of every editor I'm writing for, what his ideas and prejudices are.

In conclusion, most authors want an agent to get 'em better rates. I don't. I want all the rates I'm entitled to, but I want an agent primarily to make me turn out consistent work and keep my markets regularly supplied. Rates'll take care of themselves. Also when a magazine is a little hard pressed I'm anxious to see they are not pressed by me—in other words I want to play ball with the magazines that play ball with me.

Gardner and Hardy made a deal. Gardner sent Hardy all of his manuscripts—old and new, good and bad—and Gardner received an education in the hitherto unknown area of how a literary agency worked. Hardy made sales, but most of his comments on Gardner's stories had to do with how Gardner should write less material and concentrate on hitting the slicks, the higher-paying markets. There was an increase in the 1925-1926 fiscal year's income, $5,838.15

according to Gardner's figures, but he was obviously disappointed, a disappointment he expressed to Hardy in fear that the agency was not realizing sufficient return from commissions on his work.

During the latter part of 1926 the situation began to go sour. Hardy was attempting to market certain stories to magazines which Gardner had told him to avoid because he knew their editors would not like those particular stories. Actually, 1926 had not been a bad year. He made almost a hundred sales, just short of a million words. But Gardner felt his work was deteriorating because he was losing personal contact with his woodpulp markets. Additionally, Gardner learned that some of the manuscripts he sent were being forwarded to editorial offices without being corrected and retyped.

In March, 1927, Gardner declared the arrangement at an end, at least for the time being. He didn't feel he was ready for an agent. Perhaps if he ever wrote a book— It was an amicable parting, but there was a note of desperation in his letter to Hardy:

> I'm hanged if I know just what the trouble with my stuff is, but I do know that I cannot afford to put in the time writing stories to sell the percentage which has been selling during the past. I have either got to increase my percentage of sales or quit and devote my time to something more profitable.

The desperation was not without reason. The end of the five-year trial period was dangerously close and, to add to that problem, his law partners were making noises to the effect that he should either quit the firm or come back to work full time.

As soon as he could get away, Gardner made a trip to New York City to look over the situation personally. He visited editors, and he generated considerable interest in ideas for stories he would send back after his return to Ventura. The 1926-1927 fiscal year totted up to $6,627.50, a modest increase over the year before but nothing like Gardner had hoped for by the end of his fourth year. He challenged the setback by setting a new quota for himself: He would mail a novelette every third day.

For the fifth year, 1927-1928, Gardner's ledger showed an income of $9,614.25—not bad, but still not enough to permit him to chuck the legal practice. On the other hand, the woodpulps were beginning to feature him on their covers, he had a number of continuing characters going, and he was beginning to pick up a strong reader following. He did not give up his writing; he couldn't. A few years later, in encouraging beginning writers, Gardner told how it was: "Finally, I became so fascinated with writing that I couldn't quit it now to save me. If the editors quit accepting my stories, or quit paying for them, I'd keep on writing just the same."

His determination was rewarded. In both of the following two years, his sales topped the million-word mark; his name on the front cover of a pulp magazine became a prime drawing card. His income for those two years was $13,612.50 and $14,941 respectively, not at all bad during severe economic conditions.

Along the way, Gardner met such woodpulp luminaries as Dashiell Hammett, Carroll John Daly, and H. Bedford-Jones. He always addressed Bedford-Jones as "King of the Woodpulps." Bedford-Jones wrote under ten names other than his own. He turned down a chair of commercial fiction at a large university and the editorship of a national magazine. Gardner and Bedford-Jones traded letters and visits to exchange market information during those dark Depression days when magazines and banks alike were folding.

By 1930, Gardner had built a strong name with the Munsey house and Popular Publications; however, attempting to carry on a law practice while keeping the hungry woodpulp market satisfied was no picnic, as Gardner explained to Wallace R. Bamber, an editor who telephoned him in November of that year:

> The trouble with both of these markets, however, is that they require their stuff by the 20th, and the first part of the month is a veritable orgy of work so far as I am concerned. Then, this last week I had to go to San Francisco on a case, returned to find that a $30,000 jury case had been moved on for trial starting yesterday morning. I sat up with the facts of the case, got down to the office at eight o'clock to go over the thing with the witnesses, and then went into Court and tried the case all yesterday and today. The case went to the jury about 5:30 tonight and jury brought in a verdict in favor of my client, and I had just arrived home when your telephone call came in. I got up at four o'clock this morning to finish a story before Court and am dictating correspondence tonight. Next Monday I have to be in San Francisco to argue the constitutionality of the Joint Highway District Act before the Appellate Court returning on the night train to enter on the trial of a will contest involving about $80,000.00 Tuesday morning.

Bamber had telephoned Gardner at the instigation of H. Bedford-Jones to solicit manuscripts for two new woodpulp magazines he was promoting, *Far East Adventure Stories* and *Amazing Detective Stories*. Gardner could not resist another potential market. His letter of November 14 continued, "I will try and write something especially suited for you if you will outline just about the type of stuff you want, whether mystery action, straight detective, gangster or what."

Gardner's first submission was a bummer, but the second, "Dice of Death," earned a check for $240 ("Rush this through right away as banks in the big city are failing daily.") and an assignment for another yarn by a letter written December 11:

> We have taken time by the forelock and announced a second story by you entitled "The Lighthouse Murder" for our second issue of *Amazing Detective Stories*. We have helped you greatly by giving you a title all hand-made, so pick one of the forlorn lighthouses up around Santa Barbara channel and write us a good short mystery. And try to keep it down to ten thousand words—our budget is woefully small.

Gardner would soon learn how small. In the meantime he got to work on the story. His diary recorded the research and writing:

Sun. Dec. 14, 1930:
Little fiction— Talk some Chinese. Go to Lighthouse at Hueneme.

Mon. Dec. 15, 1930:
Write 40 p. The Lighthouse Murder.

Tues. Dec. 16, 1930:
Finish Lighthouse Murder and go office for while.

He fired off "The Lighthouse Murder" to Bamber on December 16, voicing a small complaint: "It is a little bit unhandy for me to turn out these stories on short notice and I am having to neglect other markets in order to play ball with yours."

The response was calculated to cheer any aspiring young writer and make him put up with a bit of unhandiness: "Your second story 'The Lighthouse Murder' has been received and accepted. . . . We want a story a month from you." But the joy was short-lived. On January 30, 1931, Bamber wrote:

> We have received and accepted both of your last stories, "The Lighthouse Murder" and "The Covered Corpse," and if we were as

exact in our part as you have been in yours, you would have your checks for same by now. But, unhappily and unfortunately, we simply don't have the money at present. So, I won't ask you to send in any more stories for the present until we are certain of how we are going to make out.

Gardner responded in February that the letter had been "duly received, and mournfully filed." During the following month, Wally Bamber visited the Gardners in Ventura with a proposition: He thought *Amazing Detective Stories* was "over the hump," but he still had no money; he was offering to pay writers in stock in the magazine.

Gardner wrote no more stories for *Amazing Detective*. On April 13, while preparing to take a trip to the Orient with his wife, he was still trying to collect. On March 24 of the following year, Bamber wrote Gardner soliciting his support for a writers' organization he was attempting to organize, acknowledging that he owed Gardner $400, "which you aren't going to get for awhile yet, I know. I am busted flatter than a carbon copy, but I haven't lost my courage or enthusiasm." There is no record of collection and, understandably, Gardner as well as a number of other writers lost their enthusiasm for Wallace R. Bamber—actually only one of many victims of the economic conditions of that time.

Both Bedford-Jones and Gardner were selling at the rate of more than a million words a year, and in 1931 Bedford-Jones recognized Gardner's reputation by asking him to write an introduction for his forthcoming book on writing, *The Graduate Fictioneer*.

In March, 1933, when *The Case of the Velvet Claws* was published, H. Bedford-Jones was high on Gardner's list to receive complimentary copies. Bedford-Jones came back with a tongue-in-cheek congratulatory letter:

> I have read with great interest your book, entitled "The Case of the Velvet Claws." (I may even say that only the earthquake compelled me to read it, since the electricity was shut off and I could not work.)
>
> You are heartily to be congratulated upon the publisher's blurb.
>
> For a first effort in the book field, this appears to be a fairly successful venture. The lack of imagination is of course to be regretted, but upon the whole, the book seems to be quite commendable, in spite of the leading character being merely taken out of real life and lifted bodily into the pages. Aside from certain evidence of haste in the writing, and the lack of any finished style, the story is very readable.

For some inexplicable reason, I should here state that the book was read in one evening—something which is very rarely my habit, since I find it most unwise to allow the reading of fiction to interfere with my regular hours. It was, perhaps, due to recurrent earthquake shocks that I finished the book without sitting down.

If you would read my chapters on the writing of detective tales, in a book entitled "The Graduate Fictioneer," I believe they might prove of some help to you in the formation of plot.

I am glad to be able to say that my wife is now reading your little tale with absorbed interest. In fact, I have been somewhat astonished by her expressions in regard to the worthwhile qualities of the book; but you will understand that a woman's sense of values is sometimes variable. She requests me to say that she will certainly write you herself in a few days. Pray do not be disappointed if no letter comes, because I must warn you that she promises much and fulfills little, in this respect.

Thank you for the book. It is greatly appreciated and the inscription, however flattering it must appear to one not acquainted with my works, is extremely appropriate. I shall have only good words for the book, and trust that the one to follow may set you firmly in the galaxy of writers.

The letter was signed "Late King of the Woodpulps" and accompanied by a pseudolegal document in which H. Bedford-Jones formally renounced the title:

That he does hereby and hereon solemnly and sincerely, whether richer or poorer, in sickness and in health, resign in favor of ERLE STANLEY GARDNER all right, fee and emolument in and within, from or through, whereby and whereas, the title enjoyed by him, said title being commonly known as

KING OF THE WOODPULPS

And that, further, he does hereby promote said ERLE STANLEY GARDNER from the position Crown Prince to that of King, as aforesaid, to have and to hold until death do him part, and may God have mercy on his soul.

The following month, *Life* magazine (pre-Henry Luce version) published a list of top-paid woodpulp writers. Following the admonition of the old Chinese proverb had finally paid off. Erle Stanley Gardner and H. Bedford-Jones headed the list, in that order, as "$50,000 a year men." Gardner could not resist bragging as he accepted the title from Bedford-Jones:

"Slowly Learn, Then You Will Know"

Modesty compels me to mention that the name of the undersigned is in the relative position of that occupied by Abou Ben Adhem in the famous poem. Second in importance is that of H. Bedford-Jones, late King of the Woodpulps. Us two share exclusively the classification of being $50,000.00 a year writers.

3
THE OLD WOODPULP
SCHOOLHOUSE

Woodpulp magazines, later shortened to "pulps" in the lingo of the trade, got their name from the cheap paper on which they were printed, of such dubious quality that readers often found splinters pressed into the pages. Direct descendants of the dime novels and yellow-backs of the nineteenth century, woodpulps were fathered by Frank A. Munsey in 1896. That year he completed conversion of *Golden Argosy*, a children's magazine, into *Argosy*, an all-fiction action-adventure publication appealing to adults, by printing it on rough woodpulp stock. In the interest of economy, Munsey decided the story was more important than the paper upon which it was printed.

The woodpulps drove the dime novels out of business because, as periodicals rather than discontinuous publications, they were eligible for low second-class postal rates. Their heyday came between the two World Wars. They burgeoned and prospered during the 1920s, proliferated and struggled during the fiercely competitive Depression years of the 1930s, and succumbed to comic books and twenty-five-cent paperbacks during the 1940s. Today their successors flourish on soft-cover display racks in supermarkets, drugstores, air terminals, bookstores—and, in visual form, interspersed between sporting events, talk shows, and variety hours on television networks.

Woodpulp magazines were a breed unto themselves. Buyers did not purchase upon the recommendation of teachers. No college English Literature curriculum recognized their existence until they died and became an undeniable part of America's social and literary heritage.

They were not purchased because of glowing critical reviews. (George Jean Nathan and H. L. Mencken of *Smart Set* and *American Mercury*, two of the literary scene's most scornful critics, started the mystery thriller *Black Mask* because they needed money; however, they never allowed their names to appear on its pages. They sold the filthy thing as soon as the $500 they had put into it grew to $100,000.) A woodpulp magazine was bought solely because its escapist purchasers, attracted by the flamboyant cover, were hooked by what they found on the first page.

Regardless of personal attitudes toward the wares they purveyed, woodpulp editors made every effort to determine what would appeal to their readers. When they found a writer who could or who was willing to learn to address that audience, they quickly capitalized on the discovery. Lester Dent, who wrote Doc Savage stories for Street & Smith under the pseudonym of Kenneth Robeson, was a telegrapher for the Associated Press in Tulsa, Oklahoma, and an aspiring writer. His first thirteen stories collected nothing but rejection slips. His fourteenth sold. As a result he received a telegram from a publisher: If he was making less than $100 a week he should quit and come to New York to write. He would be given a $500-a-month drawing account.

The hungry woodpulps served as a training ground for writers, illustrators, and editors. Their contributors made up a roster including Isaac Asimov, Rex Beach, H. Bedford-Jones, Ray Bradbury, Max Brand (Frederick Schiller Faust, who really would rather have been a poet under his own name than write Western stories), Edgar Rice Burroughs, Raymond Chandler, Major George Fielding Eliot, Zane Grey, H. Rider Haggard, Dashiell Hammett, Harold Lamb, Jack London, H. P. Lovecraft, Rafael Sabatini, Marc Schorer, and Tennessee Williams—to name only a few. Perhaps the most notable was Sinclair Lewis, who served a stint as associate editor of *Adventure* under Arthur Sullivant Hoffman before going on to be awarded the Nobel Prize for Literature. And, of course, Erle Stanley Gardner was by no means last or least.

Gardner was quicker than most who graduated to other writing fields to acknowledge his debt to editors of the woodpulps. In 1967, during a moment of nostalgia, he lamented the passing of the genre in a letter to the editor of *The Author & Journalist*: "I would like very much indeed to help and inspire the flock of young writers who are coming along, but who are having all sorts of difficulties these days . . . How I wish we could turn back the clock to the days of the old woodpulps. These magazines furnished a training ground for writers which has never been equaled."

Gardner knew. He had been through the school.

He matriculated in 1923, writing under the name Charles M. Green, living and practicing law in Ventura and having his rejections delivered to a mail drop in San Francisco. He told editors the subterfuge was to keep his manuscripts separate from legal correspondence which was opened by stenographers during his absence; however, since he abandoned the practice after only a few sales, it was obviously to avoid the embarrassment of having his law partners see the high rejection rate of the young writer in their midst. Failure as a writer could not help but reflect in their opinions of him as a lawyer.

"Charles M. Green" was bombarding magazines and getting his submissions back as fast as the mail could carry them. "I thought I was writing stories. Actually, I didn't know what a story was." At last, he found the usual rejection slip scrawled with a handwritten notation:

Sorry, Mr. Green—I don't like this yarn, but keep them coming. S.

The mimeographed form THE PRESENT NEEDS OF BLACK MASK was all too familiar, but the note was different: *This was from the editor himself, George W. Sutton, Jr.*

Only a writer who remembers his first personal letter from an editor can realize the feeling which flooded Gardner. He grabbed every available moment from the law office to write "The Shrieking Skeleton"—this time a novelette instead of the usual short story. "It was a major opus as far as I was concerned," he said later.

He mailed the manuscript with high hope and settled to the waiting which turned into an eternity of doubt. . . . Finally, a letter arrived in San Francisco for "Charles M. Green, Care Consolidated Sales Co.," and Gardner wasted no time getting to 1035 Polk Street to find the same brown envelope he had enclosed, still fat with manuscript pages.

Actually, although Gardner did not learn the details for many years, he was the victim of a cruel joke: "The Shrieking Skeleton" was so bad that some clown in *Black Mask*'s editorial office decided to have fun at the expense of Phil Cody, the staid circulation manager.*

---

*Later Phil Cody served as editor of *Black Mask* and went on to become vice-president of Warner Publications. A lasting friendship developed between him and Gardner.

He put the manuscript on Cody's desk with a note to the effect that the editor had purchased this novelette to use as the lead story in a future issue; Phil should plan a publicity campaign around it.

From Cody's side of the desk, his reaction is understandable. He penciled an emphatic note begging the editorial staff to reconsider. He went on to say: "This story gives me a pain in my neck. . . . It's pretty near the last word in childishness, and the plot has whiskers like unto Spanish moss on an old live oak. I foresaw the end from the beginning." The characters talked like a dictionary; the story was puerile, trite, obvious, unnatural. The note—signed "P.C.C."—was inadvertently included with the manuscript.

When Gardner ripped open the thick brown envelope, the circulation manager's note slipped out from between the pages. It would be softened by a letter from Mr. Sutton. Perhaps the editor could feel the fervent hope which Gardner had sweated into the novelette, or perhaps he saw some promise peeking out from behind the clumsy machinations of the plot. His letter, dated June 21, 1923, reiterated Cody's frank complaints, but it extended hope:

> In spite of the Circulation Manager's vitriolic remarks, I like parts of your novelette "The Shrieking Skeleton." It has several troubles. One of these is that there is no one in the story to suspect except the Japanese, and sure enough he turns out to be the culprit. You should drag in some more characters, so that the readers' suspicions could be diversified.
>
> Another thing. The conversation throughout is too long and too artificial. This is especially so on the part of the Irish policeman, but all of the characters talk more like dictionaries than human beings.
>
> In other words, this story needs careful editing, cutting and revision. If you have the patience to do these things, we would be glad to see it again.

This was Gardner's first taste of editorial criticism, the first of many lessons in the informal correspondence course he was to receive from the old woodpulp schoolhouse in faraway New York City. On June 28, Gardner fired back a response:

> I want to thank you for your criticism of my story "The Shrieking Skeleton," . . . I am revising the story as per your welcome suggestions and will re-submit it when finished. Knowing what you want, I believe I can fill the bill.

I also wish you would extend my thanks to your Circulation Manager, whose pencil note accompanied your letter. There is something genuine and human about his exasperation, and he expresses himself so much to the point that I have chuckled over it all day, in spite of the fact that I am the target for his remarks. I have been in the law game long enough to keenly appreciate the fellow who can "hand me one"; and any man capable of registering so much disgust on so little paper is an artist.

I am going to try to revise this story so it will "get under his skin" and wish you would try it out on him when I resubmit it.

Undoubtedly Gardner's initial reaction was not really such unbridled gratitude and glee, but it didn't take much study of the now cold story for him to realize that Phil Cody had ample reason to complain. Gardner took up a pencil to brief its deficiencies: 1. Plot trite; 2. Plot unconvincing; 3. End obvious; 4. Characters talk like dictionaries . . . Before he finished, the list stretched to touch just about every feature of the story except its title.

Finally he turned to his typewriter. "I was up just about all night for three nights hammering away at the thing": The story had to be replotted as he introduced new characters to divert suspicion from the Japanese, and they all had to be motivated. It took several trips through the typewriter to make sure everybody talked like a "human being." All in all, the revision turned the yarn into a fresh treatment of the original idea, and that required a new ending. It was a painful session:

> My typewriter didn't have rubber keys. The technique that I had was a two-fingered technique which caused the pounding on the hard typewriter keys to pull the flesh at the ends of my fingers away from the fingernails. I got to spattering blood on the typewriter keys, so I covered the ends of my business fingers with adhesive tape and kept right on hammering away.

On July 9 he again addressed "The Shrieking Skeleton" to George W. Sutton, Jr., "as per your suggestions of the 21st ult." He explained the changes he had made to be certain his labor would be noticed. Years later, looking back, Gardner admitted, "The story was a pretty mediocre story. It was amateurishly written." His grade may not have been high, but Erle Stanley Gardner, *alias* Charles M. Green, had completed his first lesson and passed the examination. Editor Sutton bought "The Shrieking Skeleton," and Writer Gardner received a check for $160.

"That did it. There was gold in them thar hills and I was after it."

Gardner learned to ask editors for criticism and to indicate his willingness to meet editorial demands. However, he reserved the right to stand up for his personal beliefs, an attitude he steadfastly maintained until the end of his career:

> I want my stories to be right up to scratch and any time you send 'em back with a suggestion that'll improve them, I'll keep on re-writing 'em until the cows come home, but any time you make a suggestion that I think detracts from the story is when we have an argument.

The woodpulp school was no place for the thin-skinned dilettante. Its instructors were bluntly forthright in their rejection of hopeless material, no matter how dedicated the student, as a *Black Mask* editor demonstrated the following year:

> Dear Mr. Gardner:
> This is terrible.
>   Sincerely
>   H. C. North
>   Associate Editor

If he wanted to remain in class, there was nothing for the student to do but grin and bear it. Gardner put up his best front when writing about the frequent rejections:

> Don't feel bad about 'em. I don't. That's what I put the return postage in there for. I've got a hell of a lot of rejections from a damn sight better magazines than *Black Mask*. Some bird asked me the other day why I didn't write for the *Saturday Evening Post*. I withered him with a glance. "I do," I says.
> I do, too. Only the damn fools don't appreciate it.

And sometimes the instructors were crudely frank in expressing their opinions. It helped relieve the monotony of a constant stream of unredeemable manuscripts. In a way they earned the right to blow off steam. Rather than charging tuition they were sending checks to those students who could stand up to the hazing:

> So far as "One Profitable Night" goes, I can see no hope for it. I think it is awful, a mess, not worthy of a high school kid, one of the worst— it's the kind of story I'm glad I didn't write. When I said there was no hope for it, I was a little hasty. I think there is a chance to salvage it. My

suggestion would be that you nail it within arms-length of your toilet bowl. Another little tip—the next time you write a story like that, please type it on sand paper, lest I be tempted.

However, when the student was serious and showed promise, those same crusty instructors were willing to walk the extra mile with a protégé. In the same envelope with "One Profitable Night," H. C. North returned another story. About it he wrote:

> "Ham, Eggs an' Coffee" I think is a good story spoiled by over-writing. To my mind it is sophomoric. Do you think that you can go over it with a critical eye and fix it up? If you don't get what I mean ship it back and I'll edit it for you.

Gardner was not prone to pass up an opportunity to see a laboratory demonstration by his instructor. Two weeks later he was sending the manuscript back:

> Good God no! I don't know what's the matter with this, and the more I see of it the less I can tell. If I strike out what I think you want stricken out, nine times out of ten it'll be wrong. In the innocence of your generosity you offered to edit it for me. I don't want you to do anything except make a smear with a blue pencil where you want it cut. I do want you to do that, though, and I'll sure appreciate it. It'll give me a damn sight better line on what you want.
>
> . . . Take your time and just give me the blue pencil where it's the bunk. You said in your letter it was "sophomoric." Why in hell don't you talk English? A poor cow country lawyer can't tell what you mean by a word like that.

H. C. North went ahead to edit the story and send a check. When it appeared in the August, 1925, issue of *Black Mask*, Gardner took careful note of what the editor had done. He would later write in expressing his appreciation, Harry North "was a patient cuss with something of a sense of humor." That sense of humor showed up on the receipt of Gardner's next submission.

In addition to trying to develop three series characters he had managed to get started in *Black Mask* in less than three years, Gardner was trying to insure himself by breaking into other markets. He was beginning to fester under North's incessant revision requirements:

> I was killing myself with an impossible work schedule. I would put in all day at the law office, come home at night, bolt down a hurried meal, go up to the study and hammer away on the typewriter until two or

three o'clock in the morning. I would then grab two or three hours' sleep, get up and do a little more work at the typewriter before dashing up to the office.

He had just completed "Three O'Clock in the Morning," a novelette which he hoped would be the fourth story in his new Ed Jenkins series. He thought it was a good story, the best he could write. Above all, he wanted to forestall another dose of revision. He decided upon an all-or-nothing approach. In the letter of transmittal he wrote: "'Three O'Clock in the Morning' is a damned good story. If you have any comments on it, write 'em on a check."

Response was unusually long in coming. Finally North scrawled a marginal note on a printer's proof of an editor's note quoting Gardner's brash statement. He was using it to introduce the story in the next issue:

> There, we'll let the whole world know just what kind of God damned authors we have to put up with. Won't hold your check up to write a letter. Am rushed ragged ass. . . . H.C.N.

As Gardner became more skilled in fictional techniques, he also became somewhat cynical in regard to editorial demands. In September, 1929, he wrote Howard Bloomfield, editor of *Detective Fiction Weekly*, regarding a request for revision on rather dubious grounds:

> Tell me what you want, kiddo, and I'll prostitute my talent to give it to you. And if I think the hussy has missed two bucks anywhere, I'll send her back after it.

Joseph T. Shaw, former Army captain, became editor of *Black Mask* in August, 1926, and Gardner served a long apprenticeship under him. Captain Shaw was not always an easy taskmaster. He viewed his regular writers as members of a football team and, on occasion, adopted an attitude that was something of a cross between a drill instructor and Knute Rockne. Reader response to Gardner's stories, particularly the Ed Jenkins series, had been good, and Shaw wanted Gardner to know that he was on the first string. He wrote to explain his editorial philosophy:

> You, Daly, Suter and Hammett are now the backfield, carrying the ball on novelettes with a few likely substitutes—punters, forward pass artists and goal kickers—on the sidelines waiting for a chance to get in . . . We need a few more short story writers, who can give us the

right sort of stuff to fill out. That's the line for offensive and defensive work; the hardest to pick, the most difficult to depend upon right through . . .

And we are building that line as rapidly and as carefully as it is humanly possible to do. We have a splendid nucleus in Curry, Whitfield, Nebel. They have taken my turn-backs in good spirit; they have set themselves to do a darned sight better, . . . There are others I'm nursing along, shooting back the off stuff good and hard, and trying to fit them for permanent positions in the line; and I think they are coming, too.

4
LESSONS FROM THE PULPS

The beginning writer could learn many lessons from the pulps. Some were maxims which applied only to demands of woodpulp readers; others were general principles of plotting and writing which laid a firm foundation upon which a persistent student could build a career.

A writer must scratch for money.

Woodpulp writers were paid by the word—from one to five cents, depending upon the magazine and the writer's ability to attract readers. Gardner quickly learned the advantage of a novelette over a short story: The writer could get three times as much for thinking up one idea. At one point, Gardner had a word counter on his typewriter, a device which registered every time he depressed the space bar.

All selling writers learned to stretch their stories. They extended action scenes to the absolute limit of reader endurance. An adept penny-a-word writer could string out a "walk-down," the Western's traditional climactic showdown between the hero and the badman, to $50 and still keep readers on the edges of their chairs. One observant editor noted that even though Gardner's characters might have lightning draws and reputations for deadly accuracy, inevitably they missed with the first five shots, barely managing to plug the dastardly scoundrel with the last round in the six-shooter. Gardner was frank in his response:

"At three cents a word, every time I say '*bang*' in the story I get three cents," he wrote back. "If you think I'm going to have a gunbattle over while my hero has got fifteen cents' worth of unexploded ammunition in the cylinder of his gun, you're nuts."

Gardner became expert at the art of padding, but he met stiff opposition, particularly from Don Moore, an early-day editor of *Argosy*:

> With regard to "As Far as the Poles," the story strikes me as intrinsically overwritten. How this plot was built up into 27,000 words is just one of those mysteries of a skilled technician like yourself, for I cannot find any piece of padding, yet do not feel the story is worth the length.

And less than two weeks later, the ever-vigilant Moore refused another padded yarn:

> This is not a rejection, it is a tribute to your genius for making a short story into a novelette . . . while I do not find any real evidence of padding in "Stamp of the Desert," it *is* overwritten, and there is not enough variety of incident for this length.

Gardner cut 2,500 words out of "Stamp of the Desert," and Moore bought it by return mail. He decided not to revise "As Far as the Poles," and it bounced from market to market, finally landing in *Short Stories* more than two years later.

Gardner was still selling *Black Mask* under the pseudonym of Charles M. Green while he was writing for other pulps under his own name. He took the occasion of dropping his nom de plume to make an oblique bid for a raise in rates:

> You will notice that I have killed Mr. Green. I am sending the enclosed under my own name. . . . Green never managed to get more than a cent a word. . . . Erle Stanley Gardner is getting two cents from one magazine and three and a half from another.

This hint enabled him to note in his next letter, "And, believe me, that dope about the tentative two-cent rate listened as welcome as a girl's 'yes, dear' to me."

Later, Gardner could afford to be more demanding, as in a letter to Harry Steeger of Popular Publications in 1934:

> I think the time has come with my work when I should be paid on acceptance, . . . As it stands, you've had it for about a year, accepted and unscheduled. If I had been paid on acceptance, the money could

long since have been spent putting expensive gowns on beautiful women. So hold your checkbook in one hand, your fountain pen in the other, think the situation over and send me your answer.

As Gardner improved and his work attracted a reader following, he insisted upon not being paid "scrub rates," as he called lesser rates than those paid to writers of similar stature. However, he had noticed that writers who reached the top rate were limited in wordage, because an editor's budget was limited to a given sum, no matter how many words it bought; thus, the highly paid writer could price himself out of novelettes into the short-story class. As Gardner saw economic problems approaching the pulps, he insisted upon being paid the average rate. "I preferred to have no limit on my wordage, to write stories in whatever length I saw fit and stay within the editor's budget."

Also, it is likely that lurking back in his mind was a brutally frank editorial economics lesson delivered by F. E. Blackwell, editor of *Detective Story*, a Street & Smith publication:

> An editor is just a buyer of a commodity called a story. Of course he tries to buy it as reasonably as he can; for this reason if he can buy as good a story for two cents as another man offers him for three cents, he buys the story for two cents.
>
> I have always said that just as an employee takes his life in his hands when he asks for a raise—so it is with an author; for, while the employer might give the employee a raise during haying time, he might immediately go out and look for another man—and so, when an author insists upon a certain rate, if that editor thinks he isn't worth that rate, but a lesser rate, he'll only buy stories worth the money—the others just go back.

In May, 1929, Gardner conceived perhaps the cleverest ploy on record for getting a raise: One of his characters pleaded his case. It was six months after the introduction of Lester Leith, and it was obvious the new character was attracting a following. Gardner opened a letter to Howard V. Bloomfield, editor of *Detective Fiction Weekly*, with "Listen in on this," and then proceeded with a 2,500-word colloquy between Lester Leith and Erle Stanley Gardner:

> "Well, well, my old friend Lester, back on the job, eh?"
> "No. Pardon the correction, Gardner. I'm just dropping in for a chat. Perhaps my visit will inspire you with an idea that'll put you back on your job. You went trout fishing this morning, you know."

"Well, for God's sake! Didn't I just finish a yarn for *Argosy* day before yesterday? Do you want me to work all the time?"

"Certainly not. That's what I dropped in to see you about. . . . I wanted to chat business with you. I notice you sold *Air Adventures* an air yarn yesterday. Then there was a Western the day before. Rather a good Western, but a Western, nevertheless."

"Yes. What's that got to do with us?"

"Ah, yes, my dear Gardner. Yes, indeed. That's what I was coming to. What *has* it got to do with us? Has it ever occurred to you that stories about me take a lot of starch out of you?"

"Well?"

"Sold a yarn to *Clues* yesterday, eh?"

"Yep. Was a bit peeved at 'em for a while, but finally decided to shoot 'em a yarn or two again. Told 'em they had to boost the price, though, if they wanted any more."

"I see. But, getting back to business, your stock in trade is your imagination, eh?"

"Yes. But the wife's going to ring the dinner gong pretty quick, so get it off your chest. What's biting you?"

"You can get two and a half cents or more from your action markets, Gardner."

"Yes."

"And you write those stories in about half the time and with a quarter of the effort you put in on yarns about me. What's more, when you finish with a yarn about me you're mentally exhausted. You have to lay off for a day or so. Your output doesn't stack up when there are a couple of Leith stories in a month to what it did before I made your acquaintance, eh? No, no, don't answer me, Gardner, I can read the answer in your face. . . . You've got to start getting more money."

Bloomfield succumbed to the lengthy analysis of Lester Leith's value to the magazine and Gardner's plight as his underpaid creator. On June 22 he wrote that he was raising Gardner's rate to three cents a word. However, it meant more work. The editor shortly wrote again: "How is your production schedule? Are you doing enough work for two men, or can you do more for us? Would like to see a Lester Leith every three weeks at least, and that detective character in between."

Whatever the pay, Gardner always retained a warm spot in his heart for the woodpulps. He continued writing for them long after he was getting much higher rates from other markets. He wrote the editor of *Black Mask* in 1935:

As long as *Black Mask* has its present ownership, the question of *rate* isn't going to keep you from having enough of my work to keep my name tied up with your magazine.

That isn't a sacrifice; it's business. Ten years ago I was unknown. Editors bounced my stuff back as though it had been a handball in a gymnasium. *Black Mask* picked me up and published me. If my name has any value as a magazine asset today, it is due partially to what I have written and partially to the fact that the magazines who published me gave me a chance to write, and it's damned hard to say just how much of the credit goes where.

Write the editor a good letter.

Gardner's earliest letters to editors were timid, brief, and banal—or he followed the oft-repeated advice, "If you don't have anything to say, don't say it," and sent his manuscripts without letters. But Gardner was too much of a salesman, a hail-fellow-well-met type, to continue this. He became a prolific correspondent with an ebullient, outgoing approach. One editor expressed relief that he wasn't paying for Gardner's letters on a per-word basis and probably never realized that he really was.

Gardner letters seemed to reach out and clap the recipients on the back. Seldom was he long getting on a first-name basis, and never was he lacking words. He begged information on editorial needs, about readers, and about the editors and their work. He told of his adventures gathering material and of his troubles getting it onto paper.

Most writers try to project confidence in their ability. Not Gardner: He was completely honest. "You know, I'm more or less green at the game, and I don't know all the rules." . . . "Dog-goned if I know much about my own story analysis." . . . "Maybe other writers have my same problem, but are such good liars they don't admit it, or maybe I'm just mediocre." . . . "I can't judge my own work."

Most pulp writers were chary of letting editors know their submissions had been written for the slicks and sent to the pulps only after rejection by the likes of *The Saturday Evening Post* and *Collier's*. Not Gardner. For example, he sent "The Betraying Emotion" to Howard Bloomfield of *Detective Fiction Weekly* with a full confession:

> And then this yarn got rejected three times straight by the snottiest glazed paper magazines that ever gave an author the ha, ha! And so, my

dear duke, it comes to you with the flush of shame upon its tinted cheek. Not a virgin, nor yet a wife; but a humble bit of beauty that went to the big city and was pawed over by unappreciative hands, soiled and sullied, stripped of its outer envelopes by office boys, its pages riffled by calloused hands. And now there is nothing left for it to do but sell its soiled beauty at two cents a word. But the tragedy ends not there. Its aspirations for a higher sphere may have unfitted it to be clasped to the bosom of an honest-to-God magazine. And so I send a return envelope, its history, and my blessing.

As every good writer should, Gardner got the sympathy of his reader. He challenged Bloomfield to see something good in the story; if he was going to reject he had to find a good reason. The thought which went into the letter of transmittal was rewarded:

> Putting through a check for "The Betraying Emotion." We feel this bit of beauty, which was pawed around, no longer belongs to the amateur class.
>
> A good yarn, by the way. What was the matter with those other editors?

It is highly probable that had Gardner sent "The Betraying Emotion" out cold, accompanied by nothing but a return envelope, it would have come back posthaste.

Good facts don't make good fiction.

On November 21, 1924, Arthur E. Scott, editor of *Top-Notch*, laid down a maxim that is the hardest lesson for most beginning writers to comprehend: "Truth makes bad fiction, although fiction must read like truth."

There had been trouble before with a story called "The Third Flower." Gardner concocted it from the raw material of one of his trips. Scott returned it with a note, "You say you liked it because that's the way such an adventure would have developed. Undoubtedly you are right. A real-life mystery is all mystery until the solution is arrived at; but real-life mysteries do not make good reading. The reader has no interest in being kept guessing what it's all about until the final pages."

Gardner wrote back: He recognized the story's problems; nevertheless, he had faith. He believed he could revise it:

> "The Third Flower" needs a plot conflict to hold the reader's attention. As it is, the reader is chased all around Northern California until he gets all out of breath without having any well-developed conflict of interests marching toward some orderly climax. . . . I'm going to send it out to another magazine and if it doesn't sell as it is, I'm going to revise it a bit and have the elements of plot begin on the boat.

He spent considerable time on revision and submitted the story to every potential market he could think of before regretfully consigning it to the morgue.

Gardner prowled the desert, finding odd places and collecting in-the-flesh characters. However, actuality proved no guarantee of editorial agreement with the facts he uncovered. This was driven home by "The Lord Mayor of Rhyolite."

Gardner found the ghost town of Rhyolite, Nevada, a charming anachronism with an elaborate railroad station dating back to 1906. He took pictures. He researched and found the city charter still provided that any three men who resided in the town for a specified period could "elect themselves to office, vote city ordinances, levy taxes and, in general, have themselves a ball."

He put together a yarn in which a spurned cowpuncher quit his job and went to Rhyolite to become its duly elected mayor and pass ordinances which gave the mother of his heart's desire her comeuppance, resulting in wedding bells. It was a funny story—or at least Gardner thought it was: "I tried to give it a happy-go-lucky lilt and wind it up with a bang. I like it better than any yarn I've turned out in a long while."

However, Eastern editors unanimously decreed that it would be impossible for any city of that sort to exist. Readers would not accept it. Gardner sent photographs of the railroad station and other buildings, and the proof backfired:

> The editor was good enough to answer me, stating that he was evidently in error about Rhyolite but that the story had technical defects aside from the reference to Rhyolite and he didn't want it on any terms. That was the last word I ever received from that editor except a flood of rejection slips, which continued without a break.

After being offered many times upon editorial altars, "The Lord Mayor of Rhyolite" still languishes in Gardner's file of unpublished Westerns.

About a year later Gardner took up with an old prospector in the desert mining town of Randsburg, California, where a crooked assayer and a claim jumper had been at work. He wove the facts into a story and learned from a New York editor that an assayer would "starve to death in Randsburg"; desert prospectors knew their ore and had no use for assayers. Gardner took pictures of the numerous buildings in Randsburg with weathered signs over their doors: ASSAYER.

But he remembered "The Lord Mayor of Rhyolite" and thought better of sending the photographs East. Instead, he dug an old Western out of the morgue, brushed it up with a new title, and mailed it to the editor with a letter to the effect that since he had an encyclopedic knowledge of the West, he would undoubtedly appreciate this story.

> Within a week I had received a check for six hundred and fifty dollars—and I had learned something about corresponding with editors.
>
> From that time on I sold this editor story after story. His magazine became one of my big markets. The readers liked my stories, the editor liked my stories, and I made many thousands of dollars.

Don't poach on the preserves of other writers.

Beginning writers most frequently learn by imitation, a practice sometimes abetted by editors who want to capitalize upon the current popularity of a character, a style, or a story type. When Gardner began writing for *Black Mask*, Carroll John Daly had just created Race Williams, a tough, impatient, aggressive private detective who used rapid-fire vernacular to narrate his own battles against gangsters, crooked politicians, and any master criminal who happened past Daly's mind. Race Williams's name was beginning to flash across the covers of *Black Mask* in large red letters.

Gardner immediately began to pursue the pulp writer's insurance policy, continuing characters who would attract a reader following and guarantee the writer a market. His first two tries were Bob Larkin and Ed Jenkins; both were soon in a fair way to earn positions on *Black Mask*'s pages. Editor North noticed similarities to Race Williams and issued a warning to Gardner:

> I want to caution you about your characters. Be careful not to tread on Carroll John Daly's toes. Both of your characters are very similar to

his Race Williams. So far, you have handled it very nicely, but I think you should read some of Daly's stories and consciously avoid duplicating any of Race Williams' stuff. Please don't misunderstand me—I know you won't. The similarity which I refer to is merely that both you and Daly tell your stories in slang, and Race Williams, Ed Jenkins and Bob Larkin all have contempt for law and take justice in their own hands. You can readily see how easily confusion might result, and how both you and Daly might some day be at each other's throats. I have already spoken to Daly about it. As I have said, at present all three characters have distinct personalities—Williams, a private detective; Jenkins, an outlaw; Larkin, an adventurer with no desire for gain.

Gardner immediately admitted that he had already studied Daly's stories "pretty carefully," but with the idea of making his characters different. "It's the style of telling that is similar. Now, of course, the first person present is a recognized style, used by lots of authors." Nevertheless, if there was any question of poaching "I'll be glad to either kill off both Bob Larkin and Ed Jenkins, or I'll switch to the third person."

That would not be necessary. "All we have to do is be careful," said North.

Not only were woodpulp editors wary of internecine warfare between their own authors as a result of imitation, in those early days they were jealous of the individuality of their magazines and did not want characters who were pale copies of those in rival publications—a scruple which does not bother present-day television, where the only difference between channels is likely to be the names of the actors who play the roles. On January 3, 1927, Editor Shaw of *Black Mask* wrote Bob Hardy, Gardner's agent at the time, asking him to issue another warning:

> Among the stories you recently sent me was one by him entitled "Tell-Tale Sands." This parallels closely—too closely I think—a long series which has made [W. C.] Tuttle well known in *Adventure*. Tuttle had Hashknife Hartley and a companion, wandering through the old cow country as more or less knight errants, seeking to adjust wrongs and help out the weal. And here are Fishmouth and Deuces Wild in the same role.

Hardy sent the story back to Gardner for rewriting "to make them less like the Tuttle yarns." Gardner wrote Shaw that he was junking the story; however, it was eventually rescued from permanent interment in the morgue and showed up three years later in *Complete Stories*.

Critics would subsequently charge Gardner with imitation of Dashiell Hammett's private detectives and his objective style, a charge which Gardner highly resented and hotly denied for many years.

Don't be hackneyed.

Most beginning writers who learn of their art from reading and imitation tend toward hackneyed ideas and style, and Gardner was no exception. Harry North, of *Black Mask*, was first to attack the problem.

Perhaps because Gardner looked upon himself as something of a lone wolf during his desert ramblings, he so dubbed one of his early series characters. North protested, a letter which not only helped mold Ed Jenkins but had a salutary effect upon Gardner's hackneyed tendencies:

> Calling Ed Jenkins the Lone Wolf is bad dope. The name is hackneyed. It has been used for Indians, Western bandits, underworld characters, detectives, and every one of the fifty-seven varieties of characters—on the stage, in the movies, in fiction, and in the newspaper headlines—ever since God was an editor. Can't you give him a more distinctive handle? . . . I'm willing to start him off right by going through your manuscript and changing the thing throughout. That's merely my best advice to a struggling young author.

Gardner quickly replied that Jenkins would be known as "the Phantom Crook." The character lived to inhabit seventy-four short stories and novelettes before it was all over.

That same year, Arthur Scott of *Top-Notch* registered a similar complaint on a larger scale. He greeted Gardner's first story of Speed Dash, the Human Fly, with such a spate of criticism that a less hardy writer would have immediately retired it to his morgue. The only thing Scott liked was the title:

> "The Case of the Misplaced Thumbs"—an excellent title, by the way—has a very stereotyped opening; the long description of Homer's training gets very tiresome and eventually the story develops into a dope-smuggling scheme, a subject . . . so over-written that we have practically banned it. . . . I would suggest revising it to open with

Homer's first lesson in observation in which he must succeed in order to eat. A very small part of the material you have might follow, bringing in the point about the man always joining his thumbs when considering, and then Homer's detection ability might be used in solving some other mystery than dope smuggling.

Gardner was not to be rebuffed. He bellied up to his typewriter and confessed his ignorance:

> I like the title and the central idea (and I wasn't old enough at the game to know that dope smuggling was trite), but the story as it stands is Rotten with a capital "R". I'm going to tear it all to pieces and send it back to you. . . .
>
> So don't forget me, and let's see if I can't ring your bell right square in the middle after this. I sure appreciate your courtesy, but you aren't running a correspondence school and it is an imposition to expect you to wade through mss. which aren't suitable.

Scott did wade through it again . . . and again. It took two revisions before Speed Dash, the Human Fly, was born.

Archie Bittner, an early *Argosy* editor, was death on trite plots. In June, 1930, Gardner sent him a Western and got it back in a remarkably short time:

> ["One-Man Law" is] nothing but another quite usual Western story. This yarn of thirty crooks being licked by the combination of the old time sheriff and the desert is hoary with age. Probably one of the Western magazines will grab it but I don't think we want it.

The story finally sold to *Clues*, but in the meantime the ever-persistent Gardner was back at Bittner. The following month he sent him another offering with his usual frank delineation of its previous rejection. Mr. Corcoran, of *Everybody's*, "says he doesn't like it for reasons hard to define." Bittner was painfully specific in his definition:

> "Both Barrels" strikes me as an average, fair to middlin' Western. It is none too easy to follow and in spots becomes decidedly dull and tedious. Likewise, the central idea seems to be the usual standard stuff with nothing new or inspired about it. We use Western stories all right, but I want them to be especially good. At least outstanding in some respect. I don't feel this can be said of "Both Barrels."

Gardner was continually having trouble with his "Whispering" stories for *Argosy*, a series of stories about the desert. By 1932 Don

Moore was editor, and he was no less a taskmaster than his predecessors: "You have been running too much formula in these, having almost always the same cast of characters acting on the same motives, with the same complications in their pasts." . . . "Frankly, it sounds too much like a rehash of a couple of other desert stories of yours." . . . "Strong tricks based on desert knowledge, real variation in the intrigue and double crossings based on plot invention, novelty of situation, and really varied quirks of character, will give you the variety you need." . . . "You have been letting yourself fall into a routine of finding a rock stuffed with gold."

Bittner's most scathing criticism came in September, 1932, when the woodpulp professor was obviously irritated that past lectures had apparently fallen on deaf ears:

> I am not saying that you work harder on your detective yarns than you do on these, for I feel you put better atmosphere and color into the yarns you write for us, and just as good characterization. But you definitely and absolutely do not plot them as sharply. I wish you would think this over, putting aside your rationalizations about how you cannot combine atmosphere and plot—that is, I feel positive, merely an after-explanation to yourself of a certain never-admitted laziness in working out your adventure climaxes. I do not mean that they have to be tricks, such as made your whispering stories so strong; but there has to be a certain amount of invention, of necessity and inevitability of outcome, and of ascending climax. Read over these last few pages and see if you do not get my point—you have made your normal climax (the method by which the villain was forced to confess his fraud) into a weak, casual, accidental, not convincing anticlimax—the villain could just as well have died without confessing, and the hero had no reason to believe that he could be broken physically.

The sting was taken out of the long castigation by a postscript: "I really want to see this story back as soon as you can build up this climax." Gardner took the criticism in good spirit. He revised the yarn and returned it immediately, maintaining the problem had really been lack of knowledge of Bittner's editorial desires; however, his future stories, particularly for *Argosy*, were noticeably less trite in plot structure.

Later that year, Captain Joe Shaw was holding forth on the shortcomings of writers who had ruined the reading public by hackneyed treatment and of other editors who had let them get away with it: "The reading public grew tired of planes and of six-guns simply because of the utterly ridiculous use of these and other props, and the fact that the majority of writers were telling stories of mere dressed-up symbols and not of men."

Gardner's response revealed the coming maturity which would shortly raise his work above the pulp level:

> In my opinion it is an absolutely correct diagnosis of the situation. On every hand we hear that the public has grown tired of gangster stories, whereas, as a matter of fact, what the public has grown tired of is a senseless repetition of stereos that might just as well have been written with a rubber stamp as with a typewriter, and I think that your comment really goes to the fundamental reason of the public's attitude.

Don't give your readers a headache.

Woodpulp editors did not necessarily buy stories on the basis of personal preference for literature, as Harry North pointed out to Gardner shortly before he moved on to *The New Yorker*: "I really enjoyed 'Hard as Nails,' which is more than I can say about some of the stories we buy. Damned tiresome always reading stories with the idea of pleasing imaginary readers." A good editor was one who kept his finger on the pulse of his audience and could sense the faintest change in attitude before it happened. North elaborated upon the situation in response to Gardner's next story:

> Regarding this story, I think it's a peach, but I do not know where you are going to get it published. If you could once appreciate the fact that the publisher of *Black Mask* is printing the magazine to make money and nothing else, perhaps you would be able to more nearly guess our needs. "Greed of the Gods" is too much of an incentive to think to be of interest to our readers. Now I am sure that you wouldn't want to cause them any headaches.

Arthur White, Jr., of the Frank A. Munsey Company, was more specific in rejecting "Terror Island":

> The start was rather intriguing, but after one got interested in the queer wolf-like animal, one felt rather cheated at the finish by having so little attention paid to this phase of the yarn. The whole latter portion of it seems too confused. You know our motto has always been good, easy

reading. He who wants to study out what the author is driving at buys *American Mercury* or *The Atlantic Monthly*.

Harry Steeger of Popular Publications was brief and to the point:

> I believe the stories in *Dime Detective* are unusually good for a detective magazine, but don't want to get them too high hat. A pulp magazine caters essentially to those seeking entertainment, and they don't give two hoots in hell about style, psychological problems and other what-not.

Gardner relegated all three stories to the morgue. So much for "Art for art's sake"! His next letter to an editor reiterated the lesson he had learned: "You say that you think the readers would rather be excited than interested, would rather have their emotions appealed to than their intellects. In this I entirely agree with you."

In 1929 Captain Shaw had been laboring to put across the magazine's policy to *Black Mask* writers. He had explained it to Dashiell Hammett, and the urbane San Franciscan had come back with a summary which was obviously better than Shaw's explanation. On July 30, 1929, Shaw quoted it for Gardner's benefit:

> So I am going to give you my own slant on things as Hammett expressed it.
>
> "What's wanted of me now in your scheme of things—as I understand it—is both-feet-on-the-ground stuff that asks no credulity of the reader. What isn't inevitable—gets the air. The attempt should be rather to make vivid, dramatic, for the reader that which he will accept without proof than to try to convince him that some outstanding situation is not impossible."

Many would-be pulp writers fell short of the audience because they let slick-paper techniques and writing style invade stories destined for the pulp audience. Woodpulp readers did not cotton to either mixed drinks or mixed stories. Gardner was beginning to get the idea when he submitted "The Gems of Tai Lee" to Archie Bittner. He wrote:

> "The Gems of Tai Lee" is a good yarn, but it's a combination of the white paper and the woodpulp. The final touch of having the gems lost might appeal to white paper, but it wouldn't to woodpulp so much. I should revise it and make two stories out of it. However, having a woodpulp market that I think will be glad to take it, I'll probably be too damned lazy.

Gardner was right; he should have revised the story. Bittner summarily rejected "The Gems of Tai Lee" and—after revision—it finally landed in *Clues*.

Gardner began to see the distinction between the two audiences as early as the mid-1920s, but he had not yet absorbed sufficient story and character know-how from the pulps to crack the more lucrative slick markets. In a left-handed way, this was responsible for Perry Mason.

The seed for the popular lawyer-detective was planted in 1926 when Captain Shaw, *Black Mask* editor, casually suggested Melville Davisson Post's *Country Gentleman* stories might be a good model for Gardner. Post was a lawyer and writer, best known for detective stories about Uncle Abner, a Virginia squire. Gardner responded with an idea which has a familiar ring to Perry Mason fans:

> How's this? A third person series of a lawyer whose sense of justice is a lot stronger than his sense of legal ethics who habitually outsmarts the district attorney, with the action taken from court before a reader's eyes *or*, a first person series of a lawyer who is always consulted by crooks, gets into lots of action outside of the courtroom and then comes into court (the reader being familiar with the facts) and drops a legal bombshell.

Gardner had second thoughts as to the suitability of such stories for *Black Mask's* action-oriented readers. As he laid the idea in abeyance, he wrote to Shaw:

> The only argument against a good legal series is that they all have to be founded upon some clever trick, some original twist which involves reader thought in order to follow it. I am wondering if your readers don't prefer the type of story in which everything is action and they don't have to think to follow the yarn.

You can't flout your readers' morals.

An editor is a guardian of his readers' morals and beliefs. If he is to remain an editor, he must understand that a reader does not spend hard cash to have his beliefs—or prejudices—deliberately flouted, even if he is a militant liberal with a firm conviction that everyone should be broadminded and listen to that which he doesn't believe or understand.

This is one of the most difficult lessons to get across to traditionally Bohemian writers and crusaders who want to display libertine yearnings or hide messages in their fiction. Editorial taboos are maintained on behalf of readers. In a few rare cases, a no-no stems from an editor's personal prejudice. In either case, the writer needs to know and conduct his characters accordingly.

Although the pulps were replete with blazing guns, stabbing daggers, slashing swords, and assorted poisons and tortures, it was an inviolate rule that deliberate murder or innate cruelty by a hero was unthinkable. This was Gardner's earliest lesson in the matter of morals. In 1924, Harry North had promised to buy the first Ed Jenkins story after certain corrections were made; however, upon getting the manuscript back, he discovered to his editorial horror that murder had been committed by the hero:

> It did not occur to me on the first reading that the Lone Wolf deliberately planned a cold-blooded murder in sending Shero to the electric chair. To heroize a man who plans such an act (even though Shero had it coming to him) does not seem to me to be the sort of thing we should publish. We do not object to murders in cold blood by the so-called villain, or to killing in self-defense by the main character; but I think that you can readily see the objection to murder as planned by the Lone Wolf.

Gardner got the point, repaired the plot according to suggestions which North gave him, and a properly heroic Ed Jenkins was off and running in "Beyond the Law" in the January, 1925, issue of *Black Mask*.

Way back in 1594, Thomas Nashe's *The Unfortunate Traveler, or The Life of Jack Wilton* was published, the first English historical novel and picaresque tale. It was a precursor to many such stories which supplanted the chivalrous heroes of the age with likable but knavish scamps who exploited those in elevated positions. From that date, literary history has been studded with captivating rascals, such as O. Henry's Gentle Grafter series.

However, by the 1920s "Crime does not pay" had become an editorial tenet. In spite of blood-dripping covers, the woodpulp stories were morality tales of the first water. True, the perennial Robin Hood type could steal ill-gotten gains and redistribute the wealth to worthy causes, but it was unthinkable that he should personally profit thereby. It took a series of editorial rebuffs to drive home this fact to Gardner, who liked the irony-of-fate story as well as the next writer.

Don Moore of *Argosy* wrote:

> "An Iron-Clad Out" is a little too obvious, and I am not keen about the idea of the crooked cop's getting off scot-free.

Howard Bloomfield of *Detective Fiction Weekly* was not happy with the popular Lester Leith:

> Here she comes back again. . . . you have taken Lester Leith out of character. The hotel thief gets away intact with all his loot and Lester indirectly robs not a crook, but Mrs. So-and-So. The effect is that Lester Leith loses his justification and the crook gets away clean.

Furthermore, as Bloomfield wrote on another occasion, every story should have a hero:

> I don't buy stories in which everyone is some kind of a rat, on the theory that we want a nice shining hero somewhere to take the reader by the hand.

Just one time Gardner got away with an out-and-out villainous hero, in an exceptionally well-written yarn, but the acceptance was accompanied by a stern warning from Archie Bittner that there would be no more of it in *Argosy*:

> I do not care for stories of frustration—where the reader is asked to follow the fortunes of a villain. Your Chinese short (forget the title) is that sort of yarn. It has no hero, and presents a pretty shoddy set of characters. So—I am buying the yarn.
>
> We can use it for a change—it is nicely worked out and written. But don't send us any more like it.

Furthermore, officers of the law should be respected, as George Briggs Jenkins pointed out in rejecting a story:

> I did not like the idea of arresting a sheriff, even though it's done for perfectly good reasons. Holding an officer of the law up to ridicule happens in real life, and it will probably happen sometime in *Top-Notch*, but this story just did not make the grade with me.

Most woodpulp readers liked to identify with he-man, hard-drinking, hard-fighting characters who could hold their liquor, particularly during the Prohibition era when drinking placed one daringly outside of a law which was not universally acclaimed. However, there was a limit, as Bittner pointed out in rejecting a story entitled "Tequila":

> This yarn certainly reeks of tequila. That's about all I can see in it. The plot itself is far too wild and wooly and depends altogether too much on the hooch to put it across. Many of our readers would not care for as much booze as this, in the first place. And a good many others who like to believe their fantastic stories would resent having this one put over as the ravings of the drunken man.

Gardner consigned "Tequila" to the morgue: "When I wrote it I was all chuckles over the thing, but after a couple of days when I cooled off I realized I'd written something that appealed to *me*, and that it wasn't what your readers wanted at all."

During the earliest days of the pulps, women were unto plot as furniture is to a room: helpmates as evidence of respectability or fair maidens to be rescued. However, during the post-World War I period, sex was definitely rearing its head and posing a thorny issue: Judge Ben Lindsey advocated trial marriage, Mrs. Bertrand Russell defined "the right, equally shared by men and women, to free participation in sex experience," and "true" confession magazines appeared on the newsstands. Gardner sent his series character Señor Arnaz de Lobo to join the trend, and Howard Bloomfield's letter reflected the pulp viewpoint:

> I have just read your Lobo story "No Rough Stuff." It is a swell job. He is a very horny character, by the way, rapidly turning *Detective Fiction Weekly* into *Snappy Stories*. And of course it is all-right because it will be obvious to everyone that these girls he meets aren't virgins anyway. And it is not necessary to remind you that we cannot have him rape any of them right in our family magazine.

In the mid-1920s, when Captain Shaw took over the editorship of *Black Mask*, he was wrestling with the fact that women existed in the real-life world and, consequently, were going to have to inhabit the pages of his magazine. He wrote Gardner's agent in regard to the treatment of women:

> I have been studying our best writers on our main theme—stories having to do with crime detection—for the purpose of discovering the one most qualified to handle a female character. In some he [Gardner]

has "used 'em rough"; in another, he has overstressed the flapper type, and in still others he has suggested an intimacy of relation that I would not care to see in *The Black Mask*. I don't want too much femininity; rather a masculine treatment of female character.

Black Mask was to exert a considerable influence over Gardner's handling of fictional women. In his Ed Jenkins series he had Helen Chadwick, rich and socially prominent, fall in love with Ed. The Phantom Crook was wanted by the police and hated by the underworld; he knew that a wife would lead a life of constant danger. However, readers began to clamor for Ed to do right by Helen. Gardner performed the ceremony.

He started the next story with Ed and Helen in a hotel room, happily married. Ed was surveying the street below for enemies while Helen ironed her dress. Shaw did not view this domestic scene as "a masculine treatment of female character." Later Gardner told of the repercussions:

> Captain Joseph T. Shaw, editor of *Black Mask*, sent the story back with a gasp of horror. The idea of having Helen Chadwick without a dress in a hotel room with Ed Jenkins—*Black Mask* would never stand for such a risqué situation as that.
>
> So I got mad and killed Helen off.
>
> It was a horrible thing to do. My daughter wouldn't speak to me for a month.* Readers wrote in quivering with indignation.
>
> Captain Shaw accepted her death with equanimity. He probably felt it served the girl right for removing her dress in the presence of her husband.

This experience crystallized Gardner's attitude in regard to the marital status of his favorite female character. For thirty-seven years Della Street and Perry Mason worked side by side, but Gardner kept them too busy with legal problems and murders to give serious thought to marriage—in spite of public clamor. Gardner explained his position:

---

* Years later his daughter remembered, "My father didn't think a young girl should be reading *Black Mask* and other woodpulp magazines, but I was a great fan of his Ed Jenkins stories, among others, and I used to sneak into his study and read all his carbon copies while he was practicing law."

As an author I am in love with Della Street. I am not going to kill her off. And when better authors than I am find themselves unable to cope with the problems of a married hero, I'm not going to paint myself into that corner again.

5
LEARNING THE BASICS

The woodpulps were at the bottom of the pay scale, the last stopping place for the work of accomplished writers. Those dregs of the literary marketplace were capably written but generally unsuitable because they were slanted toward slick-paper audiences. Good stories *which appealed to their readers* were the lifeblood of despairing pulp editors, who had to increase circulation or see their magazines suspended in favor of more profitable publications—usually under other editors. Therefore, the practice of latching onto promising tyros and teaching them the basics of story writing was not entirely altruistic; it was, in fact, self-preservation.

Erle Stanley Gardner was one of the most eager beginners who ever came along. He freely admitted his ignorance, he begged for criticism, he questioned any points he did not understand, he kept a "fault book" in which he recorded problems and solutions, he practiced what he learned in revisions so that editors knew he was paying attention, and his published stories almost immediately began to attract readers by the score. In short, he was an editor's dream come true.

After he had attained some measure of success, Gardner was attracted to the literary agent route: Even if an agent didn't make more sales, he relieved the writer of reading letters of rejection and re-mailing manuscripts. However, Gardner shortly noticed that he was not getting as much criticism. He seemed to be losing his touch and getting more flat rejections which the agent brushed off with noncommittal remarks such as "Damn!" and "Their loss!" or cheerful forecasts of sales to other markets.

In 1925 Gardner asked Arthur Scott of *Top-Notch* his attitude toward agents. Scott replied somewhat circumspectly: "As a general rule an editor does not take up stories with an agent in the same way he does with an author and point out things that may be corrected, unless it is something he needs badly."

That was enough for Gardner. He immediately severed connection with the agent. He would get back with him if and when he ever wrote a book. Later, Gardner turned book and slick-magazine marketing over to an agent, but he continued to deal directly with the pulp editors who had taught him the fundamentals of fiction.

First-person narrative is not an easy way to go.

Virtually all beginning writers are attracted to first-person narration. The writer feels as one with his character, and words just naturally flow easier—"like talking." However, the narrow viewpoint restricts plot mobility, and the technique generally arouses editorial rancor because of tendencies toward egotism and rambling verbosity. The former alienates readers and the latter weakens suspense and slows action. Gardner liked first person because much of his background material came from personal experience while roaming the California and Nevada backcountry.

Shortly after George Briggs Jenkins took over editorship of *Top-Notch* in 1926, he wrote Gardner a gently warning letter:

> Some people object to first-person stories on the ground that the person who tells the tale says "I, I, I" and consequently is as much of a bore as the person who says "I, I, I" in real life.

Gardner took issue, pointing out the popularity of his first-person stories in *Black Mask*, particularly the Ed Jenkins series. He tested the water with a story entitled "The Hidden Clue." Editor Jenkins displayed the sincere fairness which endeared him to writers:

> I've arranged to get a copy of *Black Mask* which contains one of your Ed Jenkins stories, and I'm going to read it, and then write you what I think of it. As I've written to you before, generalizations are tricky; few hard-and-fast rules apply eternally. I do not glow with enthusiasm when thinking about first-person stories; the yarns that stick in my mind are usually third-person. Honestly, I wish you'd convince me that your first-person yarns are better than your Speed Dash stories. I was not won over

by "The Hidden Clue," but you're going to have another chance, and as many chances as you want.*

When Jenkins died on October 11, 1932, the woodpulp school lost one of its best and most dedicated instructors, and Gardner lost one of his most respected editorial friends. Whereas Gardner quickly got on a first-name basis with other editors, George Briggs Jenkins was always "Mr. Jenkins."

Gardner labored at perfecting first-person narration, and he was obviously successful; however, continuing notebook entries show that he never ceased to worry about it. Even after the team of Donald Lam and Bertha Cool had proved themselves in book form—in the first person—a notebook entry reveals that Gardner was still concerned:

> Check up on this—
> I get better writing in my first-person stories because the characters take charge of things better. Bertha in a taxi says "Not a damn thing" and drives away. Whereas my characters are too inclined to all act as they should to advance the story—the minute I get them into the third-person narrative. Let them take things into their own hands.

First, get your reader's sympathy.

There was general editorial agreement that the principal character in a woodpulp story had to arouse reader sympathy, but there was sharp division of opinion as to the best way to achieve this all-important factor in reader identification. Joe Shaw of *Black Mask* summed up the advantage: "The single quality which makes an action story effective lies in an appealing character who instantly gains the sympathy of the reader, awakening the desire which holds the reader's enthusiastic interest to the end to see this appealing character come through his or her difficulties successfully."

George Jenkins believed motivation was the key:

> Once again you've the conflict of individuals, a villain battling for his own selfish, sordid ends, with Speed battling merely to solve a mystery. We appear to lack, in this synopsis, the sympathetic motivation that you've had in other stories, . . .

*"The Hidden Clue" was published in *Top-Notch* May 1, 1927, under the title "The Hope-So Hunch."

By all means have Speed in danger of being shot, stabbed, hung, trapped in a mine, etc., for then our readers will read to see how and if he escapes. They want Speed to survive. They want him to survive because they like him, he's battling against crooks, and so on.

Don Moore of *Argosy* thought the secret resided in a combination of understandable conflicts and clarity of presentation:

The other thing that bothers me in this is that the aims, problems, conflicting schemes, and even the action are so remote, devious, obscure, and cryptic that the story is hard to follow and does not arouse much urge, or suspense in the reader. . . . I feel that a conflict over a scrap of paper, no matter how important the treaty, is hardly important enough to warrant a serial.

Howard Bloomfield, *Detective Fiction Weekly*, was convinced no reader could identify with a character unless he could place himself in the same situation:

The reader can visualize himself as having an eggcup, an ashtray, a Rhode Island Red rooster and wondering what the hell can come of that conglomeration. But organizing committees and companies goes into more or less vague and indefinite affairs beyond his depth. . . . I have a notion the average boob draws back from a chess playing character.

Phil Cody was certain braggadocio destroyed reader sympathy:

My own reaction to the *Buzzards* story has been keen regret that nobody killed Black Barr. No man as proud of himself, no man as lost in admiration of his own prowess, no man as convinced of his own greatness should be allowed to live, when Heaven cannot help but mourn his absence.

Harold S. Goldsmith of Popular Publications maintained that reader sympathy derived from the principal character's involvement in story circumstances:

To my mind, character sympathy is built in two ways: 1. It is developed because of the betrayal of a very likeable character. 2. It is strengthened in proportion to the opposition that the main character receives.

More than thirty years later Gardner would reflect this idea in his notebook in reference to a Perry Mason story he was plotting on December 5, 1958:

Regardless of the market I plan to reach, the Perry Mason story must deal with character conflicts—human emotions and situations which flow out of the relationships, rather than characters used merely to support the situations. Menace and suspense must flow naturally from what the people do and what they do must be logical.

Such diverse editorial reactions launched Gardner into a lifelong study of the problem of arousing reader sympathy for his characters. He consulted readers and critics, he read authorities, and he studded his notebooks with observations and conclusions. He became a self-made expert in the field and—eventually—when economic difficulties and competition were besetting the pulp-magazine industry, served as an ex-officio adviser to his old woodpulp editors.

Start with the story.

Failure to engage the reader at the beginning is one of the most common deficiencies of unsuccessful fiction. Every writer longs to turn back to those "Once upon a time—"days when an author could tell all about the characters, the setting, and the situation as a prelude to starting his story. Gardner was no exception, but editors were dead set against it. Arthur Scott had frequently mentioned slow openings and Gardner had corrected the problem, but "The Haunted Hallway" had a large cast of characters and a complicated situation to introduce. It came back:

> You have again fallen into the error of the long introduction. Getting together the characters, as you call it, takes about twenty pages, none of it particularly interesting. The main thing in a story is to get a grip on the reader at once. Hugh MacNair Kahler, the *Saturday Evening Post* writer, says he sweats blood over his opening sentence, and he learned that trick *here*. If a person's interest is not held at the start, the chances are he will not continue to read the story. That's one thing you would do well to bear in mind.

Archie Bittner had the same complaint on behalf of his *Argosy* readers, though he thought the story started a bit sooner: "The story doesn't really start until page sixteen. Perhaps completely rewritten, starting off with the crime."

Gardner filed "The Haunted Hallway" in the morgue and moved on to other ideas. Captain Shaw delineated the reason for the problem: "The movies and other things of our hectic life have educated the public to quick reading. You have to catch their interest with the first line and keep 'em moving to the last." Shaw cast an ever-jaundiced eye at the philosophical openings which so many writers were borrowing from an earlier, more leisurely day of writing. He cautioned Gardner:

> It would be a pretty difficult task to interject meditative bits and not slow up the action. However, every now and then, but not too often, it might be done but not at the very opening of the story.

Gardner loved the desert and he particularly enjoyed writing "Whispering" stories for *Argosy*, a series based upon personal exploration of "secrets" and "mysteries" upon which he lavished description. Archie Bittner kept sending them back for revision. He could have saved considerable time and trouble by having the following typical complaint printed up in bulk:

> There is just one point about the yarn I want to call your attention to and that is the somewhat excessive atmosphere with which it opens. For our purposes it will be better to get into the story a bit more quickly. Atmosphere is good stuff but not when ladled on too thickly.

Shortly after this, under the heading "Action," Gardner entered a maxim in his notebook which would guide him for the rest of his writing life: "Smash 'em between the eyes right at the start, then rush 'em off their feet, and don't let 'em up until the end of the story."

Action! Action! Action!

No matter the type of magazine—mystery, detective, Western, fantasy, adventure, war—the watchword among woodpulp editors was "action," as Gardner was constantly reminded until he began to get the hang of it. The always outspoken Captain Shaw wrote him:

> Now I will state very clearly what I feel about "Push-Over." Throughout, it lacks vitality, any appeal that grips, sensation and, therefore, suspense. You will observe there is movement but no action until page 40.

And Anthony Rud of *Detective Story Magazine* said:

> I like Barney Killigen very very much. The only fault I can possibly find with the story is that Killigen is off stage so much. We do like to see

In search of ideas for his "Whispering" stories, Gardner explored such places as Afton Canyon, a tributary on the Mojave River about twenty-five miles east of Yermo, California.

him follow through his mysterious actions a little more than to be told about them after they occur.

At Popular Publications, Harold Goldsmith was pleased when he thought Gardner's problem had been alleviated:

> On your last Paul Pry story I was very glad to see that you had injected more action scenes in this particular yarn than in your previous ones. Considering the type of reader that is buying *Gang War*, I think each Paul Pry story should have a goodly amount of action-conflict.

Putting it all together.

Like every good lawyer, Gardner prepared a brief of what he had learned. As an admonition to himself, he reduced the *res gestae*—the facts pertaining to "The Case of the Well-written Story"—to a single index card which he could prop up in front of himself while he sat at his typewriter:

> Work on every plot until you have
>   1. Unusual opening incident
>   2. Complete character conflicts
>   3. Some emotional appeal
>   4. Some unusual slant of characters and situation
>   5. All stock situations eliminated
>   Make a genuine reader suspense in which he doesn't know
>   what will happen next and is surprised either by
>   (a) What does happen
>   (b) The way in which it happens

And then Gardner shared his information with Les White, a beginning writer and neighbor who lived in Ventura:

> The main criticism I ever had with your stories was that your characterization wasn't clear and that you wrote the whole thing as though it *had* happened. The reader wants to feel it *is* happening. In other words, don't step outside of your plot and write it as history. No one gives a damn about history. Write so that the reader is sucked into the swirl of the action, build up suspense.
>
> One good rule is to get an attractive hero in the first sentence, get him into trouble in the first paragraph. Have a villain in the second paragraph. Then put in three pages getting the hero in a worse

predicament. Have him grasp a solution which gets him out of the frying pan into the fire. Introduce a heroine. Get the hero out of the fire and have him pull the heroine out.

But the woodpulps want a hero. For the most part they want a manly, young, attractive hero who possesses almost superhuman qualities, either patent or dormant. They want their yarns in the third person for the most part, and they want action.

Try to write a story without a single cut back. That is start it and have it sweep along, one thing to another, with every single detail told by action. Don't say that the villain is a mean man with a wicked wallop. Show him sliding from his horse in a rage because the animal jerks away from him. Show him swing a terrific fist and crash the horse on the nose. That gives the reader the idea of the wickedness in his wallop. Then when the villain advances toward the hero with doubled fist the reader gets some suspense because he's seen what happened to the horse. But if you tell the reader the villain is bad and has a mean wallop it's history, and the less history you get in a yarn the better your chance.

6
THE READER'S SERVANT

Erle Stanley Gardner's philosophy of writing crystallized one day in 1926 when he forged all of the editorial criticism he had received to date and all he had learned about writing up to that time into a single short entry in one of his notebooks:

> My own approach to the question is different from that of the critic. I am a writer. I serve the reading public. The reading public is my master.

After that, he became an outspoken exponent of the idea that the publisher of a magazine was simply acting as a middleman in purveying merchandise—stories supplied by writers—to readers, the ultimate consumers:

> Any time we think it's Warner's [Eltinge F. Warner, of *Black Mask*] money that's paying us, we're cuckoo. Warner is merely the broker who offers our services to the reading public. It pays to be entertained, and it's the one that's paying us, paying us for doing our component bits in offering it a medium of good clean entertainment. This goes for the whole bunch. It's the public's money that pays our compensations. We manufacture and dress up the merchandise. The public buys it. Warner sells it at a profit. The more of it the public demand, the better prices they pay, the more profit Warner makes, and the more he can afford to pay us—you, me, all of us.

Early on, he explained his approach to Arthur E. Scott:

> In my stories I try to figure myself as a prospective buyer of a magazine standing in front of a hotel newsstand. Would my story title make me pick up the magazine to look at it? Would the first hasty

glance through the story make me buy the magazine, and would a reading of the yarn make me a regular subscriber? I know it can't be done, not right at the start anyhow, but there's no harm in being ambitious.

From time to time, it seemed to Gardner that editors were judging his submissions from the viewpoint of objective literary critics, rather than on the stories' qualities for exerting a subjective hypnotic effect upon woodpulp readers. The first editor he accused of this was George Briggs Jenkins, the highly literate editor of *Top-Notch*. Jenkins replied by return mail:

> I disagree with you that an editor does not read a story from the viewpoint of a reader. That is, this particular editor tries hard, sincerely, to get the reader's viewpoint. Just as you write stories to sell magazines, so I try to select stories that will make each reader want to buy another copy. If I don't get the reader's viewpoint, I'll edit a magazine that will appeal only to me.

Gardner pursued the subject of reader appeal, and discovered that Jenkins was not only conversant with his new theory but prepared to give lessons:

> Your analysis of stories is, in my opinion, founded on fact. I agree as to the development of individuality being the big thing, that we rebel against the monotony of our daily life. If things weren't so easy for us, if life was a struggle for food and against enemies ready to destroy us, we'd be so busy staying alive that we wouldn't have a chance to read. The urge for adventure, for "something to happen," drives us to the movies, the theater, to magazines and books. We like to see a character develop, grow; experience teaches a man; we add to our knowledge of men by hearing of, by reading of, the behavior, thoughts, and actions of fiction characters. Since we are dull and lead dull, stupid lives, we seek, in fiction, dare-devil, nonchalant, keen-witted fellows, who have interesting things happen to them. We find ourselves helpless in the net of circumstances, so (I quote from your letter) "in every type of stories that endures there seems to be a swift variety of events where the individual is dependent upon himself to master those events." Our fiction heroes *must* master events. He *does* master them. That's a big point, an important point, and I wish more writers realized it.
>
> Now if a reader can identify himself with a character, say to himself, perhaps not knowingly: "That's the sort of fellow I am, or would be, if I were in his shoes, and—that's what I'd try to do, and that's what will get

him out of his difficulty!" the author has caught and held the reader's attention. And that's an author's job—to rouse the reader's curiosity, interest, attention, whatever you want to call it, and—in the case of a serial or series—to make the reader want to read more of that serial or about the central character in the series.

As to things that will interest a reader, that depends upon the individual, therefore, we have different magazines, with different policies, trying to interest different minds. *The American Mercury* is aimed at one target, *Breezy Stories* at another, *Top-Notch* at a third, etc.

Although Gardner was convinced of Jenkins's sincerity and editorial ability, experience taught him over the next several years that all editors were not as knowledgeable. In 1933 Robert J. Hogan, a Texas writer, made a tour of New York editorial offices. Erle Stanley Gardner—the newly crowned King of the Woodpulps—came up for discussion, and Hogan wrote Gardner to pass along criticism he had heard:

"Gardner, if he wanted to spend more work to develop a smoother style of writing, could go over in a big way in big time. He has excellent plots and handles the story construction admirably, but his style detracts. He could write big time stuff for the best of money if he would work now to smooth out his style before he gets in a rut. Later it will be too late and after that he will never be a really fine writer in all probability because it will be harder to get out of the rut. It's too bad."

In only a few years this editorial soothsayer would discover he had put his saddle on the wrong horse, but right then Erle Stanley Gardner was pretty sure he knew what he was doing. He wrote Hogan to thank him for his letter and to expound his own views:

. . . a writer should slant his stories at his reader, rather than at his editor.

Editors are an educated class. They generally read visually. That is, they merely glance at a sentence, and it crystallizes in their minds. The bulk of the woodpulp readers do not read so readily. They are interested, primarily, in plot, secondarily, in intriguing character combinations, and not at all in style.

That which might seem more smooth to an educated mind, reading visually, would be slowed down in the reading to an uneducated mind until the action of the story would be lost.

Much of what is taken by competitive writers and many editors to be a general sloppiness of style in my stories, or a lack of polish, is, in reality, the result of careful thought on my part, and an attempt to get my stories across so that they will reach the average reader.

You put in your time going around to editorial offices, and finding out what editors want, and writing stories to please them, and you will gather a certain amount of acceptances. You will never build up a sufficient following to insure a continuation of those acceptances, and very shortly you will find your sales actually falling off. But if you start talking to readers to find out what it is that the readers want to read in a story, and then incorporate those factors in the stories you write, you will probably find that an increasing number of editors buy your stories, perhaps with an attitude of weary resignation, perhaps with a critical attitude, but because they have to do it because "the readers like your stuff."

From the very beginning, Gardner was solicitous toward his fans, taking pains to answer their letters and respond to any persistent criticism. He told H. Bedford-Jones about it:

As you probably know, I have always been a great believer in reader fans helping an author with his circulation. On the other hand, I consider fans the best barometer an author can have for an impartial test of how his work is getting across, and I have, therefor, not only not encouraged fans to write to editors, but have tried my darndest to keep anyone who knew me personally from writing to an editor, so that I could use the fan mail to see what the readers wanted and what they didn't want.

Gardner established "listening posts" among his reading audience. This practice started by accident when Gardner met one of his fans, an impecunious disabled World War I veteran whose spirits were as low as his meager pension. Gardner wanted to do something for the man, but out-and-out charity was not the answer; so he "employed" him to read magazines containing his stories and to pass them around among his buddies, soliciting comments not only on his stories but on the work of other writers. This bread upon the waters paid big dividends.

Gardner found the reports so valuable in assaying reader reaction that he recruited other typical readers; additionally, he began interviewing newsstand proprietors regarding their customers' buying habits. He shared the results of his studies with writers and editors whose stories and magazines were involved. For example, during the early 1930s when pulp houses were fighting economic troubles and each other by issuing new magazines, he warned Harry Steeger and Harold Goldsmith of Popular Publications that bringing out new titles without careful attention to quality of content could be a risky way to go:

> Fellows tell me around the newsstand that there is a certain limited circulation, or there was during times of prosperity, which would attract itself to any new title. There was a certain amount of what we might call curiosity buying. This lasted for one or two issues and then dropped off. That if the magazine was good there was a sufficient repeat business, and a sufficient additional business which came along to get the magazine going.

As the Depression deepened, the financial difficulties of the pulps were compounded by declining advertising revenues. Pulp publishers attempted to meet the problem by printing increasingly salacious and sensational material, "horror" appeal it was called, to bolster sagging circulation. Even though Gardner was by this time firmly established in the book field and well on his way in the slick markets, he could not silently sit by and watch the woodpulps work their own destruction. The indefatigable researcher located an advertising analyst in New Orleans during Mardi Gras. By judicious application of drinks, Gardner wangled from him the results of his studies. Again, he reported to Steeger and Goldsmith, as well as to other pulp editors:

> Briefly, the conclusion of these people, without knowing particularly or caring particularly why, was that there is convincing evidence to indicate that during the past few years the pulp market, while suffering some loss in circulation, *has changed the character of its circulation radically*, and is catering to an entirely different class of people which has only a small percentage of the purchasing power of the woodpulp customer of a few years ago.

As Gardner saw it, Steeger and Goldsmith were trying to "invade the cheap field and meet the cheapest competition":

> . . . Hell, in doing that, there is no need of having editors or even reading mss. Buy them by the pound, insisting only that there be a naked woman by page 3 who is threatened with a whipping with a cat-o'-nine-tails by page 7, and is about to be branded on page 29.
>
> The point I am making is that it is very apparent the better class of reader is being steadily alienated. There is evidence that not only has he quit buying the magazines, but that he has even quit looking them over

on the newsstand. It's all right to fight fire with fire, but eventually someone's got to put out the joint conflagration.

The situation finally got so bad that United States postal inspectors were looking askance at *Argosy*, one of Gardner's most beloved old woodpulp markets. Eventually, Popular Publications took over *Argosy* from the Frank A. Munsey Company. It is difficult to gauge how much Gardner had to do with it, but *Argosy* was soon converted into a highly-respected slick-paper men's magazine. With Harry Steeger at the helm, it published many Gardner articles and launched the Court of Last Resort in 1948. By 1953, Gardner was giving Steeger advice about how to appeal to this new breed of high-quality adventure-loving readers:

> . . . Too many times the adventure is described in synthetic terms. For instance, they will say that, "We made our camp that night by the banks of the stream, and early the next morning threw our sleeping bags into the automobile and started on up the winding road that went up the canyon," or "put our bedrolls on our horses, had a hurried breakfast and were off."
>
> Now what is needed is to give the reader the feeling of participation in the adventure.
>
> Camping is fun.
>
> Adventure is fun.
>
> Travel is fun.
>
> The article should describe the making of camp, the campfire, the warm bedroll, the thrill of lying on the ground and seeing the trees silhouetted against the stars, while the stars march silently by, the campfire dying down to coals, the sound of the stream, the noise made by a screech owl, and the general feeling of being out in the open. . . .
>
> The entire field in the magazine market is wide open in that the readers are being given all the time a series of adventures as those adventures are seen through the eyes of New Yorkers and edited by New York editors who are not themselves the adventure types. This makes a situation that is recognizable in the magazine stories themselves. There is not enough reader participation, and the idea should be to have the readers participate in every single thing in which the readers are interested.

Early in the 1930s, Gardner foresaw the decline of the pulps and readjusted his sights to bear on the book market. One book was probably responsible for this foresight: *The Reading Interests and*

Habits of Adults by William S. Gray and Ruth Monroe (New York: The Macmillan Company, 1929). It was a stuffy, highly academic study dealing with library patrons and readers of the "better class" of magazines. The only mention of pulps intimated that their readers were at the very bottom of the intellectual scale. Gardner mentioned this book to several editors. After reading it, he began to use the term "better class" in reference to readers and to slick magazines, and he began to experiment with the novel form in preparation for building a bulwark against the collapse of the woodpulp market. Erle Stanley Gardner always liked to have a second economic string to his bow.

7
LURING READERS

Gardner's most important discovery—the key to his success—was the "lowest common denominator of story interest." He marked the idea in an embryonic state in one of his earliest textbooks as James Knapp Reeve explained it:

> The plot is the machinery to be devised by the author to carry his idea or motive forcibly to the mind of his reader. . . . In such construction you are trying to work out the method by which Self-sacrifice may be accomplished, and the reader impressed with its nobility; or, the beauty and nobility of Love triumphant over all adverse factors and conditions that may come into the lives of your hero and heroine; how Justice must prevail even though the heart breaks; how a supreme regard for honor glorifies the individual, as does courage; and Loyalty is a motive related to these two, . . .

Various other literary analysts attempted to get at basic universal reader appeals, coming up with a vague mélange which left most beginning writers little wiser for their studies. It was nothing new; the search for a literary touchstone had been going on since Aristotle. But the task did not dismay Gardner. He took the trail in earnest—asking, reading, analyzing, contemplating, making entries in his notebooks, and experimenting.

His first attempt at definition resulted in the isolation of three universally popular character types: Robin Hood, who illustrated that "power lies in the people"; Cinderella, "good magic will reward virtue"; and Sherlock Holmes, "the easy learning, the masculine environment." But this was merely a rehash of the observation of others with the addition of an attempt to explain the popularity of

Sherlock Holmes, one of Gardner's favorites. There had to be more to it than that. Next he went at it from the direction of story type:

> Every story, or rather, every type of story that has succeeded has the common point of a single man, unaided, overcoming difficulties by the inherent power that is within him and attached to him. The western story gets by because the cowpuncher depends only on his gun for his law and order, for his safety. He is apart from the machine, away from the routine. The air story shows a pilot up in the air, away from civilization, fighting. The crook story shows a lone wolf fighting the law. The detective story features a hero who stands apart from the forces of law and order as represented by the cops, and fights his own battles against the crooks.

But this did not explain everything, stories appealing to women, for example. Next he began to read, carefully analyzing successful stories and reducing their basic appeals to themes. He came up with an admixture of old proverbs which readers seemed to enjoy seeing proven and character types which they apparently liked to have come out on top of the heap—or see defeated:

> 'Tis sport to see the engineer hoist by his own petard (the villain who overreaches himself)
> Man in position of power abusing that power and tripped up
> The old man who is still young
> Man who champions the underdog
> Why don't you speak for yourself, John?
> The ugly duckling who becomes beautiful
> Man who renounces reward and is doomed to independent loneliness
> Downtrodden person suddenly asserting himself
> The race is not always to the swift
> Virtue is its own reward
> There's many a slip twixt cup and lip
> Haste makes waste
> He who hesitates is lost
> Faint heart never won fair lady

As Gardner studied, he applied his findings to work at hand. For example, in August, 1929, when he was introducing a potential new series character to Howard Bloomfield of *Detective Fiction Weekly*, he explained the character's appeal as he saw it:

> As you know, I play a game with myself. Perhaps I merely kid myself. But I try to study stories that the readers like, reduce them to the lowest

common denominator of reader interest, and collect notes on reader psychology; that may mean something, or it may be just another method of kidding myself.

At any rate the reader should react to the psychology of a detective who is different. Here is no freak detective who goes about the solving of mysteries for the orthodox reward of having solved them.

. . . He has a contempt for the law and the lawyers. He regards the inequitable abortions of the law with unwinking amusement. He is interested in the inside story back of every crime, and he does "substantial justice." . . .

Deeply imbedded in the subconsciousness of the American people is a contempt for law and law enforcement. When the newspapers strut sayings like "You cannot convict a million dollars in an American Court" and when a citizen can walk the length of a downtown block and violate the United States Constitution half a dozen times in making the rounds, and finds the police virtually chaperoning the place. When he sees clever lawyers taking criminals and twisting and turning the very laws themselves until they snarl themselves in a hopeless maze and the criminal walks free, then the average man has a feeling of the law's futility.

Let's embody that feeling in a character who is a blond giant, supple, athletic, unwinking, stern, unyielding, but essentially human. He will be able to solve mysteries by swift thought, logical deduction. He'll work substantial justice in every case, and he'll gaze at the officers of the law with violet gray eyes in which there's just a trace of unwinking scorn, a twinkle of sardonic amusement.

Gardner's next step was to equate reader appeals with the satisfaction of basic human desires. He entered the list in his notetook:

Wealth
Happy sex companionship
Justice
Food
Happiness of environment
Opportunity to get ahead
Self-improvement
Wisdom . . . knowing more than another man
Influence
Put the overbearing boss in his place
Physical perfection or improvement
Domination of environment—mastery of others
Triumph of the underdog

He harked back to those early comments by George Briggs Jenkins, the old maestro at *Top-Notch*. These desires did not apply universally; they appealed to various segments of the total reading audience, depending upon individuals and what their environment was doing to them. From time to time, Gardner added to his list, updating to meet the changing audience.

Gardner's notebooks reveal that he seldom sat down to outline a plot without making a note of the lowest common denominators of reader interest which applied to the particular audience which he had in mind. For example, in 1951 he was editing a plot for a Perry Mason comic strip, tentatively entitled "The Case of the Braying Burro": "The old prospector is arrested and all he can give Mason by way of fee is the burro." A change in the color of ink shows a period of contemplation. Then Gardner noted the audience and pointed out to himself that the potential plot would satisfy his requirement for reader appeal on several scores: "Common denominator kid and adult interest. Animals—Adventure—Pursuit—New strange country. Mystery if not too complicated." The common denominator of interest was at the heart of every Gardner plot.

When it became evident that Perry Mason was prime television material, Gardner decided to organize his own production company, Paisano Productions, Inc. Past problems in obtaining adequate plots for radio plays and comic strips convinced him that he must exercise close supervision over story selection and portrayal of characters in order to maintain the integrity of his valuable literary property. Gardner did not write the scripts, but every one passed under his eagle eyes and almost inevitably he had suggestions for changes. As time went on, good stories became increasingly difficult to get.

Finally, in May, 1959, Gardner called a conference at Paisano Productions of all concerned with script preparation, selection, and production. It was a two-day session. On the second day, May 13, Erle Stanley Gardner held forth on the lowest common denominator of public interest, a discourse which turned out to be one of the finest dissertations yet on mystery plotting, the culmination of more than thirty years of study and practice.

Fortunately, Jean Bethell was there to be sure that it was recorded. It was transcribed and the copy was placed in the carefully guarded brown zippered notebook which Gardner kept close at hand in his study and carried with him wherever he went. Its pages show the wear of usage over the years which followed:

> In my opinion a good plot never hops into a person's mind. Nor do I believe it is possible for a person to sit down and think up a plot. I know I can't do it.
>
> A plot has to be built.
>
> If we know the necessary ingredients which go into a plot we can start taking those ingredients and fitting them together one at a time. If we are sure of the stability of our building blocks we know that by the time we get done putting them together we are going to have a structure. It may not be the structure we want but it is enough of a structure so that we can start remodeling here and there and get the type of structure we want.
>
> The first thing we need in connection with any story is a story situation which appeals to the public.
>
> The public wants stories because it wants to escape. We talk about escape literature, yet we don't stop to think of how we escape by the use of escape literature, what we escape from, and why there is this yearning for escape.
>
> Writing stories is a great profession and to be able to write interesting stories is a great privilege. The writer is bringing moral strength to many millions of people because the successful story inspires the audience.
>
> If a story doesn't inspire an audience in some way, it is no good.
>
> Any story which really inspires an audience has some basic appeal and for want of a better term I have assembled some of these and called them the lowest common denominator of public interest.
>
> Every successful story, and above all every successful character, has as his very foundation one or more of these lowest common denominators of public interest. Therefore whenever a writer reads a story or sees a character that appeals to him he should start looking for the lowest common denominator of public interest which is in that story or in that character and which has appealed to the public.
>
> There are three major characters who have been virtually indestructible in the course of fiction: Robin Hood, Sherlock Holmes and Cinderella.
>
> Bear in mind that it is not always easy to determine exactly what is the lowest common denominator of public interest. It is quite possible that the person will think he has it but find out that he doesn't have it. Therefore, as far as possible, the person should never try to get the interest germ or kernel out of one story or out of one character and think he has found the lowest common denominator. He must find

"This case has everything sex, sophistication, mystery, melodrama," he told detective Drake.

Television production of Perry Mason crystallized the appearance of previously undescribed characters in readers' minds, and *Saturday Evening Post* serializations began to use illustrations depicting actors who played the roles.

something which appears in almost every story that appeals to the public. Sometimes it is one denominator, sometimes another, but there probably are very few of these really lowest common denominators of public interest.

Take the case of Robin Hood. There are two lowest common denominators here. One of them is championing the underdog and the other one is the very subtle assurance given to people that the people themselves can oppose tyrants if they have the courage.

Our job of separating lowest common denominators is simplified because public reasoning instinctively recognizes these things and many, many of these lowest common denominators are expressed in terse sentences which are little proverbs.

For instance, the common expression, "Faint heart never won fair lady" is a very good indication of one of these common denominators.

Our whole progress of life is predicated upon the desire of the man to select a mate who can give him what he wants in his children and the desire of the female to get the man who can improve the race.

We have drifted far away from this in our present civilization, although the instinct remains. We now have erected so many safeguards that our civilization may be becoming the survival of the weakest, rather than the survival of the most fit.

However, in more primitive tribes we find this basic human instinct manifesting itself and it is still one of the best of the common denominators of public interest.

It is possible to bring certain ramifications of this principle into a story in such a way that it causes people to think.

For instance if we have a woman who is courted by a man who has great physical prowess but a low standard of ethics and his rival is a rather bookish individual who has no physical stamina whatever but does have great moral courage, we can create a story in which the superman makes the little man the laughingstock of everyone until a situation arises which requires a great showdown, where sheer guts and moral courage count, and then the bookish man comes through and the girl marries him.

This leaves a very satisfactory feeling in the minds of the audience because it has pointed out another common denominator of public interest which is also expressed in a proverb, that the race is not always to the swift.

However, to get back to Robin Hood.

People are oppressed in many ways. They are oppressed in many instances by the civilization they themselves have created. In other words, if they want sewage, police protection, and schools, they have necessarily harnessed themselves with taxes. If they are going to have taxes they have to have tax collectors. If they are going to have tax collectors they have to have penalties for the persons who hold out on taxes, and so it goes.

Yet people instinctively desire freedom and there is a vast yearning on the part of the people to be reassured that God is in His heaven, that all is right in the world and that justice will triumph over tyranny; that the blithe, debonair adventurer who sets aside all of the onerous laws which oppress the common people, yet who does it with a philanthropical and therefore beneficial idea in mind, is a hero.

In other words this person is doing what the average man yearns to do and has wanted many, many times to do.

In a good story the audience identifies itself with the hero and when the audience feels that it is identified with the hero and the hero does something truly heroic the audience feels inspired accordingly.

We have all had dreams in which we have been able to fly and there is a feeling of power when we waken before we quite realize that we have been dreaming, but while we still think we can fly.

This brings us to the Sherlock Holmes stories.

I have had a lot of people analyze in print and in conversation the charm of the Sherlock Holmes stories but I don't think I have ever heard any one of them who has given what is to me a convincing explanation of the common denominator of public interest which has made the character of Sherlock Holmes immortal.

It is my opinion there are two common denominators of public interest in the Sherlock Holmes stories.

One of them lies in the extreme masculine atmosphere and the yearning for freedom.

As pointed out, people want certain things. In getting them they have to pay a price. They don't want to pay the price but it becomes necessary. People don't want to pay taxes, they want schools and sewers. But schools and sewers go hand in hand with taxes.

The average man wants to get married and raise a family; at least, he wants to get married and then the family starts coming along because that is nature's way of carrying on the scheme of life. But when the family begins to come along there are doctors' bills, nurses' bills, the necessity to find a baby sitter when a person wants to go out; dirty diapers, teething problems; then later on, schools and schooling, clothes and clothing, and the problems of adolescence where the parent has to assume responsibility while at the same time pretending ignorance or innocence.

Sherlock Holmes and Dr. Watson were delightfully free from all of these. They had a bachelors' quarters so thick with acrid tobacco smoke any woman would have thrown them out on the sidewalk. They lived and reveled in this atmosphere and I think it is a big factor in the popularity of the Sherlock Holmes stories.

However, if we want to find the real basis for popularity I think we need to look at the advertising of the day.

The advertiser pays a lot of money for writing. He isn't paid for writing, he pays for writing. He has to buy the space in which he puts his copy and of necessity that copy must be good enough to bring in returns which more than justify the cost of the space. Therefore whenever we find any basic trend in advertising we can be certain that it is paying off, and if advertising is paying off it is paying off because it is getting public response. And if it gets a public response it is because it has touched a responsive chord in the minds of the public. Therefore by watching advertising we can get a pretty good idea of certain common denominators of public interest.

Sometime ago one of the advertisers started the idea of self-improvement without work: Play the piano in six easy lessons, "Imagine their surprise when I answered the waiter in French." The girl who got engaged wasn't the one with the charming personality and the good figure but the girl who washed her face with Woodbury's Facial Soap. The man who dominated the directors' meeting had been given Sanka Coffee the night before. The life of the party, with a wealth of information, was one who had had the foresight to subscribe to Elbert Hubbard's Scrapbook, and so on, down the line.

This trend of advertising is alarming, but it can't be discounted. It represents a growing trend on the part of the public to get something for nothing and to acquire culture while drinking Sanka Coffee or beauty while rubbing the lather of Woodbury's Facial Soap on the skin.

Sherlock Holmes had this common denominator of public interest and I think it is the big factor in the Holmes stories.

The reader identified himself with Sherlock Holmes to such an extent that Holmes' mental feats of observation and deduction appeared so easy the reader became convinced that he could go out and duplicate the processes. At least for a time, the reader thought he could fly and had the sense of power which went with it.

The Cinderella story has been told and retold many, many thousands of times. It is a common denominator which has the greatest public appeal. It is a soothing syrup to the unfortunate. It leads people to believe that there is somewhere a magic power, a fairy godmother, which will make their dreams come true—therefore it isn't simply a waste of time to have dreams. People love to dream, people love to yearn. If they can be convinced that the yearning and the dreaming have some solid foundation in fact they are going to love the media by which that belief is inculcated in their minds.

There are various modifications of the Cinderella story.

How many times have we seen in pictures the story of the young woman who wore her hair slicked back, had unsightly spectacles, dressed in a dumpy manner, and lost out or all but lost out to a female vamp who had curves and wiggles? Then suddenly there was a transformation. The girl got the right idea. She had her hair fluffed out, she put on spectacles which didn't show or used contact lenses, and became the ravishing beauty.

These things have a basic foundation in the human mind. The girl who is ugly yearns to be beautiful. If she is convinced that perhaps she can become beautiful she has received a terrific lift. It has helped her character. It has helped her master the problems of life.

There are many of these common denominators of public interest and yet probably fifteen or twenty of them would cover the whole gamut of successful story writing.

The point is that a writer in starting a story should first decide what lowest common denominator of public interest, or what combination of common denominators he is going to put in the story. Once he puts them in the story he knows he is starting on a firm foundation. If he doesn't have them in the story he doesn't have anything.

Therefore, when a script comes in, one of the first things to look for is whether we have satisfied our common denominator of public interest which must exist in the Mason stories.

Primarily this is the vision of the knight charging to the aid of the damsel in distress. It is the fairy godmother touch of Cinderella, in which justice is brought to the downtrodden. And it also has something of the Robin Hood because Mason's mind is about the same as Robin Hood's bow and arrow.

Therefore when I see a script where the characters are first presented in a disagreeable manner and Mason is given the job of representing someone who is unworthy of the benefits to be received from Perry Mason's activities I feel that we have insulted the character. We have reduced Perry Mason to the status of a mouthpiece.

It seems to me that the first thing we must strive for in every story is to have some character represented by Mason who is threatened with an injustice, who would be engulfed by circumstances were it not for the legal ingenuity and the moral courage of Perry Mason.

The only way to make an audience take a real interest in a person is to present a likable person in a sympathetic manner. The audience first has to know that person. Therefore, it seems to me that in creating a Mason show on television one of the first things to do is to start with some character who is to become Perry Mason's client and to make the audience like that character. And of course since the story is a Perry Mason story and we have to switch to Perry Mason so early in the story, we have to do some fast writing in order to get the attention of the audience, the interest of the audience, and the affection of the audience so that by the time events threaten to engulf this character and Mason enters the picture the audience is inclined to cheer.

This is the same lowest common denominator of public interest which on a physical plane was manifested by the beautiful woman kidnapped by the redskins and about to be taken off to a life of shame and torture when someone would summon the United States Cavalry and we would see the Cavalry galloping shoulder to shoulder, with the flag waving and the horses pounding over the road.

Everyone wanted to get up and cheer.

Mason has to do the thing mentally which the Cavalry did physically.

Therefore when I see these scripts come in where the first characters are disagreeable, where there is slapping and physical violence and it is hard to become interested in any particular character, then we see a crime committed and know that Mason is expected to solve that crime, I feel that we are selling our character down the river. I want to vomit at the idea of the great Perry Mason with his sense of justice, his basic faith in human nature, descending so low as to be hired to represent a person of that caliber.

In short, it seems to me that we can say to all writers that it is a basic rule of the Perry Mason stories that the audience must want the character to be represented by Perry Mason to come out on top.

If this is done too obviously we simply burlesque the whole situation. It must be done in a subtle manner.

The Mason stories are stories of mystery. It seems to me that in addition to a lovable character we should start with something in the line of a mystery which intrigues the audience.

I think there has been a tendency to start scripts from time to time with acts of violence and a little toughness. I think we should have a mystery.

What is a mystery?

When the story is finished all of the events must have a logical explanation. Therefore when we know the facts there is nothing mysterious about the opening events. In other words it is the job of Perry Mason to correlate those opening events and the subsequent events in such a manner that they do fit into a logical pattern, and this logical pattern points to the culprit in the case.

My definition of a mystery is that it consists of a series of interesting events which have sinister implications and the logic of which cannot be instantly comprehended by the audience.

Therefore it seems almost essential to me that we should open our stories with some event which attracts the interest of the audience, which seems to have somewhat sinister overtones because they know they are going to be watching a murder mystery, and which simply intrigues the hell out of the audience.

Obviously, getting such a situation is not an easy matter and if we try to conjure one up without knowing the basic rules pertaining to such a situation we are simply wearying our minds by trying to climb a mental greased pole.

There are however certain basic laws for getting such a situation and once we understand those laws we can build the situation into our story just as we can start with a common denominator of public interest and build that into the story.

In a mystery story the opening situation can best be understood by referring to what I have called the murderer's ladder.

Understand that it is not always necessary for the audience to see every step in this ladder but the writer should have each step in mind when he starts to think about the murder. He should know the motivation for the murder, he should understand the temptation, he should know the over-all plan.

However, the basic story situation comes when the murderer starts to climb from the rung of the ladder which represents the first action which can't be withdrawn. In other words, at a certain point the murderer has committed himself; he has started his action; he has broken into the house where he intends to commit the murder; he has surreptitiously boarded the yacht where his victim is sleeping; he has put the poison in the glass. He has done something which he isn't supposed to do and which, if detected, will expose the fact that he has murder in his mind. It is the point where he can't back up. In the motivation of murder it is the point of no return.

Once the murderer reaches this point it is only necessary to provide some event which makes his plans go awry in order to bring about a story situation. The murderer can't back up. He has to go forward. His plans have been knocked into a cocked hat. Therefore he has to improvise. He starts improvising with an image of the hangman's rope dangling over his neck. He has to improvise in a hurry. There is this terrific element of urgency which is crowding him.

Therefore he does something which brings about a sufficiently paradoxical situation as far as the audience is concerned, knowing only what it knows at that time, so that the audience is intrigued and sees a pattern of interesting or perhaps exciting events taking place with the unmistakable background of urgency, yet those are events which puzzle the audience, which arouse its interest and which bring about an atmosphere of mystery.

If we simply have characters thrown into a story, we have them push each other around and then have a murder and call on Perry Mason to solve that murder in the courtroom, we have insured ourselves an eventual ticket to oblivion.

Perhaps the best illustration that I can think of offhand of this necessity for a mystery lies in *The Case of the Borrowed Brunette*, although there as I remember it, it wasn't a question of the murderer's plans going astray but it was all a part of the murderer's plan.

In any event the murderer wanted a brunette of a certain description. He didn't want to have the persons who didn't answer that description get a good look at him. Therefore he put ads in the paper by which brunettes who had the necessary physical attributes were brought into contact by correspondence or by telephone and each brunette was told to be at a certain corner one block apart at a certain time so that the man who wanted to employ them could ride slowly by in an automobile and size up each brunette as he went by to see if she had the physical characteristics and the physical appearance that he wanted.

Now this is what I mean by starting the story with a mystery, by encountering a subordinate act of villainy but not the crime itself. In other words, in place of being called upon to solve a murder, Mason, driving down the street following the schedule of the murderer was astounded to find that on each street corner of a somewhat deserted residential district (that is, a residential district which was devoid of traffic at that hour of the day) there was a striking brunette very similar in appearance, each one waiting expectantly on the corner.

This aroused the interest of the audience. It had sex, it had mystery and it was a paradoxical situation which impinged upon the life of Perry Mason.

Please bear in mind that I am not laying down arbitrary rules or trying to put the imaginations of writers in a straitjacket, *except* insofar as the lowest common denominator of public interest is concerned. On that point I am adamant. I think that our stories must have one of the lowest common denominators of public interest or else they simply can't hold the attention of the audience.

As to these other matters, the murderer's ladder and all of the other aids which I brought out and demonstrated yesterday, the point I am making is that these are means by which a writer can build mystery and suspense into his plot. I don't claim they are the only means by which mystery and suspense can be built into the plot. I don't claim they give a good plot.

As I mentioned before, they do give a structure because we know we are using building blocks that are sound and we know we are putting them together in a construction of ideas which is going to give us a house. As I remarked before, it may not be the house we want but it is much easier to take a house and then start tinkering with the interior than it is to try to build a house without materials that will stand up, such as putting sand in the foundation and expecting it to bear the weight of a superstructure.

All I am doing and all I try to do with my methods of plot building is to stimulate the thinking along constructive lines so that ideas are being put together so as to make a cohesive whole.

Once I get my plots I nearly always revise the hell out of them but the point is that by that time I have something in the nature of a plot.

If a writer will start following the murderer up the ladder he sometimes will find steps taken by the murderer which can be translated into an interesting opening mysterious situation. He will sometimes find that the murderer is confronted with an emergency from which it is difficult for him to escape unless he does something and the doing of this something involves the lives of the people who are to become prominent in the story.

Then there are factors in the solution which should be taken into consideration. Chief among these factors is a division which I have made of mystery writing which I refer to in my files as "clue sequence."

It is only necessary to cite the one incident which I cited yesterday in order to show what is meant by clue sequence. On a warm, humid day a person who pours a glass of beer, if the beer is taken from the icebox, will find that the glass has left a ring on the table or that the glass has beads of moisture on it. If he finds a man sitting drinking beer and the man tells him he has just taken the beer out of the icebox and there is no moisture on the outside of the glass the detective knows the man is lying.

Another interesting clue sequence which I think I used once in a story is that a person wearing slippers and pajamas and approaching a bed, standing facing the bed, getting ready to get into bed, will kick off his slippers so that the toes are pointed under the bed. Whereas if he sits on the bed, talking with somebody, then takes off his slippers to get into bed the toes will be pointing away from the bed.

Any person who is going to write mystery stories should start looking for these clue sequences. He will find them by the dozen if he simply keeps observing various phenomena and the events which take place around him. He can then start a card file of clue sequence events and will find that he has some very interesting material.

What I am trying to do here is not try to write a complete treatise on plotting but simply to hit the high spots of the points we covered yesterday so that you can recall them to mind and to emphasize above all and to reiterate over and over again that writers must be trained to build plots. They can be told there are certain ingredients which exist in a Perry Mason story and by the time they are told to come up with a likable character, a common denominator of public interest, an opening mysterious situation, they are pretty apt to find that they have created something which so intrigues them that they will be racing ahead to finish a script. Whereas if they grope around in their mind trying to find a starting point that starting point is altogether too apt to be related too closely to some story which has been done time and time again, or some act of violence which unfortunately in the minds of many writers is the trigger by which a story comes into existence.

I don't care about having this shown to anyone but on the other hand it would be foolish to give you the material and then tell you that you couldn't use any of that material. I am leaving it up to Gail Jackson* who understands the situation and understands me to give you the green light or the red light as to how far it is necessary to go in using this material.

What we want is writers who are willing to cooperate and once we have them we should do everything in our power to train them so they can give us the kind of material we want.

---

* Gail Patrick was a coproducer of the Perry Mason series with her husband Cornwell Jackson. As Gail Patrick, she had been a motion picture star and had an intimate knowledge of the inner workings of Hollywood.

8
THE FICTION FACTORY

There is little doubt that William Wallace Cook was the major force in molding Erle Stanley Gardner's writing career. Cook was an incredibly prolific nickel- and dime-novel writer who easily made a transition to the woodpulps and, during his later years, developed the system of plotting which Gardner used to perfect his techniques of plot analysis. When Cook died in 1933, newspaper columnist O. O. McIntyre called him "the man who deforested Canada," in reference to the millions of pounds of paper which had been used to print Cook's works.

Early in his study of writing, Gardner happened upon a book by Cook, *The Fiction Factory*, "Being the Experience of a Writer who, for Twenty-two Years, has kept a Story-mill Grinding Successfully." It was not a new book. It had been published back in 1912 by The Editor Company of Ridgewood, New Jersey, under the pseudonym "John Milton Edwards." In this book, Cook recounted his experiences from September, 1889, when he sold his first story, through September, 1911. It was a mother lode of information and advice for the embryonic writer who would read it. Gardner not only read, he adopted Cook's techniques and philosophy lock, stock, and barrel.

First of all, "John Milton Edwards" commanded instant empathy from the young lawyer in Ventura who wanted to get away from office tedium. His friend and editor Phil Cody whetted his appetite in 1927 when he wrote, "I know how good you will feel when you are in the position to tell your law firm that it can go have an earthquake."

Cook, writing as Edwards, had been a paymaster who itched to extricate himself from office routine. His book recounted the doubt which had preceded his escape in a debate with his wife. She said,

> "You've been thinking it over for two years, John, and this month is the first time your returns from your writing have ever been more than your salary at the office. If you can be so successful when you are obliged to work nights and Sundays—and most of the time with your wits befogged by office routine—what could you not do if you spent ALL your time in your Fiction Factory?"

After reading that, Gardner annually compared his earnings from writing to his income from legal practice.

Cook advised neophyte writers to subscribe to the trade magazines which were available to writers: "From the beginning of his work Edwards has made it a point to acquire every publication that dealt with the business of his Fiction Factory." After that, when he was preparing for a trip into the backcountry, Gardner's packing lists inevitably included the *Writer's Digest*. Cook also advised beginners to read books on writing, particularly those on the short story by J. Berg Esenwein and James Knapp Reeve. You'll find those books on the shelves in Gardner's study, as they were transported to The University of Texas, worn volumes with pages marred by markings of the passages which he wanted to transfer to his notebooks.

Cook instilled in Gardner an attitude toward literature he would carry through his career: "A writer is neither better nor worse than any man who happens to be in a trade. He is a manufacturer. . . . If the product is good it passes at face value and becomes a medium of exchange." In view of Gardner's recent sales experience, this attitude made sense. He would preach this text many times in the future to editors, writers, and anyone else who would listen—so often that apparently he came to believe he had invented the idea.

Cook gave detailed information concerning his methods of working. He noted that he had at one time used a word-counter which was attached to his typewriter. (Gardner turned up with one.) He also believed an author should avail himself of the latest equipment: "If a typewriter appears this year which is a distinct advance over last year's machine, Edwards has it. Keeping up-to-date is usually a little expensive, but it pays."

On July 25, 1925, Gardner noted in a letter to an editor, "I'm using one of the new electrical typewriters and haven't got used to it yet." It was a Woodstock. Later he would attribute his ability to keep up with a massive self-imposed production schedule to the electric typewriter. Over the years, Gardner's collection of typewriters and dictating machines provides an overview of the state of the art.

Cook urged that an author must have faith in his work and persist in his marketing efforts, including examples of apparently hopeless stories which finally found their way into print; then he gave practical advice concerning the type of manuscript records to maintain: title, when written, number of words, amount of postage required, when and where sent, when returned, when accepted, when paid for, and how much. Gardner never stopped keeping detailed histories of his works, many of which would swell to include numerous reprints and many foreign rights. Following is his record of an early story written for the pulp market; he persisted in his attempts to market it for more than two years before finally consigning it to the morgue:

The Killers of Cottontail Canyon

82 Pages	22,000 w		26¢
May 9 [1925]	Short Stories	R.L.*	May 25
May 25	Complete Stories	Letter	June 9
	Transferred to		
	Top Notch ?		
	Western St	RL	June 16
	Revised June 23 & Remailed		
June 23	Short Stories	R.L.	Sept 10
Sep 14	Frank A. Munsey Co.	R.L.	Sep 27
Oct 15	Ace High		Oct 30
Nov 8	North-West St.		Nov 20
Nov 21	Hardy [an agent]		
June 22 '27	Complete Novel M.	R.N.	July 6
July 11	Jenkins (Top Notch)	R.L.	Aug 1
Aug 15	Brief St.		

Cook advised aspiring authors against waiting for inspiration, which he believed to be the last resort of the lazy writer. He himself had written two 33,000-word stories a week for months at a time. And this was precisely the schedule Gardner set for himself.

---

* This column indicated editorial reaction, whether a submission was turned down by a cold, unadorned rejection slip; a note scrawled on the customary printed notice; or "Received Letter."

In *The Fiction Factory*, Cook tabulated records of his sales down through the years, and Gardner established identically the same format for keeping his meticulous records. He was particularly proud of one month. When the occasion arose, he would take out his four-by six-inch index card for May, 1931:

Date	Title	Words
May 7	"On Top of the Heap"	16,000
May 11	"Promise to Pay"	14,000
May 12	"Muscle Man"	10,000
May 15	"No Rough Stuff"	12,500
May 18	"Make It Snappy"	10,500
May 20	"The Whip Hand"	8,000
May 21	"Turn of the Tide"	5,500
May 23	"The Gloved Mystery"	11,500
May 25	"The First Stone"	12,500
May 30	"The Play's the Thing"	17,000
May 31	"The Hot Squat"	15,000

Across the bottom of the card he had scrawled "No rejections—no revisions." Had it not been for a legal case that kept him from his typewriter during the first week, it could have been a perfect month. Even so, he managed to keep his production schedule up to William Wallace Cook's demanding standard. Four of the stories sold to *Detective Fiction Weekly*, two to *Detective Action Magazine*, two to *Black Mask*, and one each to *Argosy*, *Gang World*, and *Detective Story Magazine*.

Cook advised clipping plot germs from newspapers and magazines for future reference. He explained his system for alphabetically cross-indexing between his files and notebooks—exactly the system Gardner established and continued to maintain.

During the spring of 1895, Cook "had found himself literally swamped with orders":

> . . . and he tried the experiment of hiring a young man stenographer and typist to assist him. The young man was an expert in his line and proved so efficient an aide that Edwards hired another who was equally proficient. Two stenographers failing to help him catch up with his flood of orders, he hired a third.

Cook abandoned the practice except for occasional use because he believed "successful dialect cannot be wrapped up in a stenographer's 'pothooks.'"

Despite Cook's doubt, in 1930 Gardner decided to give dictation a whirl. After all, he used it in his sales and law work. Jean Bethell, office manager and executive secretary at the law office, started going to Gardner's home after hours to take dictation. At first he dictated only his ventures into book writing, continuing to peck out his woodpulp yarns with his rapid-fire "four-finger hunt-and-peck system of typewriting." Then he tried dictating stories; he sent them out and awaited reaction. Editors reported "marked improvement."

For Gardner dictation worked, dialect and all. By mid-1933 he was dictating everything. "I would use the extra time to concentrate more on my plots and character development." He set his quota at a hundred thousand words a month, doubling up for those days when law practice encroached upon his writing. Eventually he expanded his secretarial staff to three . . . then five . . . and finally as many as seven.

Cook advocated making an annual "prospecting trip" to New York City to become acquainted with the personal views of editors, to negotiate direct commissions, to campaign for better rates and, in general, to bring oneself to editorial notice. Gardner adopted the practice and usually came away on a first-name basis with the editors he visited. Future letters would refer to Bohemian activities which they had shared in the big city and plans they had discussed for stories. Like Cook, Gardner never failed to give "a prompt and hearty response" to any editorial request and "getting 'hooked up' with a big house" was high on his shopping list.

In *The Fiction Factory*, Cook told of losses incurred as a result of "the folly" of selling all rights, rather than reserving reprint and foreign rights for future sale. Immediately, Gardner recognized the legal implications of unconditional sale. He had title pages printed upon which to begin his stories. They contained his return address—Post Office Drawer Y, Ventura, California—blanks for inserting approximate wordage and title, and "by Erle Stanley Gardner." At the bottom was noted "Stamped Addressed Envelope Enclosed," and they bore the important legend: "Offering First American Serial Rights

Only Unless Otherwise Stipulated When Accepted," and from that point on Gardner insisted upon retaining all subsidiary rights.

Toward the end of his book, Cook had a word of caution for beginning writers:

> Before a young man throws himself into the ranks of this vast army of writers, let him ponder the situation well. If, under the iron heel of adversity, he is sure he can still love his work for the work's sake and be true to himself, there is one chance in ten that he will make a fair living, and one chance in a hundred that he may become one of the generals.

Gardner was not daunted by this discouraging note. He proceeded to emulate his mentor and went on to become a "general."

Borrowing from "John Milton Edwards," he forthwith referred to his own writing activities as the "Fiction Factory." Later, when he met John Milton Edwards in the flesh, he discovered him to be William Wallace Cook, affectionately referred to by his friends as "Uncle Billy." And from that point Erle Stanley Gardner encouraged one and all to call him "Uncle Erle," a term of endearment which was carried on through the years, particularly by his secretarial staff, who found it so natural that they forgot—if they ever knew—from whence it came.

Gardner's reference to his writing activities as the Fiction Factory eventually caused some bother. After a *Time* magazine article used the designation, he began to receive letters from applicants wanting to join the stable of writers in the Fiction Factory, and his secretaries would patiently respond:

> Mr. Gardner has never employed anyone to do his writing for him, and he never even reads plot suggestions and ideas which are sent to him. As a matter of fact, he has many more ideas than he has time to place on paper.

As Gardner's publications swelled in volume and reached an ever widening audience, the persistent rumor of ghost writers began to crop up in the press. At this point, Thayer Hobson of William Morrow and Company offered $100,000 reward for proof that anyone but Erle Stanley Gardner ever wrote any of Gardner's material. There were no takers.

It can be unequivocally stated that there is no evidence to support that old rumor. Gardner was definitely his own man. Perhaps the most telling evidence on this point was Gardner's violent reaction when Harry Steeger of *Argosy* suggested the magazine had a writer who was sufficiently familiar with Gardner's style to condense his work. Gardner fired off a telegram to his agent:

> STEEGER WRITES MY COPY BEING CONDENSED AND CUT BY WRITER WHO IS FAMILIAR WITH MY STYLE STOP ONLY WRITER WHO IS FAMILIAR WITH MY STYLE IS ME STOP

He followed the telegram with a scorching letter:

> . . . A hell of a lot of damn good writers have been studying my style for the last ten years, trying to imitate it in detective fiction. My style doesn't amount to much technically, but practically it consists of a pace, a change of pace and a rhythm predicated upon years of study of audience psychology. If Brown can duplicate my style so that the reader can't tell it, he's wasting his time writing for *Argosy* magazine.

In the early days, Gardner wrote whenever he could snatch time from his law practice, mostly late at night and on Sundays. He composed in longhand and made copies for mailing on the typewriter, all the while exhorting himself in his notebook to learn to think on the typewriter. It was not long until he mastered writing his story text on the typewriter, although he still had to evolve plots in longhand, a practice he continued throughout his writing life. He would "pace the floor and perspire out the psychological continuity, scribble with pencil all over a ream of paper for plot stuff, then grab the electric typewriter in a stranglehold and dash it off as fast as the fingers can work."

He longed for "some sunlight fiction writing when I'm fresh." Cadging a day from the law office hardly meant a holiday, as he explained to Joe Shaw in responding to a request from *Black Mask* for a story: "A lucky break in the law, and because I knew you were in a rush, has enabled me to put in a straight twenty-four hours with the exception of six for sleeping." By February, 1926, desperation colored a letter to Robert Hardy, his agent:

> I can't stand the double pace I'm keeping right now. I'm turning down lots of law business, and the bit I keep keeps me busy all day. My story writing is done before and after daylight. By this time next year I've got to be either making a lot more writing, or I'll have to quit.

Gardner did cut to three-fourths the time spent with his law partnership, but his study in Ventura was always within easy reach of the law office. His writing career was probably saved by the happenstance of someone coming along with a "camp wagon" that he wanted to sell. The camp wagon was a forerunner of today's self-contained motor home. Gardner bought it with the idea of going into out-of-the-way places and "writing Westerns right on the ground."

For its day, the cumbersome boxlike structure built on a 1927 Chevrolet truck chassis was quite a layout. It housed a bed, stove, icebox, pressure cooker, a lined clothes closet, water tanks, writing desk, typewriter desk, enough storage space for a three-month food supply, and of course room to stow the latest Remington Model 12 typewriter with cushion keys and a good supply of paper and manuscript envelopes.

Gardner added innovations. He routed the exhaust through a storage tank to heat water for the bathtub which was stashed under the bed and found room for a file cabinet. Along the way he picked up Navajo rugs for the floor. His bow and arrows were always close at hand, for recreation and to supplement his food supply with small game. As his interest in photography grew, he added a portable darkroom. After he started dictating, he installed a Dictaphone which ran off the vehicle's multiple battery system and, as his outings grew longer, he would ship the wax cylinders containing stories back to Jean Bethell in Ventura to be transcribed and mailed to editors. Gardner kept the camp wagon parked in front of his house, ready to go: "When I decide to go some place I don't need to do anything except walk up to the camp wagon, open the door and step on the starter." Occasionally his wife Natalie would accompany him, but usually it was just Erle Stanley Gardner—writer-at-large—and his dog Rip.

When Gardner stepped into his camp wagon, he entered a world of his own, inaccessible to his law partners; they could no longer have second thoughts about letting him escape the office routine. After this, his writing became noticeably less taut, and his letters to editors sparkled with idyllic descriptions of his nomadic life:

> If you're inclined to be envious, get your envy machine all stoked up for action under forced draft. For I'm sitting out in the middle of the desert, stripped to the waist, sunlight glittering, a blue black sky, not a

cloud in sight, not a breath of wind, air like wine, yet very warm without being hot.

And if you think that isn't the life you've just been overcivilized, that's all. . . . I can get into sections of the desert where most cars never go, and go for days at a time without seeing any humans. Then head in to some out-of-the-way mining camp and turn on the radio, switch on the electric lights, get out the drinking whiskey, and entertain characters who let their reminiscences fall on fertile soil.

His stories began to center around old prospectors and ghost towns, buried treasure and mysterious happenings in the desert, and a wealth of crusty old cowhands who were headed for distant horizons to escape the cloying influence of civilization. Not only was it a wonderful place in which to write stories, but the atmosphere and the characters he met helped him build air castles tall enough to grip any woodpulp reader's attention. He wrote editor Howard Bloomfield about one of them in 1930:

We now have a scheme on tap that should tickle your cockles. A sea captain who has adventured in all parts of the world and is commencing to write adventure fiction, an English chap who does a bit of article writing, and our esteemed contemporary, God's-gift-to-treasure-hunters, Gardner, are going to purchase a four-masted lumber schooner, fit her up, start sailing the seven seas in search of material. We air castled the thing all yesterday afternoon and it sounds feasible. This captain knows his Manila women and his salt water. We have our eye on a peach of a boat around three hundred feet and a good buy, in A-1 shape.

We will ship a Manila crew to Hong Kong and then pick up Chinese for permanent crew. Will carry a radio, a mate, a doctor and an engineer. Will write stories and adventure, have a secret booze place built in the boat by some expert Chinese smuggle artists, and then drift around through the South Seas to New York. By that time I'll be writing exclusively for you and you can give the expedition some publicity. I'll threaten to break away and free lance unless I'm kept busy, so you, Archie and Gibney will have to come and live on the boat to entertain me while I'm in port. We'll have a few imported natives, both sexes, some genuine hootch and many local curios from various savage races. When I get two drinks under my belt I'll regale you with the story of how I got shipwrecked on a savage isle of cannibals and went native. I was there a year and ate up every damned native on the place except one beautiful . . .

But right then, Gardner didn't have any more time to fritter away wandering around in air castles. As he wrote H. Bedford-Jones, "when I have the money I have just sold a story and have to write another to take its place, and when I haven't sold a story I haven't got the money with which to travel."

However, as his literary fortunes improved, the air-castled trip materialized, not aboard a four-masted schooner as he had dreamed it but second class on a Japanese steamer. Instead of native maidens he had his wife Natalie for company. Along with his typewriter, he had packed the latest writers' market list, and Jean Bethell stayed back in Ventura to handle correspondence and forward stories to editors. It was quite a trip—China, Japan, Macao, the Philippines. Not only did Gardner have a chance to exercise the Chinese he had been studying, he was surrounded by an abundance of local color including typhoons and Chinese pirates.

> During all the time I was in China and in the Philippines I kept up my steady rate of production of a novelette every third day.
>
> I wrote a novelette in Macao in the middle of a terrific typhoon which ripped out trees and wires, sent surf crashing over the sea wall and caused great destruction. I sat in the bathroom of my room, which was the only place where sufficient light came in through the window to enable me to see to type, and sitting on a stool with my portable typewriter on the seat of the toilet, hammered out a novelette.
>
> Before I left Manila for Baguio I pounded out another novelette, and when I decided to leave Baguio and take what was at that time a rather perilous trip into Bontoc, I had a novelette to write for *Black Mask*.
>
> I started the thing at six o'clock in the evening, got my plot, pulled up the typewriter, began hammering away, and had the novelette ready to mail about two o'clock in the morning. I was up at daylight and headed for Bontoc.

Gardner returned laden with souvenirs which he distributed among the various editors who had been buying his wares. His stories began to tell of foreign intrigue and mysterious doings in the Orient, with such titles as "Red Jade," "Fingers of Fong," and "The Watchful Eyes of Taiping."

As sales increased, Gardner expanded his fiction factory on wheels. He added tents, automobiles, and trailers to carry all the gear. One trailer was fitted out as "a pretty comfortable home and office." Its most important feature was a double bed in the back, "a real honest-to-God bed with coil springs, a thick mattress," Gardner emphasized. On August 5, 1933, he wrote to tell Howard Bloomfield about his new setup:

> You have the honor of getting the first story which has been written in the portable fiction factory. The fiction factory is now established at the Bar W Ranch on the Van Duzen River, about fifty miles south and east of Eureka. There's redwood forest all around us, trout streams tumbling down out of the mountains, and the Gardner Fiction Factory, consisting of five tents, a camp wagon, a trailer that's a regular house on wheels, and a couple of more cars and trailers to carry camp equipment, is firmly established and working at its best and happiest. . . . We may be here three months, or we may leave in three hours. We're just playing gypsies and following our hunches.

Gardner was sure he had found the ultimate in utopian existence: "As far as I'm concerned, I'm afraid that I'm ruined for living in houses again." But success began to pose problems.

With the introduction of Perry Mason in *The Case of the Velvet Claws* and *The Case of the Sulky Girl*, slick-magazine editors finally noticed Erle Stanley Gardner, and motion picture studios began to knock on his door. Gardner had some decisions to make. The first real pinch came in 1935: He had promised three woodpulp novelettes, but fulfilling this commitment kept him from making the deadline with a serial for a new slick market. The editor looked to another writer to fill the order and told Gardner just to send him a one-shot novelette. Gardner wrote Joe Shaw how it worked out financially. "Figuring the difference in price between the price offered for the serial if I could have completed it in the time and the price for the novelette, those three woodpulp stories cost me just a little over two thousand dollars apiece to write."

There were also problems with operation of the fiction factory on wheels. During winter, the high country got too cold for tent living; and down on the desert, winds made it uncomfortable for the secretaries on whom Gardner was now so dependent. "I like it down there, myself," he said, "but the water supply is scanty and hard." Delivery of manuscripts that had to be revised and letters that had to be answered became increasingly difficult and undependable. Always with an eye on his production, Gardner looked for something else.

Finally, in 1938, Gardner decided to move his fiction factory into permanent headquarters, at least temporarily, miles from Temecula,

California, the nearest settlement, which had 250 inhabitants if you counted the Pala Indians who came to town to shop. In 1938 he wrote a Munsey editor about the projected move:

> For the past two years, I've been traveling and living in auto trailers, an arrangement which is swell for adventure, but isn't conducive to volume output, as I can only do field work in the trailers and have to mail stuff for final copy, bookkeeping, etc. to other offices. Recently I've found a ranch property which suits me right down to the ground and I'm moving in, lock, stock and barrel, with a regular office, plenty of elbow room and my various branches all centralized under one roof, and I'm going to be able to turn out more work. I'm going to make headquarters here for the next six or eight months, . . .

The "six or eight months" stretched on and on. Rancho del Paisano, as Gardner called it, became the focal point of his writing career as he constructed buildings to house himself and his secretarial staff, quarters for those who helped him operate the 1,000-acre working ranch, outbuildings, guest facilities, and vaults to store the growing volume of papers and archives. "Altogether I think we wound up with twenty-two buildings," Jean Bethell said.

Here in his memento-littered study and across the long refectory dining table Gardner and his friends could build air castles to their hearts' content—and make them come true. Rancho del Paisano became a jumping-off place for exploratory expeditions as he branched out into travel writing with numerous magazine articles and books such as *Hunting Lost Mines by Helicopter*, *The Hidden Heart of Baja*, and *Mexico's Magic Square*.

Rancho del Paisano became a mecca for the stream of editors and publishers whom Gardner invited, and they left angling for a return invitation. Erle Stanley Gardner was an unparalleled host, and what he didn't think of Jean Bethell did. Guests were shown to a cabin with a living room, bedroom, and bath. An Indian girl brought refreshments consisting of a big bowl of fruit and a fifth of whiskey. Secretary Peggy Downs always kept track of preference.

Understandably, the stream of visitors swelled to a flood, particularly of other writers who wanted to sell articles describing how Erle Stanley Gardner lived and worked. Others were just curious to see how a fiction factory operated. Rancho del Paisano began to defeat its purpose. Gardner could not get any work done because of the people who came to see him work. So, when he had a deadline to meet, he fled to a "hideout."

Over the years he had several. There were Paradise Camp in the northern California timber country; a house at Oceanside, only forty miles away from Temecula and close to the beach; a desert retreat at Yucca; a date ranch; a place at Shasta Lake with boats and another at Port Orford, Oregon; "Camp Hood" on the Hood Canal in Washington; a house in Palm Springs and another near the village of Idyllwild; later a fleet of houseboats in the Sacramento Delta—and if none of these suited his purpose or mood, he would set up the fiction factory wherever he happened to light, such as the French Quarter in New Orleans, where he found Wood Whitesell, the real-life inspiration for Gramp Wiggins in *The Case of the Turning Tide* and *The Case of the Smoking Chimney.*

Needless to say, such activities soon attracted the attention of Internal Revenue Service auditors who had little talent for understanding the ways and needs of creative people. In 1956 Gardner's accountant wrote to tell him that a new man had arrived at the audit office in Ventura; he was being investigated again. Gardner tried to arm his accountant to forestall a personal encounter:

> It is no easy matter to get up each morning and think of new ideas. It is no easy matter to write mystery novels. You can't do it unless you have a certain type of imaginative mind and unless you are free from nagging interruptions. I think this is something that perhaps the average person fails to take into consideration. I am not like a beginning writer who can write at his own convenience and as he pleases. I have to turn out a certain number of stories each year. Every one of these stories has to be ingenious, novel and interesting, and all of these stories have to be delivered on time. They are contracted for by my publisher and he in turn has bound himself by contracts with reprint houses.

It was a futile effort, and in less than two weeks Gardner was trying to explain to the Internal Revenue agent how the fiction factory at Rancho del Paisano worked, as he had explained to the one before him and the one before him.

> Please bear in mind that I keep five secretaries busy, sometimes to the point of nervous exhaustion. In order to do that I have virtually no social life and my recreation is confined to ways in which I can exploit the sale of my books through advantageous publicity, or gather material for articles.

I have never measured statistically the floor space that is devoted to desks, dictating and transcribing machines, duplicating machines, reference books, files, manuscripts, etc., but it is enormous.

The business is in an isolated location which enables me to avoid many interruptions, but does require more employees than would otherwise be the case. My secretaries who live on the place have to be given a place in which to live, have their housework done, etc., and a cook to prepare their meals. . . .

I dictate my stories to a dictating machine without punctuation and only the most competent, highly trained literary secretaries can do the work. . . .

As you can readily understand, the fact that I keep five secretaries busy, that I write the number of books I do a year and carry on the volume of correspondence which flows through this office, means that I have no personal life at all. I never go anywhere except on business. I sleep in a small sleeping porch attached to my office. [This porch later grew to five rooms.] I put in every minute of my time on some form or other of work. I am, in short, never away from my business. The result is reflected in the fact that I sell more books than any other writer in the world. This result is due to a good many things. I owe a great deal of my success to the relations I have been able to maintain with publishers and editors, to my experience in the field of salesmanship, to the loyalty of secretaries who have made this business their life work. (Three of them started working with me some thirty-five years ago.) . . .

I don't know how to try to explain this in a letter because we live in different worlds and from your letter I am afraid we are talking a different language. . . .

Indeed, many of the problems of a best-selling mystery writer were beyond the ken of the uninitiated. For every fictional murder there was a murder weapon, but the weapon could not be fictional. Realism demanded that when a gun was introduced as evidence during a courtroom scene its make, specifications, and serial number be given. If Gardner invented a number which could not be real, the many firearms experts in his audience would spot the hoax; if he contrived a number which could be real, some time, somewhere, a reader was going to show up owning that murder weapon, and there could be repercussions. So, for every fictional murder with a firearm, Gardner had to go out and buy a gun of that type so he could use its serial number, thereby acquiring one of the largest collections of modern handguns in the State of California.

Someone had to keep track of all the automobile license numbers he used in his books and stories and maintain a log to avoid duplication. For the most part he used numbers from plates on vehicles which he, his employees, and relatives owned. Then there was the business of naming characters. Magazine editors became perturbed when a reader wrote in objecting to having been dubbed a murderer in *The Case of Whatever.* To avoid this, Gardner used the names of communities taken from an atlas so that he could always point back to his source as being disassociated from real people. From time to time he would make up alphabetical lists of cities and towns. With such a list at hand as he plotted or dictated, he added appropriate Christian names. Even so, a secretary had to check every character's name against a telephone directory for the community which served as a background, and on at least one occasion two names had to be changed throughout a final draft because they showed up in the Los Angeles telephone directory. The character list for *Fools Die on Friday* is typical of those for all books. Of course the names of continuing characters such as Donald Lam and Bertha Cool were already established:

Adell		Newton
Gerald Ballwin	*Daphne, Beatrice*	*Ruth* Otis
Candor		Parnell
Dilworth		*Dr. George L.* Quay
Elmore		Ridgely
Jim Fordney		Stetson
Glasco		Tilden
Carlotta Hanford		Underwood
Mary Ingram		Villas
Carl Keetley		Wellford
Lancaster		*Ethel* Worley
Manville		Yermo

After fifty or so mystery novels, the possibility of subconsciously duplicating a plot was increasing by incremental giant steps. Someone had to maintain a notebook of synopses of past stories so that when an idea erupted into Gardner's notebook he could check immediately for past usage before wasting time on completing plot development. For example, on June 17, 1954, he started a "Plot for a new Perry Mason" and began to toy with a series of events in which a man disappeared from a cruise steamer; then he noted to himself: "Look up a case of disappearance from a yacht or some place in one of my books. Guy overboard in thunderstorm?" Looking it up took long enough for the ink to dry on his penpoint before he stabbed the paper to print and underline a warning to himself: *"This has been used."*

With thousands of lawyers looking over his shoulder, watching for Perry Mason, Donald Lam, or Doug Selby to commit a legal faux pas, Gardner had to research every legal point which he used, and most of them were obscure, depending upon carefully researched but untested legal theory. He had to have a brief in reserve from which to answer the letters which were bound to follow the publication of every book.

A notebook entry for Tuesday, August 23, 1955, reflects this concern as he examined a first draft:

> Mason from about p. 50. Try to bring this whole story within sec. 1023 Penal Code & Peo vs. Krupa 64CA2nd & Peo vs. Hunckler 48 Cal. 331. The body can be found near the driveway of the house. . . . Mason's desire is not to get the murderer cleared by a technicality but to get a delay so he can make certain investigations . . . thanks to Mason's tip off and the court finding the benefit to the defendant, dismisses the case, discharges the jury, and holds the defendant for murder.—Better not rely on the dismissal in view of Penal Code 1387. Better go ahead and have a verdict or get the judge to grant probation. . . .

And it wouldn't do for a continuing character to change from book to book; so there had to be master lists of characters to keep track of character traits, physical characteristics, mannerisms, speech habits, telephone numbers, addresses (realistic but not identifiable), specifics of office arrangements, and myriad other details. Even so, there was an occasional blooper, bringing letters from sharp-eyed readers that had to be answered. For example, Mrs. Fay Sellers, of Montreal, Missouri, noted in *The Saturday Evening Post's* serialization of *The Case of the Mythical Monkeys* that Paul Drake's office was on the same floor as Mason's, whereas in the previously published *The Case of the Curious Bride* it had been on the floor below. It took two pages to explain this away:

> *The Case of the Curious Bride* was published in 1934. That is exactly twenty-five years ago. Now personally I can't remember that far back

and it may be that twenty-five years ago Drake had his offices a floor below Perry Mason's.

But I have a vague recollection that around January of 1935 the landlord raised the rent on Drake's office to about twice what it had been and Drake got mad and told him he'd move out. So the owner of the building came to Paul Drake and said, "Now look, Paul, don't get mad about this. We've had to raise the rent of your offices because Madam Curlicue who has the beauty parlor in the adjoining offices has expanded her business to such a point that she needs these offices and said 'If you don't dig me up more room, I'm going to move.'

"Now look, Paul. We've got a wonderful suite of offices on the floor above, right next to the elevator, on the same floor as Perry Mason. It will give you more room and since the offices were used for a stock brokerage firm that bucket-shopped all its orders and went broke, we can give you space that is suitably designed and let you have it at less rent."

Drake was still mad and didn't like this kind of tactics. He said, "I just don't like being pushed around. And who the hell is Perry Mason? I never heard of the guy until two years ago in 1933. Why should I change my office to be near him?"

Well, the agent for the building, who was a fellow named Smooth-inplush and was a glib-tongued, sweet-talking salesman, came to Drake and said, "You think it over, Paul, because I think Mason is going to have a career. He's a comer. You don't realize it now but he is going to become one of the greatest criminal attorneys in the United States and you better get your office up on the floor next to him. But don't say anything now while you are still mad. Just think it over."

Then Smoothinplush took the elevator up to Mason's office and went to see Della Street, and said, "Miss Street, would you do me a favor?" Della is good natured and she batted those big eyes at him and gave him that sweet Della Street smile and said, "Why certainly, Mr. Smooth-inplush," and Smoothinplush said, "You go on down and get Paul Drake in an amiable mood and tell him you'd like to have him with his offices up here on this floor so that when he rides up in the elevator with you he isn't always getting off on the floor below and leaving you to complete the ride in mid-sentence, so to speak."

So Della did and Paul did, and he's been up there for some fifty books and now whenever Della Street comes into the room, he says, "Hi Beautiful."

The letter to Mrs. Sellers was eventually published in *The Saturday Evening Post* under the title "The Case of the Dislodged Detective." Then there was the fan mail. Marlene Dietrich wrote about reading his books while she was in an Italian hospital suffering from viral pneumonia during World War II:

> In that hospital I began to see what the boys did to use up time. I found that they have a God—Erle Stanley Gardner. I've never read mystery stories. In my life there hasn't been time for them. But there I read Erle Stanley Gardner and loved him. Those boys read his books, all they can get, two and three times each. They pass them from ward to ward via the ward-to-ward mail service they always arrange. When those boys say that Erle Stanley Gardner saves their lives, they mean it. "Tell him when you get back home," they said, "that he should write more and fast. We need them."

And an officer serving "somewhere in New Guinea" wrote:

> Since we've been overseas, several parents and loved ones of my boys have passed away—many of us have joined them. In this situation, there is so little that can be done, so little that can be said, to assuage grief.
>
> From your pen into the mouth of Perry Mason I remember the most beautiful passage on death that I have ever read. As I remember, Paul, Perry and Della were around some woman who had recently lost someone. Perry started talking to the effect that life and death are as day and night, the sun, a storm, evening, etc. Would you be so kind as to copy and send that particular quotation to me?

Letters such as these had to be answered, as did mail from obviously intelligent readers asking for more information on some point, those sincerely offering constructive criticism, and some simply writing to tell how much they had enjoyed a story. There were letters from writers pleading for help, so many that Gardner eventually prepared a "Memorandum to beginning writers" which answered the most frequent questions. And there were letters from those with asinine questions who were obliquely angling for an autograph. (They usually got answers signed by secretaries.)

During the early days, Gardner told Phil Cody of one correspondent who got letters which were prize Gardneriana:

> Great kick. Letter from a girl in Chicago. She's been reading my crook stories, notably Lester Leith, and thinks that I'm a crook like Lester Leith. She wants to know "how much truth is based on my stories," and I write her a guardedly mysterious letter in which I tell her, "hist, I don't dare commit myself. You're the only one that has

penetrated my mask and knows me for what I am." She writes back, sends pictures, and wants to "transact business for me," there in Chicago. When I get done with it, it's going to be some hot bunch of fan mail, particularly by the time I get the sheriff here to write her and ask her for a detailed explanation of her relationship with me.

After Gardner became involved with the Court of Last Resort, championing the cause of falsely accused or misjudged persons in magazine articles and on television, his mail reached mountainous proportions as hopeful prisoners and their relatives and friends wrote. With travel for investigation, making personal appearances, writing, and answering correspondence, the project consumed eighty percent of his time for a decade. Outgoing correspondence reached a volume of 20,000 words a day. He did a hasty computation and wrote Thayer Hobson: "During the past ten years, as you are so evidently aware, I have averaged 462.5 pages of single-spaced correspondence for every 225.7 double-spaced pages of book ms."

Additionally, the subsidiary media in which his characters appeared—radio, movies, comic strips, and television—increased activity at the fiction factory to a fevered pitch which no prosaic regulation-bound Internal Revenue agent could comprehend.

More and more requests came in for information about the working habits of the world's best-selling author. In 1959 A. S. Burack, editor of *The Writer*, unable to get an article by Gardner himself, wanted "a brief hour-by-hour description" of Jean Bethell's typical working day. She replied, "I must admit this might prove interesting, but in the first place no one would believe it, and in the second place no two days of his life are alike and never have been in the twenty-five or more years I've been with him. . . . There's nothing 'typical' about Mr. Gardner. He never fits into any forms we have to fill in; he never fits into any ordinary mold of life; in fact, it's quite impossible for him to fit into any mold. He makes his own—and breaks it regularly." Finally, she consented to describe some of Gardner's activities:

> For instance, a week ago Sunday another secretary and I drove to Tucson with Mr. Gardner. We had a conference Sunday afternoon and evening with Mr. Thayer Hobson of William Morrow and Company, Mr. Gardner's publisher. Monday morning we left in chartered planes for the west coast of Mexico (gathering material for an article which, when it appears in a travel book, will be very exciting), were flying all

Sam Hicks, manager of Rancho del Paisano, stacked Gardner's books to dramatize his output for a biographer who visited the ranch.

day. The next day we transferred to other planes and went into the deep mountain country, were in there all day Tuesday, flew part way out Tuesday afternoon and the rest of the way Wednesday morning to Tucson, where we caught a plane for Hollywood to engage in a television conference which lasted until almost midnight. Then Mr. Gardner took an early plane for Fresno where he had agreed to put on a talk, got back to the ranch late at night in order to meet a man from Mexico City, who is working with us on a matter of importance.

Of course, it became common knowledge that Jean Bethell was the custodian of Gardner's secrets, including his coveted plotting methods. She was obviously the prime fount of information about his activities, and many came to pry; but, as Gardner often said, "Once you take a secretary into the business and let her feel she has an interest in that business, she develops a loyalty for it that is far more than can be purchased with money."

When Jean Bethell was contacted to write an article about her boss, Perry Mason's Della Street could not have phrased a better reply: "Thank you for your complimentary letter of August 8th. My first contact with Mr. Gardner was in his law office where I quickly learned to see all, hear all, and say nothing—in less than 500 words."

The bane of the fiction factory was writers and columnists who imposed upon others to do their work by sending out questionnaires to assorted public figures, broadly hinting that the resulting publicity would be of immeasurable value. They callously sold the responses, in or out of context, as articles and columns. Erle Stanley Gardner was a frequent target for this ploy. Most such requests generated profane inner-office memos and received short shrift.

However, in 1959 writer Erle Stanley Gardner could not resist responding to newspaper columnist Hy Gardner with a "Memo from Gardner to Gardner": "You want to know what it is that makes male stars in the late fifties still attractive to young girls. That I wouldn't know. I suppose it is because their names are associated with romantic ideals. If, however, the result of your questionnaire shows any means by which males of sixty-nine and eight-tenths years of age can become attractive to the opposite sex, wire me at once."

As pressure from the Internal Revenue Service increased, Gardner often told Thayer Hobson and others of his temptation to give it all up and "kill the goose that lays the golden eggs"; but he couldn't do it.

Too many loyal members of the fiction factory were dependent upon him, and too many readers looked for his books.

"I have become chained to my fiction factory," he said, "because my audience can't get enough of my stories, no matter how fast I write them."

9
SEARCHING FOR A PLOT MACHINE

During his earliest days of writing, Gardner's most persistent problem was plotting. Books on writing skirted plotting as a technique. No one dared a set of directions. Most merely analyzed various types of stories; they told what was there but not how it got there. Gardner expressed his frustration: "I bought books on plots and plotting. I read and studied, and I couldn't find out what a plot was. I couldn't find out how to create a plot, how to expand an idea into a plot."

Nevertheless, he was still doing remarkably well as a woodpulp writer, mainly because he had the fortitude to withstand a ninety percent rejection rate. When one wrote that many stories, some of them were bound to click. He had to conjure up ideas by the score, hoping they would turn into plots, or that a friendly editor would tell him what to do to them. Creating such a monumental volume of wordage gave him little time to refine his work or to study stories in such publications as *The Saturday Evening Post* to determine how to make the "big time."

Then he read an advertisement in *Writer's Digest*. The product sounded like just the sort of manna to stoke a fiction factory such as Erle Stanley Gardner *alias* Charles M. Green and Robert Parr was operating:"TEN MILLION STORY PLOTS! No Two Alike. Can be developed for either short stories or the Movies by ROBOT, the most amazing device ever invented for writers."

Plot Robot "The Mechanical Brain" had been invented by Wycliffe A. Hill. It was distributed out of Los Angeles by the *Creative World Magazine*. The publishing house also plugged a land development deal—a subdivision upon which it hoped to settle a colony of writers, inventors, and the like. By the time Gardner learned the price and got his order in, distributorship had been taken over by the Gagnon Company, at the same address, and the name of the device had been changed to Plot Genie.

Gardner must have been sorely disappointed when he opened the package and examined the merchandise. It consisted of a large cardboard wheel of fortune, numbered from 1 through 180, peeping through a slot in a caricature of a mechanical man—hardly an approach calculated to lend dignity to the art it was advertised to further. Accompanying the spinner was a booklet, the *Plot Robot Index*. The cover was brown paper, only a shade better quality than wrapping paper. Inside the printed cover were mimeographed sheets, poorly reproduced and rife with typographical errors.

The Plot Genie—"change of name from Plot Robot demanded by enthusiastic professional writers who are using it"—was based upon an 1895 analytical study by Georges Polti, a French literary analyst, which had been translated from French to English under the title *The Thirty-six Dramatic Situations*. Monsieur Polti's study purported to fit the motivations of every possible story into one dramatic pigeonhole or another and furnish the "dynamic elements" necessary to create drama from each situation. Supplication, the first situation, generated from three elements: a Persecutor, a Suppliant, and a Power in authority whose decision is doubtful. Supplication divided into three subgroups:

A. The Power whose decision is awaited is a distinct personage who is deliberating.
  1. Fugitives imploring the powerful for help against their enemies.
  2. Assistance implored for the performance of a pious duty which has been forbidden.
  3. Appeals for a refuge in which to die.
B. By means of a contraction analogous to that which abbreviates a syllogism to an enthymeme, this undecided Power is but an attribute of the Persecutor himself—a weapon suspended in his hand.
  1. Hospitality besought by the shipwrecked.
  2. Charity entreated by those cast off by their own people whom they have disgraced.

3. Expiation: The seeking of pardon, healing or deliverance.

4. The surrender of a corpse, or of a relic, solicited.

C. The Suppliant element is divided between two persons, the Persecuted and the Intercessor, thus increasing the number of principal characters to four.

1. Supplication of the powerful for those dear to the suppliant.

2. Supplication to a relative in behalf of another relative.

3. Supplication to a mother's lover in her behalf.

Later, Erle Stanley Gardner would apply his legal mind to plot materials and greatly profit from analytical study, but Wycliffe Hill did not fool with such tedious detail. Inventor Hill freely admitted starting with Polti's material, which he had improved: "I contend there are in reality only thirty-one basic dramatic situations. . . . I reject seven of the accepted list and add two new ones."

All dramatic plots, said Hill, are composed of certain ingredients. Plot Genie would bring combinations of dramatic ingredients together by chance, thus freeing the prospective writer from the deadly hackneyed plots usually resulting from human association of ideas. "The mechanical brain is superior to the human organ. . . . Robot tells you what happened and it is up to you to figure out how it could have happened."

Hill thoughtfully provided mimeographed forms on which to list ingredients and left space in which to write a brief synopsis of the resulting story. There were ten steps to Hill's scheme. Entries on the first two "recording sheets" show that Student Writer Erle Stanley Gardner followed instructions religiously—through the first nine steps:

"As you repeat the words 'The locale of our story is—' turn the disk. . . . Now observe what number shows through the slot and then refer to Section 1 in the index book, and ascertain what locale or background carries this number."

Gardner flipped the pages and discovered that No. 163 prescribed a "wagon train" as the setting for his burgeoning yarn.

Next, "Select your first character by the same method, repeating the words 'and the first character is—'" The second character was designated a "beloved," to provide love interest. She would be the "daughter of" whatever character turned up next.

Plot Genie was obviously a male chauvinist; however, if for your principal character the whirling disk happened upon one of the few feminine roles among the 180 potential characters, on the third spin the magic words were "She loves a—" and Genie would conjure up a male. And so it went through the remaining six lists of Problems, Obstacles to Love, Complications, Predicaments, Crises, and Climaxes or Surprise Twists.

When Gardner finished the selection of ingredients, his tenth step was to write a synopsis for a story from:

LOCALE	163	Wagon train
CHARACTER	167	Statesman
LOVE INTEREST	11	Apache. Love with daughter of Apache
PROBLEM	53	Relief from pursuit opposed by legal procedure
LOVE OBSTACLE	31	The match is opposed by a sister
COMPLICATION	53	Revenge is sought against an immortal for having brought loss of riches
PREDICAMENT	92	Madness or mental derangement threatens loss of health
CRISIS	135	About to be obliged to sacrifice a parent to country
CLIMAX	14	Wherein a witness proves to be mad or deranged

Gardner desperately needed Western plots to supply such markets as *Argosy*, *Western Adventure*, and *Top-Notch*, but he did not bother to write a synopsis in the appropriate blank—in spite of Mr. Hill's admonition in "A Personal Word from Author and Inventor" that "Not every Robot plot will appeal to you, but you will find that the development of even those which do not will provide exceedingly interesting and valuable exercise for your creative imagination."

Gardner decided to forgo the exercise and move on from the hapless statesman on a wagon train who was smitten by the attractions of the daughter of an Apache. Perhaps it was too reminiscent of yarns which had recently been rejected. However, he would give the Plot Genie one more chance.

He started spinning the Robot's disk and noting down the new plot ingredients on the next recording sheet:

LOCALE	Monastery
CHARACTER	Magician
LOVE INTEREST	Nomad
PROBLEM	Desired liberty opposed by lack of information
LOVE OBSTACLE	Lovers are mental rivals and one is inferior
COMPLICATION	Illicit love affair threatens loss of achievement
PREDICAMENT	Madness or derangement threatens loss of achievement
CRISIS	About to permit an unrecognized father to perish in fire
CLIMAX	In which enemy is forgiven by hero after having submitted evidence to clear problem

So much for the Plot Genie!

Wycliffe A. Hill had something for everybody. He explained that this particular model of the Plot Genie had been developed specifically for the "melodramatic love story." Four new formulas were in preparation for mystery stories, comedy, romantic stories without melodrama, and adventure stories with or without love interest. There is no record of Gardner's making further inquiry. The remaining recording sheets rest among the Gardner Papers—fragile, yellowing, unused—along with the shipping container in which the whole mess arrived at Post Office Drawer Y, Ventura.

Shortly thereafter, Gardner learned that William Wallace Cook— author of *The Fiction Factory*—was in Long Beach. He wrote inviting him and his wife to Ventura. Cook declined: "I came out here, last fall, because of poor health, and it is necessary for me to remain in one place and keep to a very rigid diet." However, he "would be glad to shake your hand and have a little visit" if Gardner could drive over to Long Beach. He added a high compliment, coming from possibly the most prolific woodpulp writer in the country, "I am keeping track of your work and find it uniformly excellent."

But there was something of even greater interest. Cook's letterhead advertised *Plotto*, "A NEW METHOD OF PLOT SUGGESTION FOR WRITERS OF CREATIVE FICTION by William Wallace Cook." Gardner wasted little time getting to Long Beach.

It developed that "Uncle Billy" Cook had spent five years developing his plotting system. Gardner came away with a copy of *Plotto* and letters of introduction to other California writers, including H. Bedford-Jones whose father lived in La Jolla: "This will introduce you to a man after your own heart, a man whom I want you to know—Mr. Erle Stanley Gardner, of Ventura, California. I want you two to meet and be friends."

The first thing Gardner wanted was to get at Cook's book on plotting. We do not know if he stopped to look at it along the way back to Ventura, but we do know it was the subject of immediate concentrated study. Later he told Bedford-Jones:

> At the time I purchased *Plotto*, I was groping around, writing stories which were rejected as being too weak in plot, and not having enough story in them. I determined to build my plots, and couldn't get to first base because I was unable to find out what a plot really was. It's easy enough to strip plots from stories and tell how the various parts have advanced the story. But that isn't constructing plots. I felt that I could solve the problem sufficiently to make my stories click if I could once find out the basic law of plot and the rules governing the development of plot. I found *Plotto* exactly what I wanted.

Cook's *Plotto*, like Hill's Plot Genie, traced from the work of Georges Polti, but there the resemblance stopped. This was no hastily contrived gimmick designed to make a fast buck. This was a fat 300-page book compiled after years of careful analysis and on the basis of millions of words of experience.

Cook admitted that theme, of which other analysts made so much, was highly important, but he refused it as a starting point in plotting. Theme would come along, consciously or unconsciously, if the creator attended to writing from a sound plot. Emphasizing that his method was a "system of suggestion" to be used as a catalyst to stimulate the individual's imagination, Cook first reduced plot construction to bare-bone simplicity.

If Gardner stopped to read between Long Beach and Ventura, he quickly came to the basics—on page 1. The system derived a plot from three clauses: An initial clause ("A") defining the protagonist in general terms, a second or middle clause ("B") initiating a carrying-on action, and a final clause ("C") carrying on and terminating the action. Desire or motivation in the principal character was responsible for awakening purpose. However, "Purpose alone never made a situation; Obstacle alone never made one; but strike the flint of Obstacle with the Steel of purpose and sparks of situation begin to fly."

Here, Gardner must have gotten the first insight on his past problems. Then Cook went on to state that this whole business of story construction was founded upon a law: *"Purpose, expressed or implied, opposing Obstacle, expressed or implied, yields Conflict."*

This was more like it! There was a law after all. From that day forward, Gardner never violated that law if he could help it, and when he got into trouble with a plot, he always harked back to William Wallace Cook's ABCs.

It is safe to say that Gardner sat up all night with *Plotto* at the first opportunity. First of all, Cook laid out the whole business in a chart. There were 15 "A" clauses (protagonists or heroes), 62 "B" clauses (basic varieties of conflict), and 15 "C" clauses (things which could happen in the end). Clauses could be interchanged to make virtually an infinite number of plot variations, and clauses could be "compounded" or strung end-on-end to produce a story of any length. In simplest form, a plot would be phrased in the broadest generalities:

> ("A") A person subjected to adverse conditions, ("B") seeking to overcome personal limitations in carrying out an enterprise, ("C") meets an experience whereby error is corrected.

Cook went from generalities to specifics, subdividing his categories into literally thousands of event sequences; and as a result the above plot might grow into:

> A is crude, unhandsome and repellent to the ladies, although he desires to be a gallant. A receives from A-7 (a male inferior) a small object of mystery, X, which A-7 declares will make him redoubtable in

love. A takes X and fares forth to try it. A, involving himself recklessly in matters he does not understand, succeeds only in making himself ridiculous. A, staring at X, a peculiar idol that has a strange fascination, falls under a spell which leads him to believe certain events are transpiring—events that are partly true but mostly grotesquely false. A's imagination leads his mind astray, and in seeking emancipation from fancied misfortune he is plunged into real misfortune; however, given all he thought necessary for his happiness, he finds there is still something lacking—something in himself.

Obviously, *Plotto* did not write stories for the aspiring author. It did provide a skeleton which the writer had to visualize in human terms. The "Plottoist," as Cook called the user, did not arrive at story ingredients by chance, and he was not told to write a synopsis out of whatever came up. Instead, he had to page back and forth from number to number through various complexities of the subdivisions until some combination of suggestions struck fire in his imagination and sent him into a story in which he should change and amplify the suggestions, taking care to adhere to the basic structure of plot.

After going through the routine and turning out a couple of stories according to Cook's system, Gardner used the book mainly to learn plot construction. The results were so gratifying that he wrote an endorsement, one of the few endorsements he gave:

> Conscientious use of *Plotto* by beginning writers will do more to give them an idea of what plot is and what it is not than all the textbooks in the country.

It developed that many would-be writers did not have the patience or the imagination required to use *Plotto*. Gardner ruefully described the tenor of the letters he received from irate purchasers:

> I have always admired your ability to plot. I have thought it was your forte. I learned that you used and endorsed *Plotto*. I bought it and now I can't plot like you do—that is the editors say I can't. Now, since I could ill afford to spend twenty-five dollars, I demand that you immediately and forthwith advise me just how you use this book and what is wrong with the plots I have constructed by following your advice.

Gardner did not enlighten those who complained; however, he did go into considerable detail to H. Bedford-Jones:

> A book of this sort may be used in various ways. A writer should have a constructive mind. If he uses any mechanical plot help to do his

thinking for him his stories are going to be weak. If he uses a plot device to help get his imagination working, he's saving himself time and trouble. In my own case I used *Plotto* to find out what a plot was and how to build it. I secured data from it which has been worth a great deal to me. I think any book is of greater or lesser value, depending upon how it is used. I don't think the author ever intended *Plotto* to be used by a writer as a substitute for thought. I always figured his illustrations were just illustrations and that the author who wanted to build plots from the *Plotto* method should have what I call "imaginative equivalents." Deeper than all this, however, lies a mine of pure gold in this book.

Gardner may have put Wycliffe Hill's Plot Genie out of sight, but he did not put the idea out of mind. Following William Wallace Cook's instructions in the final lesson for use of the book, Gardner "individualized" the *Plotto* method. He had been working on development of a formula for the mystery story. He converted the twelve ingredients he had isolated to date into a series of "plot wheels," one for each decision step in plotting with specific examples of facts, characters, and events radiating from the centers as spokes. By laying these wheels out before himself in juxtaposition, he could turn them to various combinations either to obtain imaginative stimulus or to analyze a plot which he had in progress. Cutting the disks out of manila file folders, he made six large wheels (approximately eight inches in diameter):

Acts of Villainy as Story Base
Contact with Act of Villainy
Simple Conflicts Against Villain
Complicating Circumstances
Further Complications
Solution

And six small wheels (approximately four inches in diameter):

Setting
Motive
Hostile Minor Characters Who Function in Making Complications for Hero
Intended Escape
Blind Trails by Which Hero Is Misled or Confused
General Incidentals to Main Plot by Which Suspense Is Obtained

It is doubtful if Gardner seriously used his plot wheels to contrive stories other than for experimental analysis of plot ingredients. We could find no evidence of stories plotted or written as result of their use. Gardner's criticism of "machine"-derived plots was that they were "simply event combinations." The plot wheels were only a step in the development of his formulae for writing mysteries, the most important of which, "The Fluid or Unstatic Theory of Plots" (*see* Appendix I, page 229) incorporated and elaborated the ingredients used in the plot wheels.

Gardner continued development of his mystery formulae, always keeping the latest versions readily available for use in writing or the study of technique. His plotting notebooks offer ample testimony that his agile mind needed little mechanical stimulus to begin creation of a story line. Nevertheless, in 1951 he wrote a two-part serial for *This Week* by starting with nothing more than William Wallace Cook's ABCs. He opened his plot notebook and took up his pen on

Sun. Sept. 2, 1951—At Ranch:

General Serial
Problem— (a) Hero meets girl in trouble.
             (b) Hero in trouble meets girl who befriends.
             (c) Girl fleeing from overwhelming doom which wrecks life.
                 Saved at terrific climax without help of law.
    Suppose we combine (a) and (c)—Girl gets off train in fog. It's a water stop. She opens vestibule door, early in morning, barely daylight. Slips out and runs away into fog. Train pulls out. Man sees open door, starts packing to get off at next station sixty miles away. Seems in no hurry as he surveys the bleak stretch of country.
    Hero is a cattle man, educated himself, tries going into business, back to west where he knows his country, etc.
    Girl meets the guy with a story that is palpably false. He is heading into the back country. She wants to go along as a cook.—Wants to learn to shoot etc. . . . .

The idea began to flounder and Gardner abandoned it to work on *The Case of the Moth-eaten Mink* which he was dictating at the time. On Tuesday, September 16, the serial came to the surface of his mind again:

    The place where the gal gets off can be a small cattle or ranching town and man can send a gloating wire—Quarry run to earth at

Pittsville seven ten a.m. mountain time, am leaving train at North
Platte—Cheyenne.

The gal has adventures. . . .

But the story was still nebulous, and Gardner laid it back in his
mind while he worked on the "Moth-eaten Mink." However, more
than a month later, Sunday, November 18, he printed in firm letters,
"Back to Serial." He noted that it was intended for *This Week* and
printed the words "Suspense" and "Ingenuity" to remind himself of
the controlling audience requirements. Obviously, his mind had been
at work on the yarn:

> The gal on the train. Club car. The man opposite, never in a hurry,
> calm, remorseless. Train stops in Las Vegas, gal looks over things, the
> fat man at her elbow, poised, watchful . . .

This time he had it: the mood, the characters, the events. Before
the plotting session was over he made a 1, 2, 3 brief of the problems
and motivations of the characters, and the skeleton of the story
emerged. He was ready to dictate.

"Flight into Disaster," a two-part serial, was published in the May
11 and 18, 1952, issues. It was anthologized in 1956 as the lead story
in *The Spy in the Shadows*, "Espionage—the deadliest game of all
. . . Great spy stories by the masters."

The story had grown out of nothing but the basic elements of plot
construction which Uncle Billy had planted in his mind. Erle Stanley
Gardner did not need to search for a plot machine; he had become
one.

10
HEROES FOR SALE

A series character is a hero who survives the first story in which he appears to live through another and another and another—as long as reader interest, or the author's ingenuity, keeps him alive. If one could trace the misty history of folklore far enough into the past, he would probably find the technique's origin in a smoky cave where some artful skin-clad *Homo erectus* figured out that he could get a free meal by coming up to a fire and grunting out a tall tale for the amusement of those who hunkered about the blaze waiting for the blood to stop dripping from their latest kill. There are those who believe the 15,000-year-old cave paintings in southwestern France and northern Spain are the world's first story illustrations.

In colonial America, Benjamin Franklin assumed the roles of Mrs. Silence Dogood in the *New England Courant*, the Busy Body in the *American Weekly Mercury*, and Richard Saunders in *Poor Richard's Almanack*. A century later, James Fenimore Cooper created a gold mine in Natty Bumppo, who lived through five novels of the Leatherstocking series and was reincarnated on twentieth-century television.

The lifeblood of the pulps and slicks of the 1920s, '30s, and '40s was continuing characters and serials which accumulated a reader following to bring an increasing number of readers back from one issue to the next, making it profitable for advertisers to buy space to intersperse messages alongside the stories. Today, only the medium has changed. Television abounds with continuing characters. They live to attract audiences who are exposed to the commercials which interrupt the programs.

The writer's ambition was to create a character so popular that he became indispensable to the magazine, and Erle Stanley Gardner started pursuit of that ambition early in his writing career. His twelfth sale was a Bob Larkin story, the beginning of a series character. From time to time when writing an editor to project a new hero, Gardner would say, "Character is my forte." He did not speak lightly.

Erle Stanley Gardner's performance has to be a record. During his writing life he created forty-nine characters who made two or more appearances. This does not count the many hopefuls who did not reappear after the first story or the score or so of carefully conceived heroes who did not make it into print at all.

The Fiction Factory's busiest year was 1934: He had thirteen characters running simultaneously; he published twenty-eight novelettes and three novels starring them, not to mention numerous other works. To fully appreciate the feat, one must remember that Gardner did all of his own writing. He did not merely create characters and farm them out to teams of writers, as do today's television entrepreneurs.

Bob Larkin, adventurer-at-large, first appeared in a *Black Mask* short story in September, 1924. It was also Gardner's first appearance in *Black Mask* under his own name, as the editor explained: "Mr. Gardner was formerly known to *Black Mask* readers under the nom de plume of Charles S.* Green. He now makes his bow, flying his true colors, with a fast-moving story, the hero of which is taken from life."

Gardner had claimed in his letter to the editor, "The character who fought with the butt end of a billiard cue was a real man. He had been a juggler all his life, and the way he could lay 'em out in a rough and tumble was a caution." The model has not been identified, but a line in one of Gardner's earliest notebooks proposed a story about "a man whose only weapon is a billiard cue."

Bob Larkin was an "ordinary, everyday sort of adventurer." He had a phenomenal memory for faces. His speech was highly colloquial and he tended to drop word endings. Since the author employed first-person narration, we have no physical description except for Bob's own comment, "I'm no sheik." His appearance with only a pool cue as a weapon was unique in the woodpulps of the day where blazing guns were virtually *de rigueur*:

*This was a typographical error. Gardner's pseudonym had been Charles M. (for Montgomery) Green.

That billiard-cue cane, by the way, may need a little explainin'. For fifteen years, startin' as a boy, I've been a juggler, and a good one, too. I'm the one who originated the act of sittin' down at a table and startin' throwing the plates around, mixing in the cups, and keepin' 'em all in the air at once. I never pack a gun. I don't need to. A gun makes people suspicious, and gets you into all kinds o' trouble. Nope, just give me a billiard-cue cane, and I'm all set.

As a juggler, with eyes trained to see and interpret motion, Bob deftly performed such feats as catching a thrown knife on the end of his trusty billiard cue.

During his debut in "Accommodatin' a Lady," Bob Larkin went to Tia Juana, Mexico, in search of adventure. There he spotted a girl from Kansas, a tourist without escort and thus a prime prospect for an "ordinary, everyday sort of adventurer"; every woodpulp reader knew she would turn up later. Next, Bob saw a man abusing a beautiful girl with a mole on her cheek. No self-respecting hero would put up with that sort of thing. Bob engaged him with his billiard cue and knocked him out—and then discovered he had polished off Pedro Sanchez, a local bigwig.

Bob pursued adventure to Mexicali, where it turned up in the form of none other than that same girl from Kansas, who told him she was looking for her sister. Sis had sent her luggage ahead from Tia Juana but had not followed; she must have been kidnapped. Naturally Bob offered to help rescue the sister, who turned out to be the beautiful girl with the mole. The Kansas tourist and Bob hatched a plot, and Bob hotfooted it back to Tia Juana with Sis's luggage to rescue her from Sanchez.

Bob found Sis was actually married to Pedro Sanchez; however, she had thought better of the union and wanted to get back to the United States. Bob accomplished the rescue by persuading border authorities to let him, Señora Sanchez, and her luggage back into the country quickly and with no questions. Then Bob discovered that the girl with the mole didn't have a sister, neither had she sent any luggage to Mexicali.

Eventually adventurer Bob Larkin learned that the "Kansas tourist" was the notorious Diamond Maggie and that he had aided her in running contraband. He forsook further adventures in Mexico for the time being and returned to Santa Barbara to sit on the sand until his next story.

Bob Larkin's adventurous activities in *Black Mask* continued intermittently until October, 1932. During this tenure he appeared in eight novelettes and two short stories and was probably responsible for a rash of broken pool cues across the nation.

In January, 1925, Gardner launched another series character, Ed Jenkins, the Phantom Crook. In the first yarn, "Beyond the Law," a newspaper described Ed Jenkins as an "outlaw, desperado, and famous lone wolf." As Jenkins put it, "I'm my own law. . . . my own judge, jury and executioner, and if a fellow starts after my scalp . . . well, I'm still wearing it."

Ed Jenkins was indeed durable. Except for Perry Mason, he starred in more Gardner yarns than any other character: seventy-two novelettes and one short story between 1925 and 1943. He returned for a one-shot appearance in *Argosy* in September, 1961, a "book-length" story of World War II vintage.

Ed Jenkins *alias* Bob Sabin began his highly checkered career by getting into San Quentin for sassing a judge. While in the penitentiary he met Oliver Ludkin. Oliver had been framed on a drunk-driving charge by Shero, a detective who fancied his wife. Jenkins got out of San Quentin first and went to protect Oliver's wife. Ed was framed by the same detective, managed to escape from the courtroom, and began running. He stole a car and in the luggage found twenty dollars, diamonds, and a gun—so he was in business again. The villainous Shero was planning to decorate Oliver Ludkin with a murder rap after his release from prison. By considerable ingenuity and not a little luck, Ed Jenkins managed to turn the tables on Shero without anyone's knowing who was responsible.

In the Ed Jenkins series, Gardner began to use the Chinese lore he learned from his early clients in Oxnard. Jenkins had a Chinese friend, Soo Hoo Duck, the "uncrowned king of Chinatown," who called Jenkins Sai Yan Pang Yeu, "a man of the West who is my friend." Soo Hoo Duck had a daughter, Ngat T'oy, with "eyes as moistly black as ripe olives soaked in olive oil." She was sufficiently fond of Ed that readers could fantasize about what they might be doing between issues.

Ed Jenkins never carried a gun. He lived by his wits, an ambition vainly harbored by a goodly portion of *Black Mask*'s readership. He always carried a makeup kit and changed his appearance frequently with a trick mustache and hair dye. He spent his time reading crime

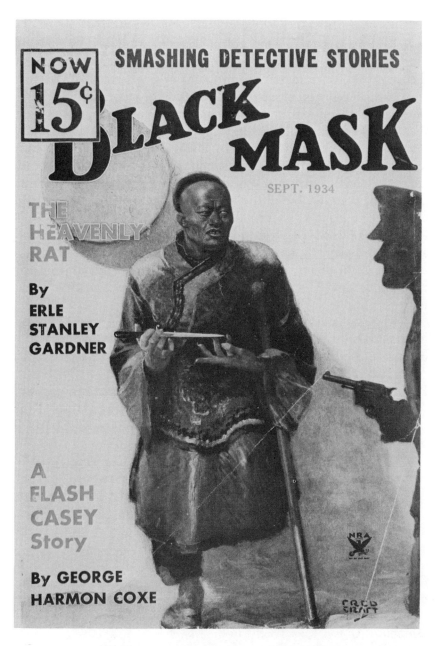

The editor of *Black Mask* wrote Gardner a description of a painting which had been purchased for a cover illustration, and Gardner wrote an Ed Jenkins story, "The Heavenly Rat," to fit the painting. Gardner's daughter Grace remembers, "My father didn't think a young girl should be reading *Black Mask* and other woodpulp magazines, but I was a great fan of his Ed Jenkins stories, among others, and I used to sneak into his study and read all his carbon copies while he was practicing law."

news and solving crimes the police had unjustly pinned on him. During the thirty-five years he inhabited magazines, he kept in excellent physical condition by jujitsu and boxing.

In part, the success of Ed Jenkins was due to a Gardner sales job. Since pulps sold primarily on newsstands, rather than by subscription, there was a problem with serials. Readers liked to be assured that all stories were complete in each issue. Gardner sold the editors on his writing three or four novelettes featuring Ed Jenkins in a loosely connected series. Each story was complete, but Gardner put a hooker on the end pointing toward the next issue, and enough villains were always left over for a grand finale. This enabled him to sell three or four consecutive novelettes, rather than having his character appear in alternating issues, as was usual. Ed Jenkins attracted a substantial following. The editors sponsored a contest for the best description of him. This gave them a bragging point to advertisers about the responsiveness of *Black Mask* readers.

Gardner's characters fell into categories. Early in his writing career he adapted the salty old prospectors, miners, cowhands, and lawmen he encountered in his ramblings about the California, Nevada, and Arizona desert country. He noted in an autobiographical sketch for Popular Publications, "All my life, I've collected characters. Just as some people take up the collection of postage stamps as a hobby, I've tried to collect characters. I've had some great ones, and still have some left."

There was Black Barr, Fate's executioner. No man rode behind him on the trail. In his first appearance he went to New York to be a detective rather than remain in the West as a legend. He was hired to return to Arizona and clean out a band of scoundrels. He wrought his deadly will—always in behalf of justice—in eight stories with titles such as "Fangs of Fate," "Buzzard Bait," and "Winged Lead."

Sheriff Billy Bales, Buck Riley, Fish Mouth McGinnis, and the Old Walrus, so-called because of his drooping mustache, were fresh out of Erle Stanley Gardner's character collection. The latter provided comic relief in a field dominated by death and destruction. For example, "An Eye for a Tooth" in the March 20, 1926, issue of *West*, centered around the traditional Western community Fourth of July parade and rodeo:

The local tailor, something of a joker, had offered a prize for the best-dressed cowboy. The Old Walrus's Bar C gang were sure winners, since the Old Walrus was judging the contest—until some rascals from the Bar Y stole all their finery. The Old Walrus decreed a tie between the Bar Y crew, awarding first prize to one and all, at which the tailor left town. Then the Old Walrus found costumes belonging to some chorus girls who were in town, took them into a storeroom, and sent in the Bar Y boys to claim their prizes. They shed their clothing to be measured for the new clothes. The Bar C crew took their clothes, leaving them a choice: wear the costumes belonging to the chorus girls or come out into the street naked.

Gardner's wanderings along the Mexican border furnished the background for Señor Lobo and El Paisano. Señor Arnaz de Lobo starred in twenty-three tales in *Detective Fiction Weekly*. Upon his introduction in 1930, Editor Howard Bloomfield was enthusiastic but had some reservations that readers were ready for a minority hero:

> I think you have a real one in Señor Lobo. He looks like the kind of bird who is fit to wear my Stetson. I have a hunch that the boy will make a damn popular character. How about sending me three or four shorts about him, then a novelette? . . .
>
> There might be some slight objection to this chap as a foreigner, although I have a notion that his romantic, hot tamale ancestry will appeal to most of the boys and girls. To line up the others, maybe it would be a hunch to have him, in moments of great bravery, etc., tingle to the blood of his American father. In other words, his eccentricities and strange doings Spanish, but his great heroic and admirable moments American, and, by God, you can make the readers swell with patriotic pride at the doings of the foreigner.

El Paisano was an American who enjoyed the excitement of Mexican border towns at night. He came and went mysteriously, working for a narcotics agency of the United States. He was a man of many aliases and carried papers to prove he was mayor of a Kansas town. His distinguishing feature was that he could see better at night than during the day, when he was so vulnerable that he had to go into hiding. On his first appearance in August, 1933, *Argosy* set the stage with an editorial note describing the traits of the roadrunner (*paisano* in Spanish), and a scientific explanation of night vision, straight from a short article Gardner had copied into one of his notebooks.

Minority racial themes were not popular during the heyday of the pulps. In 1930 Gardner tried to introduce Yee Dooey Wah in "Gods Who Frown," a short story in which a young Chinese boy was unjustly accused. Justice prevailed on Chinese terms, and Yee Dooey Wah complained that American law favored the white man: "White man sabbe word one white man better than word two Chinese boys." *Clues* took a chance on this, but there was not enough favorable response to warrant a second story. Gardner peddled Yee Dooey Wah in one more story to *Detective Fiction Weekly* before the saga of the Yee clan faded into literary limbo.

Gardner's interest in China led to a couple of free-lance diplomats. First, while studying Chinese in preparation for a trip to China, he came up with Major Copely Brane, an adventurer in international politics. In the initial story for *Argosy*, eventually published in 1932, Major Brane was lured into a Chinese curio shop and involved in a scheme to prevent publication of a forged treaty between Chiang Kai-shek and the Japanese. Since Gardner had not yet been to China, he quickly brought Brane back to the San Diego area, where he was on familiar ground. By the time Brane finished, the forged treaty turned out to be a bill of sale for a Chinese laundry he had bought, and the redoubtable Major Copely Brane survived a flight hanging on the wing of a plane and other vicissitudes to appear in three more novelettes and four short stories in *Argosy* during the next three years.

While in China, Gardner picked up a Chinese sleeve gun as a souvenir. This inspired *Murder Up My Sleeve*, a novel which created Terry Clane, ex-diplomat in the China service, lawyer, and habitué of San Francisco's Chinatown. Terry's hallmark was resorting to a few seconds of Oriental concentration to think his way out of situations. Gardner had made a note about this:

> If one could think about a given subject for thirty seconds he would master it. Work this out for myself and also have one of my characters proclaim it. The mind thinks for a flickering flash on the subject then turns to something else—then back to the subject in hand—then away on a long tangled chain of by-thought.

Terry Clane demonstrated his power of concentration in one more novel, *The Case of the Backward Mule*.

During the woodpulp era, widespread contempt for Prohibition helped further gangsterism. The nation's law enforcement agencies and the legal system became increasingly ineffective, spawning heroic fictional crime fighters who expressed public frustration by operating on behalf of justice but outside the law. Most were Robin Hood types who stole ill-gotten gains for redistribution to worthy causes. Others were ex-criminals living under social stigma. In any case, it was verboten for the hero to realize more than operational expenses. Gardner's favorite was the wealthy club man who fought crime as a hobby, and Lester Leith was the most successful of a varied lot.

By November, 1928, Gardner had sold a story to *Detective Fiction Weekly*. He went East to visit editors and dropped in on Howard Bloomfield, who had said in a writers' magazine that he was "always looking for humorous crook stories." Gardner must have done a humdinger of a selling job. By the time he got back to Ventura there was a letter waiting: "We have got a 'welcome sign' on the wall for the new crook in the top hat."

Thus was Lester Leith born. Gardner bellied up to his typewriter and a "slender, well-knit, athletic figure" clad in "faultless evening clothes" swaggered out onto the pages of the February 23, 1929, issue in "The Painted Decoy." He remained to star in sixty-five novelettes between 1929 and 1943.

> The police . . . They were morally certain that this suave polished man of the world was past master of the most unusual profession—that of beating the police in the detection of crime and robbing the criminal of his ill-gotten gains.

During his fourteen-year tenure, Leith had frequent use for the "chain-lightning mind" with which Gardner endowed him. Not only did he have to defeat assorted criminals to earn enough to maintain his status as club man, millionaire, and social leader, but he had to outwit a live-in police department spy whom he employed as a butler. Leith paid him almost twice as much as his police department salary—a sore point with Scuttle, since he had to turn the money over to the police department.

Like many of Gardner's characters, Lester Leith held cigarettes in front of himself to watch the smoke spiral upward. He blew smoke rings at the ceiling, and when he traced the perimeter with a forefinger it meant his mind was probing for new, exciting stimulus. About the time Gardner started dictating his stories, Leith turned up with a "dictating machine, one of those things that records the voice on a wax cylinder." Lester Leith plots inevitably concerned two conflicts, one between Lester and some criminal and the other with the police; sixty-five times, Lester emerged victorious, "a jaunty figure of assured indifference."

Sidney Zoom also showed up in *Detective Fiction Weekly*, a master of disguises as he served the intelligence departments of three nations, alternating appearances with Lester Leith. Sidney Zoom was a rich dilettante who operated outside the law to right wrong and fight jackals who preyed upon society: "I am my own courts, my own collector, my own judge." He owned a yacht and, like his creator, had a dog named Rip. He was a denizen of *Detective Fiction Weekly* through one short story and sixteen novelettes from 1930 to 1934.

The Patent Leather Kid appeared in *Clues* on March 25, 1930, in "The Gems of Tai Lee." In this story the character was in reality Stanley Beeker, a gang member who had been smitten by the beautiful daughter of a rich Chinese while at Berkeley. There was much hubbub over a jade bracelet. Then, the Kid disappeared for two years. On May 28, 1932, he showed up in *Detective Fiction Weekly*. His real name had changed to Dan Sellers. He was now a wealthy club man whose strange disappearances were a mystery to other members of his club. A banker could not account for his wealth, and a police inspector liked him but wondered about him. By his final appearance, thirteen stories later in 1934, he had found it necessary to move into an armored penthouse.

Other well-heeled scourges of the crime world who appeared from two to four times in various pulps included: Mr. Manse, who had eyes which "emitted a cold fire of concentration"; he was so mysterious police didn't know if he was really an official of the Surety Bail Bond and Indemnity Company. Dred Bart, criminologist-psychologist, who continued to flick ashes from his cigarette with a well-manicured little finger even though he was wounded. Dudley Bell was a meticulous chap who smoked monogrammed cigarettes and didn't care about money. Perry Burke lived in a mansion, one wing of which housed the Clearing House of Crime, fighting organized crime twenty-four hours a day.

Gardner's stable of less-moneyed crime fighters was a varied crew who doubled in brass: They taught Gardner his trade as a popular writer, aiding him along his way toward the slicks and the book audience, while they served to keep a generation of pulp readers entertained. The variety of gimmicks and plots which he employed is testimonial to the infinite fertility of the Gardner imagination.

Paul Pry was perhaps the most frequent and profitable performer in this category. He bore neither connection nor similarity to the nineteenth-century hero of John Poole's comedy of the same name. Erle Stanley Gardner's Paul Pry was "The Crime Juggler," the debonair type. He concentrated by beating on one or another of his large collection of drums. He held forth through twenty-seven appearances in *Gang World* and *Dime Detective* from 1930 to 1939. At three cents a word, he contributed handsomely to the Gardner coffers as he sat in front of a drum going "Boom . . . boom . . . boom . . . boom!"

No matter how hastily the stories were poured out of the Fiction Factory during those early days, Gardner always conceived his characters with an attempt to find a common denominator for reader identification. For example, there was his notebook entry for Ben Harper, "The Man Who Couldn't Forget":

> Harper can't forget anything he sees. When he drives he keeps his eyes raised above the road level so as not to see license numbers; otherwise will remember almost indefinitely. . . . He only has to turn his mind backward and scenes flow through his mind just as though a motion picture film was being run for a second time. . . .
>
> Back of all this we get the common denominator of a reader's desire for self-improvement, impressing upon him that his mind normally works at a fraction of its potential efficiency because of the fact that he forgets what he should know, thereby dissipating the power of knowledge.

"The Man Who Couldn't Forget" ran in the October, 1934, issue of *All Detective*. Not only did Ben have his phenomenal power of memory, but he could see during the blackest of nights, a convenient ability in view of the dark deeds which were afoot. Ben gave one theater performance a night. While blindfolded he described from memory members of the audience as their seat numbers were called out. As might be expected, this involved him with criminal types and led to murder. His only other performance was for the readers of the March 9, 1935, issue of *Detective Fiction Weekly*.

Dane Skarle, a sleight-of-hand artist and former carnival man, moved from town to town with his assistant Vera Colma solving cases in which a reward was offered. Vera kept pleading with him to quit this tenuous existence and go back to the carnival. Their brief tenure of three novelettes in *Dime Detective* in 1932 and 1933 may have been a response to Vera's pleading but, more likely, it was because readers of the day took a dim view of the liaison between Dane and Vera.

Rex Kane escaped from San Quentin in a 1931 *Detective Action Stories* yarn. Rex always smiled because of plastic surgery. The surgeon had informed him that if he frowned or looked worried the corners of his mouth would pull against tightening skin and he would revert to his former appearance. He smiled through two more stories without attracting enough readers to warrant continuation.

Edward Charles Migrane—Ed Migrane, "The Headache"—was an ex-soldier of fortune who operated with the help of Duke the Dip, a light-fingered companion who had once saved his life. . . . Then there was Jax Keen. Keen's operational background was more novel than his character. He worked for Blitzmount Studios as an alibi fixer for movie stars who got into trouble, supposedly giving readers a backstage look at the Hollywood scene.

The Man in the Silver Mask was strictly a potboiler, although *Detective Fiction Weekly* introduced him with a loud fanfare:

> He hunts the biggest game of all—public enemies that even G-men cannot reach. Only a deaf and dumb Chinese has seen his face without its mask of metal, and even those he rescues know nothing of him—save that he is rich, and fearless, and has a debt of vengeance to pay back to Crime. His past and his face are unfathomable mysteries, but the world knows and the underworld trembles at his terrifying and amazing deeds.

The Man in the Silver Mask lasted for three novelettes before Gardner turned his talent to better things.

Gardner had said he was going to reserve portraying members of the legal profession until he gained enough writing know-how to do a bang-up job of it. By 1930 he apparently believed he had acquired sufficient expertise. His first book-length efforts were about lawyers. He wrote six novelettes for *Black Mask* featuring Ken Corning, a young lawyer trying to get started in New York; the partnership of Small, Weston and Burke dealt in cases that generated horror tales for *Dime Detective*; and Pete Wennick, who was supposed to be reading law, operated as an undercover agent for his firm in *Black Mask*.

Barney "Want-Ad" Killigen was the most colorful of the lot, apparently a sort of warming-up exercise for Bertha Cool and Donald

Lam, who were to burst upon the literary scene under a pseudonym the following year. Barney Killigen was a criminal lawyer who stayed one jump above his declining bank balance. Like so many Gardner characters, he had a "chain-lightning mind." His operational gimmick was placing classified ads in newspapers for a number of incongruous items to be employed in solving the case at hand. He spoke in a "rumbly voice" and spent a great deal of time thinking out loud to Wiggy, his secretary. This was convenient, since Wiggy had to know what he was thinking in order to narrate Barney's adventures.

Though some critics might disagree, Gardner deliberately eschewed the all-powerful superman character in the interest of a mature audience appeal. As he explained in a letter:

> Unless you are deliberately creating a superman type, which distinctly appeals to the juvenile mind, the reader loses sympathy with a character who becomes too invincible. A reader likes to identify himself with the central character. A reader always feels that when he's really in training he can smash some guy on the kisser and make him stay down. He feels this, even when he is fat, fifty, and out of condition.

But Gardner made one exception.

One afternoon in 1923 he joined a number of other spectators in Ventura to watch a "human fly" climb the First National Bank Building. Gardner was impressed as the young man shed his coat, took off his shoes and socks, and hopped nimbly up to the granite sill of the lowest window. Up the side of the building he went, from handhold to foothold. Gardner made a modest contribution when he passed the hat after his exhibition. After returning to the law office, Gardner made a brief entry in his notebook:

> Start a series of stories dealing with the idea of a human fly who is employed from time to time by detectives and crooks alike and who sometimes has adventures as a freelance.

The germ would lie fallow until the next year. Gardner had been trying to crack *Top-Notch*, but he had not found an idea that satisfied Editor Arthur Scott. In June he whipped up "The Case of the Misplaced Thumbs," concerning a human fly who had remarkable powers of observation. Scott was not impressed; the story was bungling and amateurish. He was about to send it back with a rejection slip when he walked over to the window of his office on the seventh floor of the Street & Smith building. He reached out and tested the projections and indentations of the stone work:

"By George, a man *could* climb the building, if, of course, he was young, strong, and cool-headed."

Scott shipped the story back with suggestions for revision. After two revisions, he bought the yarn. Speed Dash, the Human Fly, was born!

At that time, the pulps were under attack because of trashy content which supposedly imbued young readers with criminal inclinations. One of the Street & Smith owners read "The Case of the Misplaced Thumbs" and had an idea: If this character led a pure life, his exploits could inspire the nation's youth and help whip up parental confidence in the magazine. He ordered Scott to get more stories in which Speed Dash's "pure life" was emphasized. At three cents a word, Gardner was more than willing. As he looked back on the series he reflected:

> The things he did could only have been done by one who never inhaled the faintest wisp of tobacco smoke, never touched his lips to a beer glass or looked at a woman's neatly turned ankle.

Speed Dash developed superhuman strength by crushing a raw potato every morning. His eyesight was so acute that he could sit on the roof of a building and read letters on a desk through the skylight of an office five stories below, an idea Gardner got while looking down the airshaft of the Merchants Bank Building in Ventura. Scott suggested Speed Dash's activities be expanded to the perpendicular walls of the Grand Canyon, to the steel towers of a broadcasting station, to the sheer faces of a Himalayan peak—any challenge that might come to Gardner's agile mind.

Speed climbed his way through twenty novelettes between 1925 and 1930, and generated one of the wildest files of fan mail in Gardner's collection. It seems a young sailor was inspired by Speed Dash. Although he could not yet crush a raw potato in his bare hand, leading the pure life had sharpened his reflexes to the point that his boxing was beginning to attract attention. Gardner advised him to keep up the good work and protect the purity of his life at any cost.

The young man worked up to the fleet championship, in which bout he was summarily decked by "a very wicked man who chased women, smoked cigarettes, and indulged in liquor." The sailor blamed Gardner. Gardner immediately broke off the correspondence and spent considerable time hoping he would never meet his erstwhile Speed Dash fan.

While Erle Stanley Gardner reigned as King of the Woodpulps, he festered under his inability to hit the big-time markets. Late one night he faced his notebook and tried to fathom his difficulty:

> The trouble with me in my slick stories is that I have tried to enter a field which has given me stage fright. I have tried too hard. I have tried to do the right thing, and the right thing has been the conventional thing, which has already been done until it is threadbare by people who have been doing it until they know how it is done. I enter the field with a certain amateurishness and try to compete with people who have been doing the same thing until it has become more or less mechanical with them. I should enter the field with a freshness of viewpoint, a virility and vigor which will make all of my fiction stand out, and make people remember it. If I can do this in all of my stories, I have something new to offer, and I believe the public is ready to buy something new.

Although Gardner was unaware of it as he wrote, the golden day was coming. First, three Perry Mason novels were serialized in *Liberty*. Then came the Curtis Publishing Company, the most prestigious of them all: On November 29, 1935, Ben Hibbs, associate editor of *Country Gentleman*, wrote him % William Morrow, the publisher of his Perry Mason novels:

> We have read some of your mystery stories and have been impressed with their absorbing plots and the vivacity and tenseness of your style. We are wondering if you would be interested in showing us something of yours, with the thought that we might be able to use it as a serial.

Ben Hibbs described the *Country Gentleman* audience and, in a subsequent letter, on December 12, offered $10,000 for a "successful character." Gardner wasted no time. Within three days he mailed a "Tentative Outline for Serial Character for *Country Gentleman*," describing Douglas Selby. By December 27, he mailed the first installment. On January 13, 1936, he shipped the remainder along with a revision of the first installment. On January 21, Hibbs wrote back:

> . . . we are buying your mystery novel, "The Hotel Homicide." . . . We are all delighted with the story, and I might say that we editors of *Country Gentleman* still get slightly dizzy and goggle-eyed whenever we

think of a full-length novel having been turned out in three weeks' time—particularly a script which has the quality of this one.

Your plot is a dandy and the characters stand out clearly. Most of all, we are enormously refreshed and encouraged that there is one popular fiction writer in this country who really knows and understands the small city background.

The story was serialized as "The Thread of Truth" and published in novel form as *The D. A. Calls It Murder*. Doug Selby was launched as a character and Erle Stanley Gardner blossomed as a slick-magazine writer: *This Week, American, Liberty, The Saturday Evening Post, Cosmopolitan*—they queued up to come to him for Perry Mason; Win Layton, Girl Reporter; Peter R. Quint, supersalesman; Sheriff Bill Eldon; Sam Moraine.

There is little doubt that Erle Stanley Gardner created character in his own image, or modeled upon those specimens he acquired as a character collector. In early musing, during which he attempted to detail "Rules for Development of Character," he said, "The real definition of a character is one who stands out from the common run of mankind." He went on to note that the "timid average soul" who follows group thinking, doing only the "correct" things, would "have no adventures except such as the law of coincidences may toss in his path." For Gardner there could be no worse fate.

The majority of the characters Gardner created were true to the life he lived or would have liked to live. He began his unpublished autobiography, *The Color of Life*:

> My life is filled with color and always has been. I want adventure. I want variety. I want something to look forward to, and I hate routine. If variety is the spice of life, I want cayenne pepper.

Both in his life and in his fiction, he got his desire. As a dividend— through a dozen or so common denominators—his characters gave his readers the gift of those things they wanted to do but dared not try.

After that, real-life adventures with Sutro aboard the *Spray* became more absorbing than any make-believe affair: "We sailed into strange ports. We told whopping lies. We posed as bootleggers, pirates, revenue officers and hi-jackers. We accumulated sunburn and experience." More than a year later, undoubtedly motivated by the sale of "A Landlubber's Cruise on the Yacht *Spray*," a two-part article, to *Pacific Motor Boat*, Gardner dug out his notebook. He did not take time to develop a plot; he dived into the story:

> Still without knowing what the story was to be about, I transposed those paragraphs to typewriting, added the person of an eccentric millionaire as the owner of the yacht [obviously his friend Sutro], and his daughter, Janice, his sole companion. George Sumpter, the heavily-muscled swimmer who had dropped from the steamer, came in naturally and pulled himself hand over hand to the deck of the yacht and entered the story, dripping and mysterious.

Gardner wrote some three thousand words and "got to the point where the story seemed to drag a bit." Experience had not yet taught him to start with a tightly woven plot. He chucked the floundering yarn into his file and turned to something else. A couple of months later he retrieved it, threw the initial effort into the wastebasket, and sat down to his typewriter to do a fresh version which would "ring in a bit more action." He completed "Beyond the Limit" in a single sitting that afternoon: "I hate revision, and the first copy is the final one."

His first submission was to *McClure's*, shortly before the magazine suspended publication. The editor had previously purchased one of Gardner's stories. ("Since that time checks have come and checks have gone and I've collected nearly enough rejection slips to stuff a mattress.") The story came back with an encouraging letter, but the next seven editors couldn't see it. Finally, he sent it to *Sunset*, a California publication.

Not long afterward, Gardner found the return envelope from *Sunset* in his mail, the same self-addressed stamped envelope he had sent with the story: "There were also other envelopes, all containing rejections. I opened the envelopes, pulled out the mss., chucked 'em in a drawer and left the empty envelopes on the desk. Later I swept them into the wastebasket," including the unopened envelope from *Sunset*.

After a bit, he wanted to check the date on a postmark. He dug into the wastebasket and found the envelope from *Sunset*. It contained a check. Adolph Sutro, the pragmatic millionaire yachtsman, had once read one of his stories and told him, "If you get a check for that I'll think it's a pippin. If you get a rejection slip, I'll say it's rotten."

"Beyond the Limit" had finally turned out to be "a pippin."

As Gardner refined his plotting and writing techniques, particularly after he started dictating, he ceased merely facing his typewriter to let characters and plot flow out of his mind as he involved the characters in one incident after another. He would begin a work by developing a plot germ or a character in his ever-present notebook, or on whatever scrap of paper he happened to find in his pocket.

He literally thought onto paper, recording his stream of consciousness during the creative process as he nurtured an idea, badgering it into a plausible plot which would develop logically. When he was satisfied that his characters and theme had a common denominator of reader appeal and that he had a plot sequence calculated to produce dramatic suspense, he was ready to address his dictating machine with a first draft.

"Protection," a short story which Gardner wrote in 1954, illustrates the process in all its phases. His notebook entries show the burgeoning of the story in his mind. Then he dictated a first draft, revised it, and the idea was finally forged into publishable fiction.

In contrast to Gardner's early writing, this workmanlike approach shows the tremendous development in both writing technique and concentration which had taken place during the intervening thirty years that led to publishers' putting a $1-a-word price tag on the output of Erle Stanley Gardner's Fiction Factory.

On August 10, 1954, Gardner wrote his agent Willis Wing, "We're working furiously on books these days at our hideout in Paradise. It's been hot but on the whole very comfortable." A month later, Wing wrote to alert Gardner to a possible sale:

> Magazine *Manhunt* is putting on a strong promotion campaign with the newsdealers and the public beginning this Spring and wish during that period especially to publish stories by a number of name writers.
>
> They offer $5000. for a story by you, either a short story or a complete novelette from 5000 words up. This is of course for first North American serial rights. The length is for you to decide upon and their promise to me was a reading in twenty-four hours and a cheque within twenty-four hours of that reading. Of course they want a Perry Mason

story but do not insist. I explained that I doubted very much that you would feel a Perry Mason would be desirable in view of your commitments elsewhere.

They have not set a delivery date but of course like every other editor pressed by plans like this want manuscript as soon as possible. When I asked what that would work out in their scheme as best McCloud said ninety days or by the middle of December. I pointed out that you never liked to promise delivery on any specific time but would, I know, want to know what delivery date would be desirable from their point of view.

They want to hear from me naturally one way or the other as soon as possible. Do let me know what you want me to tell him.

In his reply on September 14, Gardner was suspicious that the approach was a ploy to use his name:

> Where the heck does *Manhunt* get its financing? It has virtually no advertising revenue comparatively speaking. It started out as a Mickey Spillane type of magazine and doesn't seem to have changed its format or its editorial goals to any great extent.
>
> Is it legitimately able to pay $5000 for 5000 words, or is there a catch in it?
>
> In other words, do you suppose this magazine is being brought up before this Congressionaı Committee investigating the effect of comics, sadistic literature, etc., and has to have a Gardner story to try and incorporate the veneer of respectability, or do they really feel the story will be worth that much in reader returns?
>
> I'm a little bit concerned about this. I hate to turn down an offer of $5000 for a story, but, confidentially, I don't like this magazine concept with which *Manhunt* started out. I think it is a definite menace to legitimate mystery fiction.
>
> I'd like to have your reactions and you might talk it over with Thayer [Thayer Hobson of William Morrow].
>
> In any event, right at the moment I'm just too badly tied up trying to get abreast of this William Morrow–*Saturday Evening Post* schedule to take on any other obligations.

Wing investigated and reported back on September 24 that in his opinion the offer was legitimate. *Manhunt* was planning to publish Raymond Chandler, Rex Stout, and, hopefully, Erskine Caldwell. They were particularly interested in Gardner's brand of realism. Furthermore, the magazine regularly carried advertising for Erle Stanley Gardner's Perry Mason novels. "I don't think there's the slightest harm in your publishing a story with them." Gardner did not respond and, in a letter written October 28, Wing again brought up the subject:

> The *Manhunt* publishers have been after me to know whether on your return [from a trip to Colorado] you've reached any decision on that proposal for a $5,000. Gardner story. They realize this is a small element among your more important affairs but having made an offer as big as this—for them—they are naturally eager to know what to expect.

This letter was received at the Paradise hideout on October 30. On the morning of November 1, Gardner's "field book," a pocket-size notebook, shows work he was doing on a Perry Mason novel under the working title "Case Unconscious Accomplice," * which would eventually be published as *The Case of the Nervous Accomplice*. By the time he got back to the notebook that afternoon, Gardner had decided against passing up the opportunity to do a short story for $5,000.

The notebook reads:

Paradise, Afternoon, Nov. 1, 1954—
Story for Manhunt

The Initiative

The entry of a working title and its later echo in the plot synopsis indicate that Gardner had already reached into the recesses of his mind and brought up a plot germ. As usual, he started his plotting with basic anonymous stereotypes—"a reformed crook," "one of the waitresses," and "this egg"—who quickly began to take on personalities and names as the story idea took shape, built into scenes within Gardner's mind, and was recorded.

Gardner's handwritten notes from his field book are reproduced in the lefthand column. Ideas which were dropped in the process of writing the story are shown in italics. In the right-hand column, counterpart fragments from the completed story show how the ideas evolved from the notebook through dictation and revision to the published story:

---

* In subsequent plotting books, possibly at the time he started to dictate, this was changed to "Cautious Accomplice."

THE INITIATIVE

This guy is a reformed crook— No one knows his past. He has a rural restaurant— One of the waitresses—the evening shift is sweet for him. *She knows the score. They are living in sin because her husband hasn't come through with the divorce.* This egg shows up. He has a grudge against the owner from the old days. *The owner gets tough— won't take any chances. I'd kill you as soon as look at you. If you carry a gun I'll turn you in. Days pass. The guy lets his guard down, a night drive, air out of tire. Helper to hand him a jack and feels the cold edge of a knife. Three days later it happens again. Guy with hands full— Gradually his nerve starts failing. This is what the guy wants.* He crowds in. Going to make with Stella myself. *A word out of you and I'll blast you. Then Stella makes an elaborate set up by which the guy picks up a gun and she blasts him cold, or he is trying to pull another scare on the guy who owns the place when Stella kills him either in front of the opened safe or preferably in some other guy's place of business where she has a key in connection with her other duties.*

There must be an ingenious twist to it. *George Ollie passes the coffee across the mahogany counter. The cup balanced in just the right place to give a clattering*

PROTECTION

The . . . restaurant oozed an atmosphere of peaceful prosperity. . . . George Ollie, president of a luncheon club, member of the Chamber of Commerce had no connection with that George Ollie who had been prisoner number 56289.

• • •

The man, his hat pulled well down on his forehead, tossed the menu to one side with a gesture almost of contempt.

• • •

"Think maybe I'll go in business with you, Georgie."

Larry jerked his head toward Stella. "She goes with the joint." . . . "You need a little protection."

• • •

"I've left a hundred-dollar bill in the safe. I've torn off a corner. . . . That will enable you to get a conviction. . . ."

• • •

161

noise as Ollie's hand shook. His hand had been shaking for a week now. Three weeks ago Larry Giffen had shown up. It had taken just two weeks to get George to the point where his hand was shaking.

Or George Ollie looked across the lunch counter at his customer. He felt good, an internal warmth that oozes comfort.

When Stella was busy at the tables George helped out at the counter. Stella, smooth, soft, curvacious. He never ceased to marvel at the smooth contours of the rounded flesh beneath the silk of her nightgown.

"Curried shrimp," the man at the counter said.

Ollie was smiling good nature. "It's not on the menu today. We—"

"Fix it."

"Huh?"

"I said get it, put it on. Cook it. I want it. You heard me—curried shrimp."

Ollie looked at the man hard. There was something vaguely familiar about the manner, that assertive belligerency that was its own law.

"Larry!"

The big man grinned. "Now you got it Georgie boy."

"When—how—how long you been out?"

"Long enough to find you. Nice place you got here."

"Listen Larry you can't touch me. I'm on the legit now. I've—"

George Ollie slid down from the stool behind the cash register and walked over to look out of the window. His face held an expression which indicated physical well-being and mental comfort. . . .he had done pretty well for himself—exceptionally well for a two-time loser.

George turned away from the window, looked at the symmetrical figure of Stella, the head waitress, as she bent over the table taking the orders of the family that had just entered.

• • •

"Curried shrimp."

"Sorry," George explained affably, "that's not on the menu today."

"Curried shrimp," the man repeated.

• • •

"You heard me," the man said. "Curried shrimp. Go get 'em."

There was something about the dominant voice, the set of the man's shoulders, the arrogance of manner that tugged at George's memory. . . .

"Larry!" he exclaimed in horror.

Larry Giffen looked up and grinned. "Georgie!"

"When . . . how did you get out?"

• • •

George Ollie gathered all the

"Who said anything about touching you? I want curried shrimp. Get 'em going."

Ollie fought back the old fear. He went back to the kitchen.

Stella saw him making the curry sauce. "What's the idea, George?"

"Special," George muttered. "A special order."

"You mean a special customer?"

"Same thing—special."

The story develops to where Larry has George completely in his power by ruthless power and ingenuity. *He gets him to "visit the old friend." The lights are off and Larry seems to fumble around. He tells Georgie to find the light switch and gets Georgie's fingerprints all over the job. Then Larry is going to turn in the burglar alarm before George can remove his prints. At that point, Stella calmly shoots him, scrubs off her and George's prints.* "He's a crook, the cops won't worry about him." He looks at her. "It ain't good Stella. Now I'll have you to worry about and you'll have me to worry about. We've just swapped troubles." She smiled. "I've thought of that. In this state a husband can't testify against a wife, nor a wife against her husband."

reserves of his self-respect. "Go to hell," he said. "I've been on the square and I'm going to be on the square."

• • •

George Ollie knew from the dryness in his mouth, the feeling of his knees that was what he had been expecting.

"What's the idea?" she asked.

"A special."

Her eyes studied his face. "How special?"

"*Very* special."

She walked out.

• • •

. . . . His cheeks were stinging from the heavy-handed slaps of the big man. His soul felt crushed under a weight. Larry Giffen knew no law but the law of power . . . hoping for an opportunity to beat him up.

• • •

. . . . "Says you! You were handling the getaway car. The cops got one fingerprint from the rearview mirror . . . if anyone ever started 'em checking it with *your* file, Georgie, . . ."

• • •

"He's dangerous."

"To whom?"

"To you—to both of us."

She made a gesture with her shoulder. "You don't gain anything by running."

He pleaded with her. "Don't get tangled in it, Stella. . . ."

• • •

"... We're getting married. ... You need someone to do your thinking."

• • •

"... in this state a husband can't testify ... and a wife can't testify against her husband."

• • •

.... Strangely enough he wasn't thinking of the trap but of the smooth contours under her pale blue uniform. He thought of Yuma, of marriage and of security, of a home.

He thought of how smooth the rounded contours of her flesh were beneath the silk nightgown. For a moment he hesitated, then he opened the car door. "Get in, babe." After all Stella was right, the initiative—you couldn't always give the other guy the initiative.

After sleeping on the idea, Gardner was not satisfied with the way the plot was going. He expressed that dissatisfaction the next day in his field book as he put pen to its pages under the heading *"Tuesday, Nov. 2, 1954, Paradise"*:

The general setting and plot is all right, but I need more clear characterization of the owner as a guy who follows the line of least resistance and got into trouble because of it and Stella as the protective type who gets what she wants. The guy Larry, is tough, hard and ruthless—to hell with consequences.

I also need a more ingenious frame. The one of the killing threat isn't good enough. Larry wants a half interest in the business and in Stella—Georgie says Stella wouldn't go for that and Larry gets tough. *In the meantime Stella seems dumb. She apparently doesn't notice a thing.* Larry pulls three or four jobs. The cops get jittery and George is

.... So he had stayed in his room nights and had perforce saved all the money he made.

• • •

It was Stella who answered the question.... "Don't hurt him. You'll get the money."

• • •

... Larry Giffen ... came after him. "You're hot." ... Wham.... His cheeks were stinging from the heavy-handed slaps of the big man.

• • •

"... She's class, and she goes with the place, Georgie. Remember, I'm cutting myself in for half interest...."

• • •

"... the police ... running around like mad—those two big

nearly crazy. *Then Larry ranks** *a job and arranges to get George's fingerprints on it.*

jobs. . . . That's Larry's technique. . . . Rubber gloves. . . Burglar alarms disconnected."

The story was obviously not jelling. Gardner's notes for that day did not break into dramatic narrative form as was the case when he was visualizing the characters he met in his imagination, watching them participate in the events of the story, hearing them speak. He put the notebook aside. But the following day he was back to the trials and tribulations of Ollie and Stella with a critical eye. His mind had been working on the idea.

Paradise, Wed. Nov. 3, 1954:

The central stroke is off. How about having Stella get a crowbar and smash the cash register, *then shoot the guy.* This makes it too cold blooded. *She shoots him when he pulls the gun on George*—then opens the cash register, busts in a window etc. Or perhaps she doesn't need to do that since his fingerprints are all over the place. Then the guy is shot resisting arrest— They get out an all points bulletin on him. In order to make this convincing I have to bring in an element of grim toughness, a menace that the reader can feel. Larry has to get not only tough but rough—a banging around. *Better to have her shoot him, then put on a mask on him a nightgown on her. She heard a noise, saw a flashing light and came over. She sends George to bed.—Perhaps George kills him in a fight when he tries to take Stella and the gun goes off acci-*

She walked over to the closet, came out with a wrecking bar . . . brought it down with crashing impact on the front of the cash register, . . . jerked the drawer open . . . crunched the wood of the door jamb.

• • •

. . . After the sawed-off shotguns had blasted the life out of Big Larry the police found the bloodstained hundred-dollar bill in his pocket when his body was stripped at the morgue.

• • •

Police were still puzzled as to how it happened Giffen, known to the underworld as the most artistic box man in the business, had made such an amateurish job at the restaurant. Giffen's reputation was that he never left a fingerprint or a clue.

• • •

* Gardner was a diligent student of underworld vernacular. *To rank* was to say or do something which would implicate another in a crime.

dentally. George knows his death warrant is in his fingertips. Larry calls him on that and Stella takes it all in.

That was it! At least so far as the field notebook reveals. Obviously, Gardner laid aside the notebook with his mind still floundering among alternatives, but he must have felt he had generated enough ideas to hammer the plot into a publishable story. That day he sent Willis Wing a telegram in response to his letter of October 28:

WILL DO STORY FOR MANHUNT DELIVERY BY TWENTIETH

Wing reflected *Manhunt*'s satisfaction two days later:

MANHUNT VERY MUCH PLEASED YOU WILL DO A STORY DELIVERY DATE IDEAL

But the promising came easier than the doing. A secretary completed the typescript of a "rough draft" dictation on November 8. After reading the thirty-two-page manuscript, even with its choice of two endings, few editors would have held out much hope for the yarn; it is doubtful Editor John McCloud would have parted with $5,000 for it, no matter how badly *Manhunt* needed big names. And Gardner concurred. His opinion was typed as a finale just as he had uttered it into the dictation machine after the last sentence of the story: *"End of the goddamned thing!"*

But Erle Stanley Gardner, "working furiously on books these days," was not one to waste a short-story idea—not when the deadline for delivery was only twelve days away. That thirty-two-page rough draft shows what is known in the vernacular of the trade as "heavy editing"; interlineations, deletions, additions in Gardner's scrawling penmanship and sometimes with a stabbing red crayon. Not a page escaped clean; the backs of most are strewn with additions and changes. He changed the title from "The Initiative" to "Protection," giving thought along the way to "Without Gloves" and remembering this was the title of a Barney Killigen story he had written back in 1938. One of the endings was junked as were many of the ideas which have been italicized in the above reproduction of the original plotting notes.

The story was noticeably tightened to conform to the unities of time and place, which Gardner mentioned so often in his personal notes

Gardner emerging from a mountain hideout with Dictaphone cylinders after a night of dictation.

on plot construction. The action played out on the same day Larry Giffen arrived, with minimal time transitions necessary; the action never left the restaurant. "Accidents" were eliminated. Following is the completed story in synopsis form:

Ex-convict George Ollie owns a small prosperous restaurant. George takes pride in his success and in Stella, his headwaitress and girl friend. Larry "Rubber-glove" Giffen, another ex-con, appears to threaten George's success. Stella wants to help. George tells her not to get involved; Giffen is dangerous; he has already pulled two local safe jobs.

Giffen blackmails George for "protection" because of a former crime in which Ollie was implicated: He wants half Ollie's profits and Stella.

Giffen comes in that night after closing to get money from the safe. George resists, and Giffen beats him up. Stella comes in. She plays ball with Giffen in the guise of protecting George: She tells Giffen where the safe is, gives him the combination, and helps him to the money, including a torn hundred-dollar bill. After Giffen leaves, George accuses Stella of betraying him.

Stella turns into the protector, though George has his doubts at the time. She takes a wrecking bar from a closet, smashes the cash register, and plants evidence of break-in and safe robbery. After wiping her fingerprints from the bar, she gets George to elope with her because husband and wife can't testify against each other.

After marriage, George learns Giffen was killed in a shoot-out. Stella had planted a torn hundred-dollar bill and told local police about it in case the restaurant was ever robbed.

> Upon being advised that his place had been broken into, George Ollie, popular restaurant owner, had responded in a way which was typical of honeymooners the world over.
>
> "The hell with business," he told the police. "I'm on my honeymoon."

Gardner mailed the twenty-page final draft to his agent on November 17. Willis Wing responded by turn-around mail:

> Many thanks for your November 17 letter and for the story for *Manhunt* "Protection." I like this and I'm sure they will. It has gone over to them and I don't question they will live up to their agreement to pay $5,000. for this promptly. In case there is any difficulty there I will

let you know. However in that event there shouldn't be any problem about placing this handily elsewhere.

There *was* difficulty. On December 9, Wing wrote to report delay in payment, various stalls and excuses. He had found it necessary to threaten recovery of the manuscript for sale elsewhere. The December 9 letter was overtaken by a telegram sent the following day:

PRIED MANHUNT LOOSE AND CHEQUE IN HAND.
SCHEDULED THEIR MAY ISSUE.

The May, 1955, issue of *Manhunt* featured Erle Stanley Gardner's short story "Protection" along with a "complete novel" by Bruno Fischer and novelettes by David Alexander and Jonathan Craig. It carried other short stories by Kenneth Fearing, Bryce Walton, John Jakes, Jack Ritchie, Roy Carroll, William Logan, and Michael Zuray. The back cover was an advertisement for the Detective Book Club featuring Gardner books.

The tale of Ollie and Stella has a couple of postscripts. The 20th Anniversary Issue of *Ellery Queen's Mystery Magazine*—March, 1961—featured the story in reprint under the title "Danger Out of the Past." The editorial blurb said, "Short stories by Erle Stanley Gardner are rare—we don't want you to miss a single one." Gardner was keeping good company in that issue: Dashiell Hammett, Agatha Christie, Sinclair Lewis, and John and Ward Hawkins. Then, during that same March, Willis Wing received an inquiry concerning adaptation of the story for Japanese television.

The television deal never materialized, but as a student of Oriental languages, Gardner must have been curious about what Japanese pronunciation would have done to the many *l*'s in his characters' names—Ollie, Stella, and Larry.

12
THE BIRTH OF PERRY MASON

In 1929 Gardner was thinking about a book-length mystery. On August 6 he expressed to his agent the forlorn hope of every beginning novelist that somehow he can get guarantee of acceptance before writing a book:

> I'm going after books more than ever, and want to do some mystery stuff. But I want a publisher to tie in with before I go at it. I don't want to tie up seventy or eighty thousand words on just a blind lead. If I write a mystery yarn how about placing first serial rights? Would you like to negotiate for 'em?

Bob Hardy, Gardner's agent at that time, was not encouraging; Erle could try a synopsis for magazines, "But there isn't much use taking it up with a book publisher until we have the actual manuscript to submit—too many people are writing mystery novels."

In spite of intentions, prior to Saturday, February 22, 1930, there is no record in Gardner's diaries of serious work on book-length fiction. On that day he noted, "Experimented with book plot." During the next six months he wrote steadily for woodpulp markets, but on August 18 the project cropped up again: "Decided to start book— wrestle with plot."

Notations for August 22 and 26 show that he completed ten and six pages respectively on those two days; after that, work apparently did not go well enough to rate mention. On September 2, 1932, he wrote Bob Hardy about having abandoned the book:

> I started a book for you two years ago and scrapped it when I had it about half done because it didn't have the swing and punch that I

wanted; so I put in my time analyzing what I considered the fundamentals of a good book, trying to get away from the standardized, conventional formula in which there is a murder in the first chapter and an arbitrary set of puppets each of whom could be guilty, etc.

During that 1930–1932 period, Gardner's notebooks reveal concentrated study: notes from textbooks and articles in writers' magazines, analyses of contemporary works, his own perceptive conclusions, and work on "mystery formulae." By September 13, 1932, his labor had born fruit—a new novel 70,000 words long. Later he said that the actual writing had taken less than a week, a half a day to plot and four and a half days to dictate. He mailed Bob Hardy the manuscript entitled *Reasonable Doubt:* "I think this book has a wallop and I think it is the best piece of detective fiction I have written." At the same time he sent a carbon copy to Joseph T. Shaw, editor of *Black Mask,* to whom he was selling regularly, in an attempt to sell first serial rights. Only ten days later Gardner received a telegram from Hardy:

NOVEL WORTH BIG MAGAZINES MAY I TRY LIBERTY AND OTHERS

Gardner told him about Joe Shaw, and word came that Shaw had relinquished the manuscript, agreeing Gardner should have a chance at a high-paying market. Hardy noted in passing that Shaw said "the first part didn't hold his interest especially," but the agent brushed this disturbing omen aside with glad tidings; he would try *Liberty, Elks, Collier's,* and others for first serial rights while he was submitting the book to Simon and Schuster, Mystery League, and such. He casually tossed out $15,000 as the going price for serialization in *The Saturday Evening Post.*

This was a heady potion for a woodpulp writer who had completed only one novel. Out in Ventura, Erle Stanley Gardner immediately began to erect air castles:

> . . . . I intend to turn out a series of detective stories in which lawyers will be the heroes, because I believe that it offers a means of development which has been virtually unexploited in the detective field. . . .
>
> One of the reasons that I have been particularly concerned about getting off on the right foot with this book is that I am intending to turn them out in quantity. This is something that I wanted to ask you about. As a matter of fact, I am working on another book at the present time, and while I can't give you a delivery date at the present time, the

probabilities are that it will be in your hands within the next three weeks.

I am going to try and work out a book every month or six weeks, . . .

Gardner added a note of doubt: "As a matter of fact I can't see where the book is slick paper stuff myself. I think it has too much guts and I think the method of expression is too much in action." Despite Joe Shaw's reaction to the slow start, he had faith:

This business of having the murder come nearer the middle of the book is a trick of technique which I think will prove successful. In so many murder stories the murder is too much taken for granted and the characters are introduced to the reader merely as dummies. With this, motivation of the character is implanted in the reader's mind before the murder comes to mean something to the reader.

Gardner's doubt was prophetic. *Liberty, Collier's, Elks, The Saturday Evening Post, Chicago Tribune, Red Book,* and *Blue Book* turned thumbs down; and Bob Hardy's enthusiasm was soured by a reflection of editorial criticism:

In the line of *Collier's* criticism, and I might add my own personal feeling, I don't think it will do any harm to give some thought to making one or two of your leading characters more likeable and sympathetic. Your lawyer in "Reasonable Doubt" is pretty hard-boiled and business-like.

Bob Hardy reported Clifton Fadiman of Simon and Schuster had rejected the novel. He talked of "unloading" serial rights on one of the Munsey publications. Out in Ventura the air castles came tumbling down, just as Gardner completed his second novel:

A man can never tell just what he has done with a yarn until he gets it finally done and has a chance to sleep over it; at least I can't.

That's the way with the second book ms. "Silent Verdict" which I am enclosing herewith.

When I was writing this yarn I thought it would amount to something. Now that it is complete and I have slept over it, I am intensely disappointed in it.

In "Reasonable Doubt" I incorporated principles of reader psychology that I had worked on for some time, and as nearly as I can judge I achieved almost the effect that I wanted. Most woodpulp stories are too improbable; most smooth paper detective stories move too slowly. In the one case excitement and suspense is achieved through speeding up the event sequence to an unnatural pace; in the other case the suspense is usually achieved through character conflict and the excitement is nil. In "Reasonable Doubt" I tried to work out a yarn that would carry its own excitement without dragging in a lot of hooey and would move swiftly under its own power.

In the present yarn, I made the fatal mistake of trying to combine the two methods in order to get a slick paper formula. As a result, I have neither one nor the other. On the other hand, I believe I have a merchantable story for a certain type of magazine.

The clue sequence by which the plot is built up is, I think, rather clever. The character delineation is rotten. I wish you would glance it over and see what you think can be done with it. It is something that might sell to a magazine like *Physical Culture* and as far as I am concerned, you can sell it for whatever you can get.

Though he probably did not want to believe it, Gardner had pinpointed his own problem: In the light of mystery fiction of the day—woodpulp and popular—his novels were neither fish nor fowl. Bob Hardy was looking through the same pair of glasses, and they weren't rose-colored. He read *Silent Verdict* and wrote back, "I think it is a damned good yarn of its kind—of its kind"—but . . . Then Hardy set out to do his job as an agent, to try to correct the erring ways of his client:

I wish, however, that you would give some thought to what Wesley Stout [editor of *The Saturday Evening Post*] says about "Reasonable Doubt's" having too unpleasant a set-up. I don't want to send Stout this new story because I think he would feel very much the same way about it. Can't you write a story of this type without making your characters all so hard-boiled? Readers of detective stories are very much the same as the average movie audience. They like to get vicarious thrills out of what they read and see. I believe they would much prefer a yarn that had an innocent, wronged young heroine who was saved by a more or less noble hero. They like tenderness, heart interest. Naturally, I don't want you to inject this at the expense of the strength of your story. Dashiell Hammett's stuff is rather viciously hard-boiled, and Fred Nebel has been emulating him to some extent. Keep your air of realism, but avoid the set-up that is too unpleasant as far as you possibly can. You can help the sale of motion picture rights in this way. I think all producers like sympathetic characters, and you haven't anyone in "Reasonable Doubt" or "Silent Verdict" that is really sympathetic— unless it be the secretary in the first named story, and she doesn't figure to any great extent.

I don't doubt that writing these two novels has taught you a lot. Among other things, they should have taught you that you have a remarkable future as a writer of books. Even though we haven't sold "Reasonable Doubt" as yet, you certainly have had a lot of encouragement. You are going to write much better books than either of these you sent me. Take plenty of time with the plot of your third novel and see if you can't turn out something that will make them sit up and take notice.

Such a letter was guaranteed to be anything but cheering to a forty-three-year-old lawyer-writer who had invested so many sleepless nights in attempting to rise above the bottomless morass of words required by the woodpulp markets in order to provide a living in the style to which Erle Stanley Gardner wanted to become accustomed.

A week later Hardy reported that Frederick A. Stokes Company had turned down *Reasonable Doubt*. Bob tried to cushion the disappointment with what can only be described as a graveyard whistle: "Which in my opinion doesn't mean a thing except that they showed damned bad taste." He added, "I have just talked to Thayer Hobson, president of William Morrow and Company, and I have got him very much interested. Anyhow, I am sending the manuscript over to him at once."

William Morrow was "a young and growing house," but it was definitely any port for a writer during those stormy Depression years when "the mystery book market just now is badly shot because of the tremendous influx of cheap cloth-bound books of this character. A number of volumes are being brought out for fifty cents, and this doesn't help the $2.00 books at all."

On November 11, 1932, Hardy sent the glorious news: "Thayer Hobson, President of William Morrow and Company, wants to bring out 'Reasonable Doubt.' I am also going to show him 'The Silent Verdict,' which I think he will like just as well." There was mention of "a little minor editing. . . . He thinks the last chapter is rather bad, almost unnecessary. . . . Another thing: he doesn't like the title very well. He says it ought to be more vigorous for that type of book."

Thayer Hobson has to have credit for being one of the most perceptive and foresighted editors of his time. Even in comparison with the somewhat crudely written popular fiction of the day, in manuscript form *Reasonable Doubt* was not a standout; it reached above the woodpulp level only in plotting technique and pace. In the telling, the tightly woven plot was fraught with typical pulpisms such as "He smiled smokily" and "Rasped out the man." Somehow, beneath this dubious surface, Hobson was able to see the agile, productive mind of the woodpulp writer who sat out in Ventura teetering on the brink of chucking the writing business and applying himself to the legal profession.

But Bob Hardy had also emphasized Gardner's capacity for production, and Thayer Hobson himself had an agile mind. He put that mind to work, and Hardy reported on the results:

> . . . . Hobson seems very keen about your work and is trying to dope out some plan by which it will be easier to sell in large quantities. One suggestion of his that inasmuch as you are going to write stories about a lawyer who turned detective, it might be a good plan to use the same character over and over again a la Sherlock Holmes. The lawyers in your two books are quite different in character. He personally likes the man in "Silent Verdict" better of the two, but he thinks you might combine their qualities to advantage. The lawyer in "Silent Verdict" is not quite so hard-boiled as the other one, but he is a bit older than Hobson would like. He thought that in each case after the problem was solved you could have a brief scene between the lawyer and his secretary in which she tells him somebody wants to see him outside. He inquires who it is, or what they look like, and she tells him something like "A man with a split lip," "a girl with a crutch," or some other effective descriptive touch. The lawyer tells her to send him in and that's the end of the book. Then the publisher will put a note in and say that Mr. Gardner's next book, "The Case of the Man with the Split Lip" will be published in book form on or about such and such a time. Of course, he would have to have one book constantly ahead, but this could be done without much trouble. He thinks this would enable him to build up a very large following and a splendid sale.

On November 20 Hobson wrote Gardner directly, confirming publication of both novels and bringing up a similarity of Gardner's style with Dashiell Hammett's in *The Maltese Falcon*, a comparison which would plague and irritate Gardner for years to come. Gardner responded, expressing a businesslike philosophy toward writing: "You are a specialist in the sales end of the book field." Hobson was delighted "to find an author with an attitude toward his work such as yours." He enclosed his editor's reports covering both *Reasonable Doubt* and *Silent Verdict*.

It is doubtful if Gardner viewed the projected revisions as "minor." The problem was to combine Ed Stark and Sam Keene into one character who would star in both books. "Make your lawyer a little more subtle and a little less hard-boiled than he is . . . I remember being rather uncomfortable at some of the short, clipped, staccato dialogue when there didn't seem to be any reason for it." The Morrow editor objected to wordplay in the names of the heroes—as it were, jabbing readers in the ribs with personification of their salient character traits—one of the more blatant woodpulp ploys. The report went on to deal with plot discrepancies and weak portrayal of minor characters.

When Gardner sat down to revise *Reasonable Doubt*, he was working against the grain of his writing nature, developed by millions of words of woodpulp stories during more than a decade of writing about such lethal characters as Señor Arnaz de Lobo, The Patent Leather Kid, and Black Barr.

Woodpulp readers of that day reveled in action, particularly fights during which they could sit in their armchairs while their hero was beating the senses out of someone who richly deserved it. Generally speaking, those readers were aggressively male; their heroes were disdainful of due process of law in bringing about true justice and rather lacking in social graces. Women—if permitted between a magazine's covers—were equally rough-and-ready specimens. During the early 1930s, the characters' language was highly colloquial; profanity was usually confined to *damn* and *hell*, but readers could always tell worse was in their minds. William Morrow's editor made it clear that complaints about "rough" dialogue did not imply censorship: "If the author wants, he can get a lot nearer four-letter words than he has without running into trouble. The profanity is perfectly all right, but not quite as hard-boiled in its tempo."

During the 1930s there was a yawning gulf between the newsstands from which flamboyant magazine covers screamed violence and death and the drugstore rental library shelves where bored housewives and jaded commuters found mystery and romance for a few pennies a day. In March, 1927, Erle Stanley Gardner had peered hopefully across the gulf when Captain Shaw thought a series of stories starring Ed Jenkins would make a book. He had sent the manuscript to a friend who was an editor at G. P. Putnam's Sons. The rejection came back: "I am sorry to say we do not find them suitable for book publication.

The characterization is not good, and the general style is a little too melodramatic."

Gardner's job now was to prepare *Reasonable Doubt* to cross that gulf. As Hardy had noted in an early letter: "The stories have too little human interest as it is. I wish some sort of love interest could be tucked in somewhere if it could be done without hurting the story."

The task was not going to be easy. Among Gardner's notes are character sketches he had made for reference while dictating the novel. The principals were pure woodpulp:

> Ed Stark . . . . . Attorney, shirtsleeves, weatherbeaten face with steady eyes, five feet eight, hundred and sixty-five to seventy-five, former prize fighter and lumber man, hard and knows it but enigmatical. Hair color sandy, eyes blue, rugged, quiet voiced. Hands big and bony, wrists huge, lips well formed but mouth big.
>
> Della Street . . . . . Secretary, twenty-seven, quiet, fast as hell on her feet, been places. Worked in a carnival or side show, knows all the lines, hard-boiled exterior, quietly efficient, puzzled over the lawyer, chestnut hair, trim figure, some lines on her face, a hint of weariness at the corners of her eyes.

The original manuscript contained 264 pages, and not a one escaped emendation. Interlineations snake out from between lines and circle the margins. Entire pages are crossed out, and the backs of many are covered with rewritten passages. Gardner elaborated upon poorly developed scenes and patched up plot discrepancies. When there was insufficient room on a page—particularly in the beginning—he typed inserts. By the time he got to the last chapter it was obvious that stern measures were necessary; Thayer Hobson had been right. Gardner scribbled a note to his typist: "Margaret:—Am doing this chapter completely over— Dictating it to the machine. Better let Honey transcribe."

Metamorphosing a woodpulp hero involved more than just giving him a new name, but that was the first step. The harsh stabbing thump of the spondaic Ed Stark was discarded in favor of the rippling trochee of Perry Mason. Gardner's first inclination was toward "Stone," but that had the same sort of wordplay to which the Morrow editor objected; additionally, stone is inanimate. "A mason is one who works with stone and, to my mind at least, gives an impression of granite-hard strength." Actually, Gardner's subconscious reached back to his boyhood when he had bought a money order to the Perry Mason Company to subscribe to *Youth's Companion*. As he would learn years later, "Perry Mason" was a pseudonym for Daniel S. Ford, owner of the publication.

After settling on the new name, Gardner faced the problem of chipping away the abrasive corners of Ed Stark without destroying his vitality. On that point Gardner was adamant:

> . . . as far as editing is concerned or changing the title, that's quite all right. They can edit or change as much as they want, except that I don't want them to destroy the general character of the book—a fighting lawyer who is willing to go to hell to save a client, even when the client isn't worth saving.

As one studies the revised manuscript, it becomes obvious that transforming Ed Stark into Perry Mason was not the only change which was taking place. A woodpulp writer had reached maturity; he was stepping up to the next rung of the literary ladder as he subjected himself to the painful discipline of revision. This change of audience appeal was a far cry from his former practice of merely rewriting ailing short stories and novelettes within the loose confines of the same old slam-bang woodpulp style. When it was all over, Erle Stanley Gardner would write his agent: "revising a book is about the hardest job I have ever tackled."

The following examples illustrate how Gardner went about the transformation. Original manuscript versions of *Reasonable Doubt*, starring Ed Stark, are on the left; the same passages as finally published in *The Case of the Velvet Claws* are on the right. First Gardner gave attention to his character's physical description, particularly his hands and shoulders. This had the effect of making Perry Mason's presence more intellectual and less physical than Ed Stark's bruising personage:

Autumn sun beat against the window.	Autumn sun beat against the window.
Ed Stark sat at the big desk, in his shirt sleeves. He was not fat, and yet the man's torso gave the impression of having been too big for his coat, particularly where the huge shoulders seemed to	Perry Mason sat at the big desk. There was about him the attitude of one who is waiting. His face in repose was like the face of a chess player who is studying the board. That face

bulge out on either side of the vest. His face had a weather-beaten appearance. The man radiated competency.

Book cases, filled with leather-backed books, lined the walls of the room. A big safe was in one corner. There were two chairs, in addition to the swivel chair which Ed Stark occupied. On the back of one of these chairs, was draped the coat which Stark had removed.

•　•　•

Ed Stark fingered a paper weight on his desk. His wrists were big-boned, and his hands were massive. The fingers seemed filled with a competent strength that made it seem the hands would have a grip of crushing force.

•　•　•

He frowned, scooped up the money with his big hands, and beckoned to Della Street.

•　•　•

Ed Stark . . . His face was grim and determined, and the eyes were cold as twin chunks of ice. He radiated impatience that was held under control.

With his big shoulders and out-thrust jaw, he seemed like some pugilist seated in his corner, waiting . . .

seldom changed expression. Only the eyes changed expression. He gave the impression of being a thinker and a fighter, a man who could work with infinite patience to jockey an adversary into just the right position, and then finish him with one terrific punch.

Book cases, filled with leather-backed books, lined the walls of the room. A big safe was in one corner. There were two chairs in addition to the swivel chair which Perry Mason occupied. The office held an atmosphere of plain, rugged efficiency, as though it had absorbed something of the personality of the man who occupied it.

•　•　•

Perry Mason fingered a paper weight on his desk. His hand was well formed, long and tapering, yet the fingers seemed filled with competent strength. It seemed the hand could have a grip of crushing force should the occasion require.

•　•　•

He scowled, scooped up the money with his swiftly competent hands, and beckoned to Della Street.

•　•　•

Perry Mason . . . His face was set in lines of patient concentration, his eyes glittered. He seemed like some pugilist seated in his corner, waiting . . .

Gardner not only made Perry Mason put on his coat while dealing with his client but he rid him of Ed Stark's typically rough and ready woodpulp background without detracting from the fighting lawyer he wished to portray by the simple expedient of deletion:

"If you look me up through some family lawyer or some corporation lawyer, he'll probably tell you that I'm a shyster. If you look me up through some chap in the District Attorney's office, he'll tell you that I'm a dangerous antagonist, but he doesn't know very much about me. If you look me up through a bank you won't find out a damned thing.

"People come to me because they need me. I never went through college, and I don't run around in society. I used to be a prize fighter, and then I was a lumber-jack in the Pacific Northwest. I saw I wasn't getting anywhere, and started in to study law. I don't know how much law I know. I know enough to get by. I picked a state that had easy examinations to get admitted in. And then I got admitted in this state on the strength of my certificate in that state.

"If I had to get by on the strength of what law I know, I'd probably starve to death. That is, I know it all right, but I don't get credit for knowing it. I had specialized in just one thing, and that's getting clients out of trouble. Whenever I do get them into court, I win my case. Not so much because I know law, as because I know exactly what the

"If you look me up through some family lawyer or some corporation lawyer, he'll probably tell you that I'm a shyster. If you look me up through some chap in the District Attorney's office, he'll tell you that I'm a dangerous antagonist, but he doesn't know very much about me. If you look me up through a bank you won't find out a damned thing."

Burke opened his mouth to speak, then thought better of it and was silent.

"Now maybe that information will cut down the amount of time you're going to take to look me up," went on Mason. "If you call up Eva Belter, . . ."

witnesses are going to testify to.

"Now maybe that information will cut down the amount of time you're going to take to look me up.

"If you call up Eva Belter, . . ."

Perry Mason's attitude toward both his client and his enemies became more subtle as he took on social graces obviously lacking in Ed Stark. Mason displayed harshness as required by story conflict rather than as a matter of course because he was a male protagonist:

Ed Stark said, brutally: "How the hell did I know?"	"How was I supposed to know that?" asked Perry Mason.
• • •	• • •
He paused abruptly, and whirled, thrusting his weather-beaten face within a few inches of Locke's startled countenance.	He paused abruptly, and whirled, staring at Locke with cold, hostile eyes.
• • •	• • •
Ed Stark stared at the man with his rugged, weather-beaten features showing a certain admixture of disgust and resentment. Then he deliberately raised his feet and put them on the corner of the politician's desk.	Perry Mason's expression was a mixture of disgust and resentment. Then he took a step toward the politician's desk and stared down at the man's face.

Gardner got away from the old woodpulp formula of the extended fight scene by development of his principal character. He explained his new technique in a letter to Thayer Hobson, "The character I am trying to create for him is that of a fighter who is possessed of infinite patience. He tries to jockey his enemies into position where he can deliver one good knock-out punch":

"The hell it won't," said Ed Stark. He measured the distance, and slammed a straight left full into the leering mouth.	"The hell it won't," said Perry Mason. He measured the distance, and slammed a straight left full into the grinning mouth.
Crandall's head shot back. His face lost its leer, and twisted into a distortion of savage hatred. He	Crandall's head shot back. He staggered for two steps, then went down like a sack of meal.

thrust his jaw forward, and set himself for a terrific swing.

Ed Stark stepped in with the swift skill of a professional, and chopped a short left to the jaw, a light blow that served only to measure the distance and hold the jaw into the position that he wanted. Pivoting from the hips, he crossed his right in a sledge-hammer blow to the jaw, that sounded like the impact of a spade on wet clay.

The man went down like a sack of meal.

Gardner labored over the dialogue. Not only was he anxious to respond to the editorial criticism but, as he pointed out to Hobson, "rereading . . . I find that I have made my style far too similar to Hammett's":

". . . Get him to shadow this baby when she leaves the office. . . ."

• • •

"So," he said, "that's the kind of scum you are, is it?"

• • •

"Hell no," he said. "I was at home in bed."

• • •

Stark said: "Wait a minute, baby. You haven't seen the blow-off yet."

• • •

"You're a good kid, Della," he said. "Even if you do get funny ideas about women."

". . . Get him to shadow this woman when she leaves the office. . . ."

• • •

"So," he said, "that's the kind of tactics you folks are going to use, is it?"

• • •

"No. I was at home, in bed."

• • •

"Wait a minute, young lady," Mason warned. "You haven't seen the blow-off yet."

• • •

"You're a good girl, Della," he said. "Even if you do get funny ideas about women."

Also, Gardner polished the rough corners off Della Street's character and, by deftly turning a phrase, made her more perceptive than worldly wise. Her speech became more refined:

Della Street was slim of figure, steady of eye; a young woman of approximately twenty-seven, who gave the impression of knowing the world and being just a little weary of it.

She eyed Ed Stark with quiet insistence.

. . .

"No," she snapped, "that's not fair. And you know it. And, anyway, that isn't what I meant. . . ."

Della Street was slim of figure, steady of eye; a young woman of approximately twenty-seven, who gave the impression of watching life with keenly appreciative eyes and seeing far below the surface.

She remained standing in the doorway eyeing Perry Mason with quiet insistence.

. . .

Della Street shook her head, and said: "That isn't what I meant. . . ."

The new Della Street was not a mere female office stereotype, to be patted, ogled, and ordered about the office, as was the usual lot of woodpulp secretaries. Perry Mason developed understanding of his employee and was rewarded by her concern for his welfare:

Stark moved over toward the door and put his arm around the girl's waist, and carried her along with him.

"Okay, Della. I'm willing to take your word for it. But I'm not going to quarrel with customers. Let me know just as soon as you hear from Paul Drake. He should be reporting pretty quick either in person or by telephone."

Ed Stark stood in the doorway of the outer office while Della Street walked over to the desk, . . .

. . .

He watched her with eyes that were suddenly deep and enigmatical. "If all clients had your loyalty, Della, there wouldn't be any law business. Don't forget that. You've got to take clients as they come. You're different. Your family was rich. Then they lost their money. You went to work. Lots of women wouldn't have done that."

Her eyes were wistful once more.

"What would they have done?"

"They could," he remarked slowly, "have married a man, and then gone out to the Beechwood Inn with some other man, got

". . . . I never did trust her."

"Okay," he said. "Now forget that, and get an ear-full. I don't know what's going to happen here, and you may have to carry on if anything happens that I can't."

"What do you mean," she said, "that you can't?"

"Shut up," he said, "and get an ear-full."

"Okay," she said. "Give it to me."

He said: "This woman came to us as Eva Griffin. . . ."

caught, and had to get a lawyer to get them out of the jam."

She turned toward the outer office, keeping her eyes averted from him. Those eyes were glowing. "I started to talk about clients," she observed, "and you begin to talk about me." And she pushed her way through the door into the outer office.

Perry Mason walked to the doorway and stood there while Della Street went over to her desk, sat down at it, and slid a sheet of paper into her typewriter.

• • •

". . . . I never did trust her."

"Okay," Mason said, wearily. "Now forget that, and get your instructions. I don't know what's going to happen here, and you may have to carry on if anything happens that I can't keep the ball rolling."

"What do you mean," she asked, "that you can't?"

"Never mind about that."

"But I do mind," she said, eyes wide with apprehension. "You're in danger!"

He ignored the remark. "This woman came to us as Eva Griffin. . . ."

Thayer Hobson had worried about the "hard-boiled paternalism" with which both Ed Stark and Sam Keene treated their secretaries. He suggested, "Why not put Stark's girl in a little closer relationship to him? You wouldn't have to say it in so many words that they were sleeping together or that the girl wanted to marry Stark and Stark wasn't quite ready for it, or that Stark wanted to marry the girl and she wasn't quite ready for it. . . ."

Whatever else woodpulp characters did, they observed propriety in regard to marital relationships. Erle Stanley Gardner, of *Black Mask* fame, was the one who was not ready—not for anything like that! He barely managed to tuck in a few touches of Bob Hardy's "some sort of love interest," and Della Street waxed vehemently vocal in Perry's defense—forging a relationship that was destined to last for forty years through eighty-two novels and three novelettes:

"When any woman gets me in a jam," he said, "I'll take it on the button. I don't have to have the protection of any woman to get me out of a tight place."

"Okay," she said, "I told the detective that you wanted her shadowed as soon as she left the office. He said he'd be there to pick her up."

• • •

His face didn't change expression, but his eyes glinted. "That's one of the chances I have to take," he told her. "I can't expect my clients to be loyal to me. They pay me money. That's all."

She stared at him with a speculative look that held something of a wistful tenderness. "But you insist on being loyal to your clients, no matter how rotten they are."

"Of course," he told her. "That's my duty."

"To your profession?"

"No," he said slowly, "to myself. I'm a paid gladiator. I fight for my clients. Most clients aren't square shooters. That's why they're clients. They've got themselves into trouble. It's up to me to get them out. I have to shoot square with them. I can't always expect them to shoot square with me."

"It isn't fair!" she blazed.

"Of course not," he smiled. "It's business."

She shrugged her shoulders. "I told the detective that you wanted her shadowed as soon as she left the office," she said, abruptly getting back to her duties. "He said he'd be there to pick her up."

• • •

". . . . She's got that snobby complex."

Stark grinned at her.

"You're jealous," he said.

Della Street's face flushed.

"The hell I am," she said, and slammed the door behind her as she flounced back into the outer office.

• • •

Ed Stark gently disengaged Della Street's arm, and said:

"It's okay, baby. Don't get all worked up about it. I'm going out and chase down a few clues. . . . You can manage to let me know what's going on without letting on who I am."

"You mean that they'll be listening in on the line?" she asked.

"They may," he said. "I don't know just where this thing is going to lead."

"Oh, Ed," she said.

He shook his head at her and grinned.

"Be good," he said, and walked out of the office.

It was still dark when he walked into the lobby of the Hotel Ripley, . . .

". . . . She's got that snobby complex."

"Lots of people are like that, Della."

"I know, but she's different. She doesn't know what honesty means. She loves trickery. She'd turn on you in a second if it would be to her advantage."

Perry Mason's face was thoughtful.

"It wouldn't be to her advantage," he remarked, his voice preoccupied.

Della Street stared at him for a moment, then softly closed the door and left him alone.

• • •

Perry Mason pulled his hat down on his head and slipped into his overcoat, which was still damp enough to give forth a smell of wet wool.

"I'm going out and chase down a few clues," he told Della Street. . . . "You can manage to let me know what's going on without letting on who I am."

"You think that they'll have the telephone line tapped?"

"They may. I don't know where this thing is going to lead."

"And they'll have a warrant out for you?"

"Not a warrant, but they'll want to ask me some more questions."

She looked at him sympathetically, tenderly, said nothing.

"Be careful," he said, and walked out of the office.

> It was still dark when he entered the lobby of the Hotel Ripley, . . .

Titling turned out to be a bother. Gardner's original title derived from the legal condition for acquittal which he planted a number of times through the book, as when Perry Mason said, "I know the jury can't convict anybody as long as they've got a reasonable doubt."

Despite earlier discussion of the eventual title format with Bob Hardy and Gardner's responding suggestion of *The Case of the Velvet Claws*, Thayer Hobson now thought *case* should be the last word in the title, possibly influenced by the popularity of S. S. Van Dine's books such as *The Benson Murder Case*. He wrote, "The title is tremendously important in the mystery field. The trend is away from the 'Murder' type of thing, but it is damnably hard to find something really distinctive and original. If you have more than one suggestion, by all means send them on and let us advise you."

On December 14, Gardner sent along a spate of suggestions: *The Blackmail Murder Case, The Blackmailed Bride Murder, The Blackmailed Bride Affair, Murder in the Rain, The Bathrobed Corpse Case,* and *The Case of the Bathrobed Corpse.* He also reached into his notebook of woodpulp tricks: "If you want to get away from the murder and case angle and get a title which hints at action and detective stuff without saying so in so many words": *Hangman's Hemp, The Finger of Suspicion,* and *Thirteen Steps.* "Then there's the angle of using two-word titles as *Velvet Claws* which I would favor if it wasn't for the fact that some murder mystery fan might figure it was a story of sex and sirens."

Nevertheless, "Velvet Claws" was tentatively penciled on the revised version of the first chapter which he enclosed, but he assured Hobson that he could regulate the text to refer to any title which might be chosen.

On December 17, Hobson telegraphed Gardner to let him know the editorial decision went to *The Case of the Velvet Claws.* The die was cast, but it is doubtful if anyone involved in that decision dreamed the pattern would last for almost forty years. The revised manuscript which was then being typed in the Fiction Factory shows the insertion of a single textual plant to echo the title, a sentence at the end of one of Della Street's comments on Perry Mason's double-dealing client:

The Perry Mason comic strip was syndicated in United States and Canadian newspapers from October, 1950, until June, 1952. Difficulties obtaining adequate plots and faithful character representations made it one of the most troublesome of Gardner's subsidiary enterprises. Gardner insisted each segment should have sufficient suspense to make a reader want to get the next day's newspaper. He plotted "The Case of the Nervous Horse" (above) using his knowledge of archery as a background.

"I *hate* her!" Della Street said fervently. "I wish you'd never seen her. She isn't worth the money. If we made ten times as much money out of it, she still wouldn't be worth it. I told you just what she is—all velvet and claws."

One can almost hear the sigh of relief exuding from Gardner's letter of December 20 from "On Board the Camp Wagon, Somewhere around Indio, California." He told Thayer Hobson the revision was complete except for final typing and he was taking off to prowl his beloved desert.

Erle Stanley Gardner had graduated from the woodpulps; however, as he told Bob Hardy, he was going to do some "magazine stuff" and wait for critical reaction to *The Case of the Velvet Claws* before he tackled *Silent Verdict*. If the newly graduated mystery book writer thought procrastination would make the writing and revision of novels easier, he was sorely mistaken. His plotting notebooks show the germination and development of plots for most of the more than eighty Perry Mason stories he wrote thereafter, and seldom is one of those synopses lacking the interruption of an annoyed caution to himself: "This is too woodpulpy. . . . This is not a Mason plot."

William Morrow and Company published *The Case of the Velvet Claws* in March, 1933. The acclaim of reviewers made all of the trouble seem worthwhile. Elizabeth C. Moore of the *Philadelphia Inquirer* was perhaps the most accurate in prophecy: "Perry Mason is destined—we hazard the guess—to engage the attention of the lover of good mystery stories through many another case to follow. . . . An excellent story." And O. O. McIntyre, widely read newspaper columnist, gave it a good boost on April 23, 1933: "'The Case of the Velvet Claws' (Morrow) will keep you up—if you like curdling mystery."

Perry Mason had been born of a union between Ed Stark and Sam Keene, with Thayer Hobson serving as midwife. Erle Stanley Gardner had spent most of December, 1932, spanking life into the blustering baby, and now it was up to him to incubate and nurture the new lawyer-detective through a time when hundreds of similarly employed characters were dying for want of reader sustenance.

13
GARDNER *vs.* HOBSON

A lawyer traditionally sets aside the warmest personal friendship during the knockdown courtroom conflict on behalf of a client, and editors go about their work with cold-blooded concern for the commercial success of the books they publish, no matter what their feelings toward the authors of those books. As Thayer Hobson once put it in a letter to Gardner, "Damn it, Erle, it is tough to get really fond of an author."

At the beginning of their association in late 1932, Bob Hardy introduced Thayer Hobson by writing Gardner, "He's a terribly decent sort. I think you two men will get along together splendidly."

During the first six months, their friendship warmed slowly over distant mutual respect. Gardner wrote, "You folks know more about the desires of the book reading public than I do"; and Thayer Hobson was obviously rather in awe of an author who so matter-of-factly described Herculean activities:

> Last fall when I started to write books, I turned out that first book one month; the second book the next, and then a third book in the following month. During all of that time I was writing one hundred odd thousand words of magazine fiction every month and the output was not curtailed on account of the books.

As they traded editorial correspondence, Gardner addressed Thayer Hobson as "Mr. Hobson," waiting for his editor to make the first move toward informality. On June 20, 1933, he could write:

> Glad you have abandoned the "mister." In dealing with you New Yorkers I never know whether to bust out and act natural, so I always let

you folks make the first advance, but I have a feeling you and I have a good deal in common in our outlook on life, and have been strongly tempted to throw formality overboard some time ago.

Within a month they were on a first-name basis. While their letters were concerned with the serious business of launching Perry Mason, alongside the problems of the moment there was bantering; Hobson would write, "Give my regards to the slaves," and secretaries in the Fiction Factory would respond by adding postscripts to Gardner's letters.

In late June, Gardner submitted *Broken Glass*, a mystery novel about a lawyer-astronomer. If Morrow objected to using his name, he suggested through his agent that the book might be published under a pen name, by either Morrow or some other house. Hobson was painfully frank in his lack of enthusiasm: "I'd fight like the devil to prevent it appearing on our list or on anyone else's list over your name. . . . things drag along too long before the crime. The solution is a little bit unsatisfactory since none of the main characters in the story turn out to be guilty. Frankly, I wouldn't have finished the book if I hadn't known that you had written it." Gardner agreed and told his agent to withdraw the manuscript from circulation.

During editorial work on the first several Perry Mason novels, Gardner was a docile writer so far as accepting editorial criticism and complying with suggestions for revision were concerned. In fact, he took exception in October, 1933, when Hobson wrote that he had thought about "toning down" his editors' critical remarks concerning Gardner's fourth book, *The Case of the Lucky Legs:**

> Just let me give you Gardner's idea of Gardner, so that we won't be working at cross purposes. I think I'm green on the technique of handling books. I think that I've got a good plotting mind. In fact, I'm afraid that I'm a little too stuck on it for my own good. In other words, I think "The Lucky Legs" book may have had a little too complicated a set of circumstances in place of a straight, simple plot. I'm not certain but what the book I'm working on now is open to that criticism. Too many complications make a tangle instead of arousing interest. I know I'm careless as the devil as far as details are concerned. I know I'm

---

**The Case of the Howling Dog* was the third Perry Mason novel to be written; however, William Morrow delayed its publication to give *Liberty* magazine time for serialization. *The Case of the Lucky Legs* was scheduled in its place in February, 1934.

conscientious as hell as far as the work itself is concerned. I'll do any amount of work in order to turn out something that's the best I can do. I know that right at the present I'm faced with the necessity of getting out around a hundred thousand words of woodpulp fiction a month and that such books as I do have to be done in addition to that, which makes lots of work at high speed in place of a more leisurely development. Eventually, I hope to be able to subordinate that woodpulp fiction. But, brother, I'm one fighting son of a bitch. I've started in to lick this mystery book business and while I may lose a round or two, if any of you birds think that the ultimate outcome is in any doubt, all I've got to say is don't bet any money on it.

Since titles for the Perry Mason novels usually derived from the peripheral opening mystery which aroused interest rather than from the principal plot, Gardner could easily use a title as a springboard for starting a book. When he furnished a new title, *The Case of the Lucky Legs*, to substitute for *The Case of the Howling Dog*, he wrote Thayer Hobson that he had selected the title purely because of its promotional value:

> I am willing to admit that I haven't the faintest idea of what the lucky legs are going to be about, but I know that we are, both of us, anxious to sell books. . . . so I figure that if you are interested in the title, *The Case of the Lucky Legs*, it may adapt itself to a good deal of exploitation.

It did! Both *The Case of the Velvet Claws* and *The Case of the Lucky Legs* were runners-up for the best-seller list.* The conversion of Sam Keene in *Silent Verdict* to Perry Mason in *The Case of the Sulky Girl* put Gardner's second novel on the top list for 1933.

During the first three years of Gardner's association with Hobson and other Morrow editors, there were lively discussions over "the Mason formula" and minor editorial changes, but no disagreement of major proportion. Gardner and Hobson had their first real argument

---

* A best seller, as defined in Frank Luther Mott, *Golden Multitudes: The Story of Best Sellers in the United States* (New York: R. R. Bowker Company, 1960), was a book with a total sale equal to one percent of the national population. This represented a minimum of 1,200,000 copies. A "runner-up" was one which almost reached the required total. From 1933 through 1938, Gardner was author of ten of the forty-four books (both fact and fiction excluding bibles, hymnals, textbooks, reference works, etc.) which composed the best-seller and runner-up lists—almost twenty-five percent.

over titling. Just before leaving on a trip to Hawaii, Gardner submitted *The Case of the Dangerous Dowager*, his tenth novel. In Hawaii, he received a cablegram from Thayer Hobson suggesting that the title be changed to *The Case of the Pigheaded Widow*. Nearby residents of Honolulu must have thought a new volcano was spouting as Gardner sat down to his typewriter to pound out a steaming two-page reply:

> Your wire about The Pigheaded Widow.
> My answer "NO!"
> Pigheaded women are a drug on the market.
> Suppose you're a man looking for entertainment. You have two bucks in your pocket. You want something intriguing, something different. A friend says I've got two women friends. You can spend your two bucks going to call on either one. One's a dangerous dowager. The other's a pigheaded widow. What's your answer?
> If you don't like Dangerous Dowager kill it. But let's get a title that will have sales appeal that will have a hint of danger, of mystery, of contradiction in terms which will promote reader interest. Let's have it sinister, unusual or compelling. Pigheaded Widow is like Blonde Manicurist, Fond Parent, Wayward Child, Persistent Salesman, or Temperamental Author. . . . Who the hell cares? . . . If you want a title which will make every normal masculine reader turn away in disgust there are only two others which will have a higher disgust-producing value:—The Case of the Nagging Wife, and The Case of the Visiting Mother-in-Law.
> You wanted my opinion. That's it.

Gardner's notebooks reveal that he had been experimenting with Mason titles for some time. The margins of his plotting books are sprinkled with titles which he recorded as they came to mind. Some eventually turned up on books: "Unpaid Fiddler," "Burnt Fingers," "Eloquent Corpse," "Floating Crutch," "Duplicate Crutch," "Shop-lifter's Bag," "Matchmaker's Wig," "Tattered Typist," "Timid Typist," "Terrified Typist," "Candid Calendar Girl," "Calendar Girl," "Mystified Model"—to list only a few. He also analyzed title combinations on the basis of mystery, action, contrast, and other categories (*see* Appendix X, page 263).

After his return from Hawaii in June, 1936, Gardner carried his protest of "The Case of the Pigheaded Widow" directly to Thayer Hobson's office, where the announcement of his impending arrival created considerable consternation. Hobson circulated an office memo: "Listen, we have to take this Gardner title business seriously. He's arriving in New York next week and we have to have something to see him on, that we can sell him on. I think he's damned PIG-HEADED WIDOW too completely in his own mind ever to be able to accept it. I am attaching his last letter. For God's sake, let's get some decent title suggestions within the next week."

The memo went the rounds, and none of the appended suggestions was particularly inspired. Gardner won his case. Hobson succumbed, and *The Case of the Dangerous Dowager* was published in April, 1937.

On the final page of *The Case of the Dangerous Dowager* a young woman carrying a caged canary evaded Della Street's watchful eye to get into Perry Mason's inner office by way of the private entrance. Della was about to have the interloper ejected when Perry knelt to examine the bird and noticed that it had a sore foot. Although Perry Mason was unaware of his tenuous hold on life, at that moment there was every possibility that the upcoming *Case of the Lame Canary* would be his last courtroom battle.

The title hassle had brought to the surface all of Gardner's submerged resentment at previous editorial remarks; they magnified as he and Hobson exchanged letters. The serialization deal with *Liberty* played out, and there was no immediate prospect of another magazine market for Perry Mason. There was doubt that Warner Brothers would renew their option. As sorry as the pictures were, Gardner depended on the income. This would mean a loss of money at a time when he had been spending a lot of it.

There was a sequel to this title bout. For reasons comprehensible only to the motion picture industry, when Warner Brothers exercised their option they produced *The Case of the Dangerous Dowager* under the title *Granny Get Your Gun*. It was not released as a Perry Mason picture, thereby wasting the advertising value of a best seller and a popular character for which they had paid dearly. It is small wonder that Gardner wanted no more motion pictures for fear they would ruin his Perry Mason character.

Seeking solace and inspiration in travel, he put the Fiction Factory on wheels. By Wednesday, August 19, 1936, the caravan had reached Salt Lake City; it was time to start doing something about *The Case of the Lame Canary.* Gardner armed himself with two pens, one containing black ink and the other red, and sat down to a plotting session:

> Have a plot which will support a complete novel independent of any murder mystery. In other words the reader must be so interested in the problems of the characters that he wants to follow them and find out what happens.

He started trying to weave the events and conflicts which had brought the woman to Mason's office with a canary. The story did not go well, perhaps because Gardner's mind was more on the elusive *Saturday Evening Post* than on developing characters. He noted, "Make the whole thing more of a S.E.P. mystery requiring brains to unravel—" The plot machinations became "too pulpy," and Gardner's mind obviously turned back to discussions of the Mason formula. He used red ink to write, "Mason has always worked with a bunch of stage props. Now I want to have something definitely different." Shortly before he ended the plotting session, he noted, "*Now* we're getting somewhere." However, it didn't pan out; his diary recorded no dictation for that day, and the next day he was back at the plotting book.

Thursday did not go well either. He continued to work at the plot, but the characters were not coming to life. His diary for that day recorded, "dictated correspondence. Wrestle with Mason plot and get nowhere, but don't let it bother me."

On Friday morning he got up early, played a little tennis, and set out to "Try a more smooth mystery approach—" but the plot drifted away to trying to establish characters who were dealing in gems smuggled from Spain. Gardner's red ink scrawled his annoyance:

> To hell with all this stuff. The Mason stories must be fast moving, with guts, and with an unusual situation, motivation and development. To hell with what the S.E.P. wants. Keep Perry Mason true to Perry Mason.

By the end of the day he was able to note in his diary, "gradually getting glimmering of the fundamentals." But it was not enough with which to start dictating the story.

On Saturday he opened his plotting with "Back to first principles." It was a long session. On Sunday he started dictation, turning out six records. On Monday he got out ten records before going to a park to relax by listening to the radio. Later he recorded that he was "Dissatisfied with many things in the story." On Tuesday he had trouble working: "Fall asleep thinking, and have a hell of a time forcing myself to dictate three and a half records."

When women feel depressed they shop for hats or shoes or dresses. Erle Stanley Gardner shopped for trailers. Between recording in his plotting book, buying a new trailer, and dictating, he completed the first draft of *The Case of the Lame Canary* on September 1—only to start revision the next day.

Gardner headed the new trailer toward Bishop, California, where he worked on the revision for two weeks, shipping the Dictaphone cylinders away to a secretary for transcription. When he received the typescript a week later he recorded in his diary, September 30, "Wake up knowing I have to make a further revision of the Case of the Lame Canary."

Thayer Hobson had been writing that he wanted to try the new Mason on *The Saturday Evening Post* for serialization, which made Gardner doubly anxious to have it right. It was October 28 before he mailed the "final" draft to his home secretary for copying.

Hobson's reception of the story was not encouraging. He thought Gardner had "made Perry Mason too respectable and too soft." Probably influenced by hopes for *Saturday Evening Post* serialization, Gardner had warmed the traditional businesslike relationship between Perry Mason and his secretary considerably. Hobson was not impressed. He wrote, "I honestly got a trifle sick about the sentimental passages between him and Della Street. Pages 132 and 133, for instance. This isn't the sort of sentiment that Perry and Della would get mixed up in. If they were going to get married, they'd do it in the morning after the night before and they'd be making cynical wisecracks about it."

This was not happy news, particularly since Gardner agreed with Hobson's criticism. It meant back to the plotting book. During December he was alternately working on a final revision of *The Case of the Dangerous Dowager*, a serial for *This Week*, Doug Selby for *Country Gentleman*, woodpulps for his old markets, and a complete revision of *The Case of the Lame Canary*—when news arrived that Warner Brothers were not going to renew their contract. Furthermore, the contract constrained sale to another studio for three years.

The outlook was bleak for Perry Mason.

On December 10, Gardner wrote Thayer Hobson that "Perry Mason has run through ten or twelve books, which is damn near enough." His plan was to have Perry announce at the end of the "Lame Canary" that he was going to be gone for a year on a trip to the Orient:

> If you wish, we could have some other lawyer in the office to handle his business while he's gone, but I think it would be better, from a legal standpoint, as well as a reader standpoint, to simply quit the books while there are still some readers who want them. Then create a brand new character, similar in many respects to Perry Mason, a little more refined, a little less daring, a little more sophisticated.

When the news reached New York, Thayer Hobson called an editorial conference at William Morrow and Company. The final decision was to agree with Gardner; after all, they couldn't demand that he go on writing Perry Mason novels. On December 14, Hobson replied to Gardner's letter, but he left himself a loophole: "I think your suggestion of doing a swell job on *Lame Canary* and then disposing of Perry Mason, at least for the time being, is a sound one." He went on to suggest that Gardner might, at the end of the *Lame Canary*, have Mason turn his practice over to a "brainy, hot-headed, nervy, young fire-eater, a junior partner in a law firm."

This idea immediately caught fire in Gardner's mind. He fired back a letter on December 17, a letter which sounded awfully like a potential suicide who wanted to be talked out of pulling the trigger. The young lawyer could cable Mason when he was in a jam, and when Perry returned they could form a partnership. Hobson suggested, "By the time you roll it around in your mind for a few weeks you are going to create something that's really big. . . . I have a hunch you'll do more Perry Mason some day."

By February 25, 1937, Gardner finished rewriting *The Case of the Lame Canary* and headed for Mexico City. On March 4, Marie Fried Rodell—a Morrow editor who had been critical of the Mason formula—dispatched a telegram to Mexico City:

REVISED CANARY SIMPLY SWELL STOP ONE OF THE BEST JOBS YOUVE
EVER DONE STOP TERRIBLY PROUD OF YOU STOP HOORAY DONT STOP
MARIE

But better news was to come!

On March 7, Gardner received a telegram from his agent: POST ENTHUSIASTICALLY ACCEPTS LAME CANARY. At long last *The Saturday Evening Post* had yielded. The $15,000 was not to be sneezed at, but more important was an option on the next serial at $17,500. Perry Mason had won a reprieve. No matter what happened between him and Della Street during their trip to the Orient, they *had* to come back to make another appearance in *The Saturday Evening Post*.

In spite of the growing success of his books and sales to the slicks, Gardner was in financial straits during the late 1930s. With the purchase of Rancho del Paisano and development of its facilities, operational expenses of the Fiction Factory mounted; Gardner had to draw against his royalties. Based upon his woodpulp experience, the solution was obvious: Boost the production schedule and create more characters. But there was still another complication. He could not go to a rival house, and William Morrow was publishing as many books as the name Erle Stanley Gardner would bear; besides, another character would suffer under comparison with Perry Mason.

So Gardner decided to develop another character under a pen name—for William Morrow but unknown to William Morrow. In August, 1938, he bet Thayer Hobson that he could write a novel under a different name and Thayer would not be able to spot it. By September, Gardner had whipped up *The Bigger They Come*, introducing a detective agency composed of Bertha Cool and Donald Lam, as unlikely a pair of characters as a writer ever put together to lure readers.

Bertha Cool, owner of the agency, was in her late sixties, a woman not likely to garner much reader identification on the basis of her physical attributes and habits. She weighed more than two hundred pounds; "Her sighs ripple loose flesh of her stomach and breasts into jellylike action." She swore lustily and used corny adolescent expressions like "stew me for an oyster" and "roast me for a turkey." She had an assortment of character traits which added up to pure burlesque.

At the opening of the book, Bertha hired a scrawny, down-at-the-heels, 29-year-old disbarred lawyer named Donald Lam, whom she

THE SATURDAY EVENING POST

Founded A°D¹ 1728 by Benj. Franklin

Volume 209   5c. THE COPY   PHILADELPHIA, PA., MAY 29, 1937 $2.00 By Subscription (52 issues)   Number 48

"She'd Just Started to Clip the Canary's Claws When This Young Man Grabbed Her in His Arms"

THE CASE OF THE LAME CANARY

By ERLE STANLEY GARDNER

ILLUSTRATED BY RICO TOMASO

ANY student of character will concede that outstanding examples of class run contrary to type. The best detectives look like clerks. The best gamblers look like bankers. And nothing in Perry Mason's appearance indicated that his agile brain, unconventional methods and daring technique made him the city's most feared and respected trial lawyer.

Seated in his office, he regarded the young woman who sat in the big leather chair, holding a caged canary in her lap. His steady eyes held none of the gimlet qualities so frequently associated with cross-examiners, but were, instead, filled with a patience touched with sympathy. His rugged features might have been carved from granite.

"That canary," he said, with the quiet insistence of one who will continue to repeat his statements until he has scored his point, "has a sore foot."

The young woman shifted the cage from her lap to the floor, as though trying to keep the lawyer from seeing too much. "Oh, I don't think so," she said;

and then added, by way of explanation, "He's a little frightened."

Mason appraised the youthful lines of her figure, the neatly shod feet, the long, tapering fingers of her gloved hands. "So," he said, "your business with me was urgent enough to make you crash the gate."

She tilted her chin defiantly.

"My business is important. It couldn't wait, and neither could I."

"I take it," the lawyer remarked musingly, "patience isn't one of your virtues."

"I didn't know," she said, "that patience was a virtue."

"You wouldn't. What's your name?"

"Rita Swaine."

"How old are you, Miss Swaine?"

"Twenty-seven."

"Where do you live?"

"Thirteen thirty-eight Chestnut Street," she said, glancing across at Della Street, whose pen was busy making copperplate shorthand notes.

"That's all right," Mason assured her, "you needn't worry about Miss Street. She's my secretary. Do you live in an apartment house?"

"Yes. Apartment 408."

"Telephone?"

"Not in my name. There's a switchboard service."

"What do you want to see me about?"

She lowered her eyes and hesitated.

"About the canary?" Mason asked.

"No," she said hastily, "not about the canary."

"Do you usually carry a canary with you?"

She laughed nervously and said, "Of course not. I don't understand why you attach so much importance to the canary."

"Because," he told her, "so few of my clients bring canaries to the office."

She started to say something, then checked herself. Mason glanced significantly at his wrist watch, and his action started her talking. "I want you to help my sister, Rossy," she said. "That's short for Rosalind. About six months ago she married Walter

5

addressed variously as "Donald my love," "you little runt," "lover," and "little bastard." Donald was the principal investigator and narrator, weighing in at 127. Not many readers would envy his physical state. Bertha described him as "a pint sized parcel of dynamite with the nerve of a prizefighter and a punch that wouldn't jar a fly loose from a syrup jug."

Examination of the characters alone would brand the yarn as the sort of story a writer might produce either from ignorance or for his own amusement with little hope of mounting a successful assault upon literary bastions, particularly since the portrayal of wacky criminal types in first-person narration was at that time so completely encircled by the domain of Damon Runyon that anything similar was forthrightly dubbed a pale-pink copy. But this did not take into account Gardner's tightly woven plot which whizzed along at express-train speed.

Eve Woodburn was Gardner's agent at that time. Using a phony Los Angeles address and signing himself "A. A. Fair," he cooked up a letter to Miss Woodburn in which he posed as a rank amateur. He had heard that William Morrow and Company was a good publisher; he wanted her to try his novel there. Eve Woodburn almost blew the whole act; she submitted the manuscript to *Collier's*, who, fortunately for Gardner's plan, rejected the yarn.

Thayer Hobson was immediately enthusiastic, and it didn't take him long to penetrate Gardner's cover; Donald Lam's legal she-nanigans were the giveaway. However, Gardner did not admit to being A. A. Fair until after Morrow had accepted the book. Then he insisted on preserving the pseudonym. For a while Thayer and his secretary were the only ones who knew the author's identity. When the contract came in November, Artrin A. Fair wrote a letter to Eve Woodburn which was pure hokum, but apparently she merely thought she had stumbled onto a talented hick:

> I suppose this Morrow company is all right, but by God I hate to sign any contract like that, and one thing in it I just *won't* sign. That is the paragraph which provides that the publisher is going to put the copyright in my name and then make me responsible for all this other stuff. . . .
>
> I'm leaving things all up to you and after this don't bother me with any more business. I don't like it. You look after the business, only don't let anybody change my characters and don't tie me up on any

contracts that I don't know about. Aside from that, you sell stories as serials and hold off the books if you think that's the thing to do. . . . I want the publishers to handle my books, but sometimes I am hard to get along with and if one of those big shots would send me a telegram collect or something, I'd blow up. They say these New York publishers don't think anything of sending long telegrams collect to authors. I know an author who got a long telegram the other day about a lot of tripe. Those publishers take an author's brain work and make all the profits and give the authors just enough to buy food so they can write more books, and then if they think an author is getting a little saved up, send him telegrams collect.

When the check for the advance came through his agent, it was necessary to include Eve Woodburn in his confidence, but "Please take every precaution to keep from letting the cat out of the bag, and this means that barring some emergency, you must not even think of Fair as Gardner." In order to throw suspicious Morrow editors off the track, Gardner suggested Hobson employ an investigator to check up on the mysterious Mr. Fair. Gardner "planted evidence" at the Los Angeles address for the investigator to find. It was a plot which would have done credit to Perry Mason at his best in confusing a witness.

The Bigger They Come was published in January, 1939, and Harry Emerson Wildes reviewed it for the *Philadelphia Forum Magazine*:

> Let me now present a thriller of first magnitude. Advertised as "a startlingly original, unguessable plot, that is realistic and reasonable," A. A. Fair's *The Bigger They Come* more than lives up to its press-agentry. I have never heretofore heard of this A. A. Fair, though I suspect him to be blood-brother to Erle Stanley Gardner, the Perry Mason man. His style of writing, his choice of personality, quirks of plot, the reliance upon legal skulduggery, all stamp this A. A. Fair as one who has well learned the Gardner technique. There, in itself, is sufficient recommendation for you, for all whodunit addicts know that Gardner tops the detective story racket, but Fair, if so be he a separate personality, gives his master lessons. *The Bigger They Come*, with its unique cast of characters, its believable dames and its human sleuths, races ahead at a mile-a-minute gait. If you don't care for it, you're expelled from the ranks of mystery fans.

Wildes wrote William Morrow to learn if his deduction was correct, and Hobson stoutly denied the charge. The A. A. Fair name was maintained *pro forma* until the late 1950s, even to the extent of

Gardner's writing an article on mysteries for *The Writer* under the pseudonym, but most experienced mystery reviewers refused to be hoodwinked for that long.

Gardner usually laid the groundwork for his book-length submissions to Hobson by sending a teaser, not unlike a movie trailer. On April 13, he wrote to announce that the next Bertha Cool–Donald Lam yarn, *The Knife Slipped*, would be along in about ten days. Since most popular writers were writing with a view to movie rights and serialization, there was a sameness to the fare offered readers, many of whom were turning to magazines rather than pay two dollars for a book. Gardner wanted Hobson to understand that he was now deliberately writing a book which would be unique in the book market:

> In any event, this Donald Lam–Bertha Cool yarn won't sell to the movies and won't sell to magazines. It's going to run around 75,000 words. It deals with a highly sexed girl from the country who cuts loose all at once and comes to the conclusion she is a nymphomaniac. Bertha Cool sails majestically through its pages, delightfully hardboiled. When she and Donald call on the wife of the city official, who puts on the high-hat act when Donald tries to talk with her, Bertha Cool says, "Just a moment, Donald, let me handle this bitch." The wife stiffens into frigid indignation and demands of Bertha Cool, "What was that word you used?" and Bertha Cool says, "Bitch, dearie, b-i-t-c-h, bitch. It means a slut."

When Hobson read the manuscript he did not like it; he did not pull his punches:

> I think it is cheap—crude, without being effective. All Bertha Cool does is talk tough, swear, smoke cigarettes, and try to gyp people. . . . And I don't think much of the story itself. If that manuscript had come to me in the ordinary way, having no idea who the author was, I would have stopped reading about page 70 and the book would have been rejected without even any hope on my part that the author would ever write a really good story.

Gardner agreed the manuscript should not be published, but not too gracefully: "This is once I'm inclined to think you're getting way off on the wrong track." He voiced a perennial complaint that Hobson or someone in the organization was prejudiced against Gardner characters.

But there was no hint of prejudice in Hobson's reception of *Turn on the Heat*, the next Lam–Cool submission: "Jesus Christ, here Bertha Cool is Bertha Cool and she is somebody and she is flesh and blood and she is grand. So is Donald Lam. Now damn you, Erle, you know perfectly well that these are the characters that have been in your mind and not those stuffed shirts who came wobbling into the office a few months ago."

Examination of correspondence files reveals that over the years Gardner's contentiousness in dealing with Thayer Hobson and Morrow editors increased in direct proportion to his writing experience and expertise. He was reasonably pliant on revision which really mattered, particularly in regard to the integrity of his facts; he fought virtually every suggestion which seemed to stem from an editor's personal taste. He waxed highly profane when anyone threatened the integrity of one of his characters ("Bertha Cool has been changed Goddam near all she's going to be") or suggested alteration of text which would slow the galloping pace. He vehemently defended the right of his characters to use profanity. ("Dammit to hell I cuss. My friends cuss.")

Sometimes he resorted to his old ploy of having one of his characters speak on his behalf, as when Thayer Hobson thought Bertha Cool had been calling Donald Lam "lover" too frequently in *Turn on the Heat*:

> Listen to what happened last night after I went to sleep and the characters in the book gathered around me. Bertha Cool, as usual, dominated the picture. She read your letter and said, "For Christ's sake, Donald, he doesn't want me to call you lover so often." Donald said, "As far as that's concerned, I don't either." Bertha snorted, "To hell with both of you," she said. "It's my agency and I run it the way I God damn please." She read some more in the letter and then said, "For Christ's sake, get a load of this: I have spoiled the pet name that he called his wife—Jesus, you'd think any man in the publishing business that had any sex experience whatever could think up a new pet name to call his wife a hell of a sight easier than asking an author to change a character and rewrite a whole book. My God, Fair, tell him he's been married enough to start calling his wife, 'Say,' and 'Listen, you, where the hell's that shirt?' If the poor bastard is going around the house calling his wife lover, he'd better revise his love life— But you leave me just the way I am, Artrin Fair. I've never met this Thayer Hobson and

I'm probably not his ideal, but I haven't asked him to marry me and I don't intend to."

In spite of all the bombast, Gardner turned out a revision which answered all the complaints and drew a disgusted but congratulatory letter from Hobson:

> This morning I am thoroughly disgusted with you. For God's sake, you keep us all tearing our hair for weeks, you argue with us, you tell us we don't know what we're talking about—that your first draft is just what it should be and we are trying to get you to prostitute Bertha Cool and make her an unnatural character and we are trying to get you to write to form—you act as though your lousy book were good. Then you turn around and do everything God himself would want you to do and send in the smoothest, best-written, thoroughly rounded job that you swore you couldn't do and shouldn't do. In other words, this Fair book is just about perfect.

That was the way most of the arguments ended.

Many of the exchanges between Gardner and Hobson were sufficiently blistering to convince an uninitiated observer that the two were engaged in a blood feud. However, all of this wrangling was in reality part of an enduring personal friendship. There is every reason to believe that most of Gardner's raging at both Hobson and his editors was pure courtroom antics. Eventually he admitted to employing temper tantrums to get his favorite editor back after Hobson had replaced himself with a substitute.

Bob Hardy had been right when he said, "I think you two men will get along together splendidly." Gardner lent Hobson money during bad times, and Hobson paid advances to Gardner when unexpected expenses cropped up.

As time passed, Thayer Hobson became more and more involved in advising and assisting Gardner in marketing subsidiary rights to his work. Eventually Gardner cut a piece of the cake for him with the formation of Thayer Hobson and Company, a marketing organization to handle his numerous literary properties, particularly foreign rights. That organization continues to function to this day.

14
"START WITH A MYSTERY"

While professional snobs in the field of literary criticism were writing off Erle Stanley Gardner's books as "time killers," readers were purchasing them in record numbers and other writers were trying to figure out how he wrote them.

Gardner's method did not arrive full-blown in a blinding flash of inspiration; it was carefully forged upon an anvil of experience over the entirety of his writing career. As Perry Mason came to life, the Gardner name began to sprinkle book review pages and he exhorted himself in his notebook to leave the common herd of woodpulp readers behind:

> *The one rule of success that's so simple and elemental I have repeatedly lost sight of it*: Develop a Gardner individuality in everything I do and say. This is more than a style of expression. It's a rule of substance. Get a certain Gardner "touch." Then make every chapter, every situation, every character smack of that *individual* touch, and write about any plot I goddam please.

Once Gardner decided to enter the mystery book field—glutted though it was during the 1930s—he became the most avid student of the mystery story on the literary scene. He analyzed the construction of everything he wrote and everything he read. As a lawyer, he sought to isolate the laws, rules, methods, theories, and formulae which applied to story construction, distilling his findings into various notebooks for future reference. Freeman Lewis of Pocket Books, Inc., Gardner's paperback publisher, got at the secret of his success: "It often seemed to me that he operated as a professional in an area inhabited largely by amateurs."

Although Gardner reached a level from which he could well afford to be blasé concerning the opinions of professional critics, he never relaxed as a practical student of the mystery story. He constantly reminded himself of the basic principles of the art he practiced. On Friday, June 12, 1959—when he was generally conceded to be at the top of the heap of best-selling writers—he began the day's work by printing a note to himself in his plotting notebook: "A mystery story should start with a mystery."

This would seem basic to the point of banality, but the majority of aspiring mystery writers did not see it. As Gardner pointed out, the prime difficulty was the simplicity of the murder formula: A murders B, but the blame is placed on C, until some ingenious detective, D, clears C and puts the blame on A:

> Avoid a story in which the characters are shoved around to make the situation which starts the plot, then march through the printed pages doing exactly the things for which they have been introduced in the story for the purpose of furthering the plot until finally the hero is ready to pull the rabbit out of the hat. During the thimblerigging everything marches with dreary monotony and the hero doesn't do anything worthwhile until . . . presto!

Gardner was death on "thimblerigging"—in his own stories or anyone else's. The term derived from the sleight-of-hand swindling game in which the operator palms a pellet or a pea while appearing to cover it with one of three thimblelike cups or shells; then, while moving the cups about, he offers to bet that no one can tell under which cup the pellet lies. In the rules of writing according to Gardner, at no point should a story be mere manipulation to obscure the identity of the criminal. When he caught himself moving characters solely for obfuscation or obviously jockeying them into position for the final exposure, he would jerk himself up short, as on Wednesday, August 14, 1963, when he opened his day's plotting by abandoning the story in-progress:

> *Scrap this Mason story.* I don't like it. It is a story of thimblerigging and most of the action has taken place before the reader gets acquainted with the characters.

That was the problem of starting with a corpse. The action—the conflicts leading up to the murder—was all over. Readers didn't know the participants and really didn't give a damn whether the detective found the guilty party. Gardner started with an incidental mystery which intrigued both his detective and the reader and then—after the reader was acquainted with the characters and their conflicts—led to murder. On September 4, 1954, he was beginning to plot a Mason story which he hoped would be selected by *The Saturday Evening Post* for serialization. He discarded the first character that came to mind:

> The idea of the gal who acts as a professional co-respondent would never appeal to a family magazine like the Post. It is better to get some mystery situation which will intrigue Mason and the reader alike. *The very first element must be a mystery— Some interesting woman in a situation where Mason has to take some action involving great personal responsibility—yet where the reader can't account for certain incongruities.* Let's start with unusual situations which seem logical. . . .

The story opened with Della Street informing Perry Mason that a girl was calling; she had been robbed—"my clothes, my personal effects, my home." She was calling from a telephone at the fourteenth hole of a golf course, wanting Della Street to bring her clothes so she could come talk to Perry Mason. As usual, Perry was susceptible:

> Mason glanced at his watch. "My next appointment is at two o'clock. We can just about make it, Della. This thing has *really* aroused my curiosity. Let's go."

The editors of *The Saturday Evening Post* evidently decided the opening mystery would also arouse their readers' curiosity. They purchased serial rights to *The Case of the Sun Bather's Diary*.

Della Street brought Perry Mason most of his mysteries, although he found some on his own while driving, reading the newspaper, and engaging in other mundane activities. These mysteries, while incomprehensible to observers, were quite logical results of deviations from society's norm, in accordance with Gardner's "Departures from the Normal Theory of Story Situation" (*see* Appendix VII, page 251). In each case, there was a "point of contact" between the individual and murder—else there could have been no murder mystery.

Gardner developed his most comprehensive and reliable plotting system from the theory that certain activities and appetites are basic

Temecula Sunday Jan 20 1957

Mrs. Farrell thinks her husband killed her.

1. She has been in three hotels as Ruth Culver, doing typing.

2. Lifted alimony list from car & phoned Kennedy

3. Helen Rose went to Redfern Hotel. Mrs. F. saw her go out, leaving key on counter, so she grabbed then got room on seventh floor. This about 1.00 p.m.

1.50 Rose leaves room & leaves key on desk.

1.52 Mrs. F. picks up key

1.57 is in her room

2.40 Rose back & starts typing

3.30 Husband in & kills

4.00 Fiff in, finds woman dead & decides to make it look like suicide. (Husband had hid gun down behind bed or put in Rose's bag & it wasn't found until later) Fiff pulls trigger.

4.30 Mrs. F. starts using her key & is caught by chambermaid. (She has first gone to lobby & rung the room, then takes precaution of knocking. Can't tell

it be Ruth who is dead
then, Ruth murdered can't

New Schedule

~~12.30~~ 1.50 Rose goes out
12.45 { 1.51 Mrs. F. gets key
{ 1.55 Rents room + moves in – tries
key, sees set up.
1.15 ~~2.30~~ Rose back
1.45 ~~3.00~~ Mrs. F. out to phone Jerry C.
3.05 ~~3.10~~ Back.
Husband in + kills during this time.
3.30 ~~3.45~~ Gifford in – She hears shot
3.45 ~~4.15~~ He leaves not knowing guy
under bed trying / make
it look like suicide
3.50 ~~4.30~~ Mrs. F. in, finds gun, corpse,
gets caught is in panic
4.00 ~~4.45~~ Orders dinner. By coincidence
~~4.30~~ same as Rose had only
Rose had peas.
4.30 Has dishes removed ~~gets scheme~~
4.40 Has duplicate key made + sets
trap

Revision

10.00 Rose checks in
12.30 " out for lunch – Mrs. F. sees go
hotel dining room orders
Turkey dinner
12.31 Mrs F. has key
12.45 " " Rents suite
1.15 Rose back types
2.30 Mrs F. out to phone Jerry
2.35 Rose's husband in + kills
2.45 " " leaves

niques. He worked out the above schedule for *The Case of the Daring Decoy*
just before he started dictation.

3.05   Mrs F. back
3.30   Gifford in
3.40   Shot tries to make it suicide
3.42   Giff leaves
4.00   Mrs F. discovers Corpse (cough?)
4.30   She orders dinner same as
       Rose ate
4.50   She packs Rose's bags
5.10   Dishes out
6.12   Phones Jerry
6.30   He enters room
6.45   Mrs. F. checks out
6.55   Phones Mason
7.20   Mason arrives
~~7.40~~ ~~7.00~~   Drake + Mason to hotel
Fico ~~8.20~~   Holcomb arrives
9.20 8.40   Mason leaves
    8.30   "   arrives office
    ~~8.50~~   Gladedell Motel
9.15 ~~9.40~~   Eva Kane's apt.
9.30 10.45   Out
9.50 ~~10.45~~   Mrs. F's apartment.
10.10 ~~10.60~~   Calls Jerry to say has proxy list.

1.00 ~~7.45~~   Elsinore
1.30 ~~8.10~~   Leaves
8.10 ~~8.40~~   Arrives office
9.30 ~~9.30~~   Goes hotel
3.45 ~~6.00~~   Discovers bullet in mattress.

— Arrival at Rose Calvert's apartment
house + call to Conway.

10.20   Leaves apt.
10.25   Phones Drake
10.55   Meets Drake's man
11.45   Start Elsinore
12.50   Arrives

Temecula Sat Jan 26 1957
A.A.Fair revisions of Kept along
along. Have the woman the
one who kills & he has
caught her & does nothing
to stop her. Have a new
version of Kept Fair going to
prison & prison willing
the wants to clear the
guy. He is making a
_____ which we will
have alimony repercussions.

Temecula Tues. Jan 29 1957
Revisions of A.A. Fair yarn.

Here is what must have happened. Laura goes to his. She
knows Carroll is in Caroline's
apt. Laura leaves. Lois gets him
tells him she knows he is a
murderer & that Laura is going
to find it out. He gives her
key to his apt. she puts it
on her key ring. Or he can
give her his key. She leaves Laura
her apartment — so has duplicate key to his apt. made
after she has gone in &
taken the thing he didn't
want Donald to find. Then
he phones her & Waters & tells
her is. Caroline knows that he
keeps a thing. Donald will
have to tell the cops he knows.

human motivations: desire for sex, wealth, travel, human friendship and contact, food, self-improvement (mental, physical, financial), security, advancement, and justice. In life, each desire is confronted by conflicts—personal, circumstantial, and financial obstacles. The person with a desire attempts to overcome conflicts by a counterattack, a detour, or flight. This is the real-life workings of William Wallace Cook's law: *"Purpose, expressed or implied, opposing Obstacle, expressed or implied, yields Conflict"*—the basis of all story construction.

When the attempt to overcome culminates in murder or a deviation from the norm which is covered up by a murder, a mystery story situation evolves. From this analysis, Gardner developed "The Murderer's Ladder" which, in turn, provided the basis for "The Fluid or Unstatic Theory of Plots."

10. The necessity for eliminating the little overlooked clues and loose threads
9. The false suspect
8. The cover up
7. The flight
6. The actual killing
5. The first irretrievable step
4. The opportunity
3. The plan
2. Temptation
1. Motivation

THE MURDERER'S LADDER

In plotting, Gardner approached his story from the viewpoint of the murderer; in writing, he presented the resulting sequence of events from the viewpoint of the detective:

> The point is that any murderer, in killing a person, where the crime is not one of passion, enters upon a critical period as he climbs the ladder of motivation, temptation, opportunity, etc., to a point where he is irretrievably committed to the crime after he has taken one step which is such that he can't back up. If the murderer's plans go astray between the time of taking this first irretrievable step and the actual killing, the murderer must improvise; and when he starts improvising he does certain things which are quite logical to him but which would be exceedingly mysterious to a person who did not know the whole sequence of events.

Gardner placed the heart of story situation at Step 5, the first act from which there is no retreat; Step 6, during accomplishment of the foul deed; and Step 10, when it becomes necessary for the murderer to deal with unexpected eventualities. He emphasized that villains have difficulties to overcome which are inherent in their schemes, and every scheme contains an element of weakness, the seed of its own destruction. Suspense was obtained by having the hero make mistakes which threatened to engulf him. In overcoming these complications, the protagonist accomplished the final objective of cleaning up the villainy. It sounded very simple as Gardner explained it:

> When a detective story is stripped to its bare essentials the murder is, after all, a simple matter. A kills B and does it by a knife or gunshot at a time when he is supposed by all parties to the story to be elsewhere, or by telling a story, such as seeing a man running away, at whom he shot etc., diverts suspicion. It is the contact with the resulting incidentals which makes the story. A murderer tries to conceal his crime by false alibis, false clues, misdirected suspicions, convincing falsehoods.
>
> Each of these subterfuges must at some point or other contact *known facts* and apparently coincide with them. As a matter of fact, if all the minor facts were known, the synthetic truth would break down, since every fact is inseparably matched with other facts, like the cogwheels of clockwork. It is in the failure to assimilate minor facts that detective work falls down.
>
> For story purposes it lies in showing the failure of some one minor fact to mesh. Therefore, to plot a mystery, plot more and more carefully and in greater detail the avenues of escape sought by the real perpetrator, which may combine any and all of the basic methods of deception such as false motive and perjured alibi combined with planted clues, etc.

Gardner developed "The Fluid or Unstatic Theory of Plots" over a period of several years and many revisions as an aid to keeping a story in constant forward dramatic motion from that first incidental mystery which challenges the interest of the reader to the final "blow-off" when the protagonist solves the case in a blaze of action. In constructing a plot, the author worked through nine steps:

1. The act of primary villainy
2. Motivation for act of villainy
3. The villain's cover-up
4. Complications which arise during and after the cover-up
5. The hero's contact with the act of villainy

6. Further complications and character conflicts
7. Suspense through hero's mistakes
8. Villain's further attempts to escape
9. Hero sets solution factors in motion or traps villain

As Perry Mason aficionados scan the multitude of choices Gardner could make during the plotting of a story (*see* Appendix I, page 229), they will recognize most of the adventures of Perry Mason, Della Street, and Paul Drake.

Once he had a plot, there were definite rules for the writing. Gardner would not allow himself to start with an opening situation which was supposed to develop in and of itself into a mystery. The necessary complications for a mystery had to be fully developed but submerged under the chain of circumstances which appeared on the surface. The plot had to proceed on the basis of the "overlapping power pulse." This was accomplished by having the first plot situation lead to the second, with new actors, and the second lead to the third— but all were tied together. The first situation had to lead to the second before the initial situation was resolved, thus allowing no place for a let-down of reader interest.

The rules of the game provided that Gardner had to "play fair with the reader" by showing all of the clues needed to solve the enigma. This was accomplished by "Development Through Clue Sequence":

> Slip the clues into the story in such a way that the reader does not know they are clues. Example: when detective is in a room that has been closed for more than a day, he hears a cheap alarm clock ticking, one that isn't supposed to run more than 24 hours. Not emphasized at that time by hero or to reader. . . . Subsequently, hero pounces upon officer who was in charge of the room.
>
> Don't have clues labeled. In the traditional detective story, as soon as the detective picked something up, the reader knew it was a clue. In the new type he would discover certain things which would not appeal to the reader as clues until all fitted together.

Although Gardner gave the reader all the facts along the way, it should be noted that if any of the stenographers in the Fiction Factory was able to spot the murderer before the end of the book, he would immediately begin to revise.

Gardner would not allow himself as the author to indulge in narration of past events. He had long before discovered that readers are not interested in history. Any revelation of past events had to be made as part of the on-going story movement; thus, it was not by accident that Paul Drake and others would so frequently report to Perry Mason on past events which immediately turned into present complications or future difficulties. Gardner would allow a minimum of aftermath explanation, but he really preferred none at all.

Under the restrictions of his "Law of Subordinate Characters," he would allow no minor character to be introduced as a stereotype for the sole purpose of advancing the plot. He cautioned himself in his notebook, "The reader wants subordinate characters as human beings with their loves, hates, complications, worries and triumphs. Try to have a rounded cross section of life for every character introduced."

To produce an exceptionally fast-paced novel or a highly complicated plot, Gardner applied the "Three-Ring Circus Theory of Plotting." It had the added advantage of using up old hackneyed plots he happened to have lying around:

> Life is so complex that events are always impinging upon individuals. It is human nature to see only one's own life and the events which comprise it. But the events which comprise the life of any one individual are, in turn, the results of causes in the lives of others. Therefore, if we take three old, hackneyed plots—which are old and hackneyed because they are true to life—and start them revolving in separate groups, affecting three separate groups of individuals, and then take the place where those plots impinge upon a common ground and use the results of that impinging contact for motivation for a main plot we have something on which to work:
> *Illustration:*
> PLOT NO. 1. Man and wife are splitting up. The wife tries to make the man jealous by flirtation with a neighbor.
> PLOT NO. 2. That Neighbor is trying to get the job of the man above him and, in order to do that, seeks to discredit the man higher up with the boss.
> PLOT NO. 3. The Man Higher Up is playing around with a cutie who has gotten him to dip into company funds, on the assumption that he can pay them back.
> Now if the woman who wants to make her husband jealous goes out with the Neighbor at the time when the Man Higher Up knows that he is up against a showdown, and feels that if he can only have a fall guy he may save his own bacon there's a chance for story motivation, a situation, and characters.

"This man has got to be arrested," said Cartright, his voice rising. "The howling has got to be stopped. You hear? It must be stopped!"

The Case of the

(Reading time: 36 minutes 49 seconds.)

PART ONE—THE NERVOUS CLIENT

DELLA STREET held open the door to the inner office and spoke in the tones which a woman instinctively uses in speaking to a child or a very sick man. "Go right in, Mr. Cartright," she said. "Mr. Mason will see you."

A broad-shouldered, rather heavy-set man of about thirty-two, with haunted brown eyes, walked into the office, and stared at Perry Mason.

"You're Perry Mason," he asked, "the lawyer?"

Mason nodded. "Sit down," he said.

The man dropped into the chair Mason had indicated with a gesture, mechanically reached for a package of cigarettes, took one out, conveyed it to his lips, and had the package halfway back to his pocket before he thought to offer one to Perry Mason.

The hand that held the extended package of cigarettes trembled, and the lawyer stared for a moment at the quivering hand before he shook his head.

"No," he said, "thank you; I've got my own brand."

The man nodded, hurriedly put the package of cigarettes back in his pocket, struck a match, and casually leaned forward so that his elbow was resting on the arm

of the chair, steadying the hand which held the match as he lit the cigarette.

"My secretary," said Perry Mason in a calm tone of voice, "told me that you wanted to see me about a dog and about a will."

The man nodded. "A dog and a will," he repeated.

"Well," said Perry Mason, "let's talk about the will first. I don't know much about dogs."

Cartright nodded. His hungry brown eyes were fastened upon Perry Mason.

Perry Mason took a pad of yellow foolscap from a drawer in his desk, picked up a desk pen, and said, "What's your name?"

"Arthur Cartright."

"Age?"

"Thirty-two."

"Residence?"

"4893 Milpas Drive."

"Married or single?"

"Do we need to go into that?"

Perry Mason held his pen poised above the foolscap while he raised his eyes to regard Cartright with a calm, steady appraisal.

"Yes," he said.

"I don't think it makes any difference in the kind of a will I'm drawing up," Cartright said.

6

The Case of the Howling Dog, serialized by *Liberty* in 1934, was Gardner's first acceptance by a "big-time" slick market.

By

ERLE
STANLEY
GARDNER

AUTHOR OF

THE CASE OF THE SULKY GIRL and
THE CASE OF THE VELVET CLAWS

ILLUSTRATIONS

BY

FRANK
GODWIN

Howling Dog

"I've got to know," Perry Mason told him abruptly.

"But I tell you it won't make any difference, on account of the way I'm leaving my property."

Perry Mason said nothing, but the calm insistence of his very silence drove the other to speech.

"Yes," he said.

"Wife's name?"

"Paula Cartright, age twenty-seven."

"Residing with you?" asked Mason.

"No."

"Where does she reside?"

"I don't know," said the man.

Perry Mason hesitated a moment, and his steady patient eyes surveyed the haggard countenance of his client. Then he spoke soothingly.

"Very well," he said. "Let's find out a little more about what you want to do before we go back to that. Have you any children?"

"No."

"All right. How did you want to leave your property?"

"Before we go into that," said Cartright, speaking rapidly, "I want to know if a will is valid no matter how a man dies."

Perry Mason nodded his head wordlessly.

"Suppose," said Cartright, "a man dies on the gallows or in the electric chair. You know—suppose he's executed for murder. Then what happens to his will?"

"It makes no difference how a man dies, his will is not affected," Mason said.

"How many witnesses do I need to have a will?"

"Two witnesses under certain circumstances," Mason said, "and none under others."

"How do you mean?"

"I mean that if a will is drawn up in typewriting, and you sign it, there must be two witnesses to your signature. But in this state, if a will is written entirely in your handwriting, including date and signature, and there is no other writing or printing on the sheet of paper save your own handwriting, it does not need to have any witnesses to the signature. Such a will is valid and binding."

ARTHUR CARTRIGHT sighed, and his sigh seemed to be one of relief.

"Well," he said, "that seems to clear that point up."

"To whom did you want your property to go?" asked Perry Mason.

"To Mrs. Clinton Foley, living at 4889 Milpas Drive."

Perry Mason raised his eyebrows.

"A neighbor?" he asked.

7

For instance, in the above the husband will try to do something about the Neighbor. Perhaps something individual, such as realizing what the wife is doing and let her go ahead, merely shadowing her. The Man Higher Up will try to get the Neighbor in a compromising position where it will look as though he has taken the dough. The woman who has been running around with the Man Higher Up will be trying to get rid of him. All of these things, mixed together, make for the complexities of life.

It is only necessary in each plot to figure what the problem of the character is, what he will do about it, and where that thing he does about it impinges upon the lives of the persons in the other two plots.

Gardner maintained there were no truly new plots. The secret was in giving old plots a fresh, dramatic treatment—that Gardner "touch":

> All plots are old. The attempt to get a novel plot is what makes for strained story construction. . . . it's the piecing together of the different story characters into a new series of interlocking events which gives an appearance of freshness to an otherwise devitalized plot.

He was not averse to flying in the face of literary tradition. He wrote *The Case of the Howling Dog* because S. S. Van Dine (Willard Huntington Wright), a popular mystery writer of the day, stated "the dog that does not bark and thereby reveals the fact that the intruder is familiar" has been used too often to be effective. The novel was serialized by *Liberty*, Gardner's first acceptance by a "big-time" market. It was also his first sale to the movies.

The hallmark of the Gardner touch was a combined effect of continuously flowing plot and a pace that galloped along so fast that one felt he dared not read more slowly lest the story run off and leave him. The biggest problem was maintaining pace through the middle portion when characters were being placed in position for that final breathless sprint during which there could be no stopping. Gardner detailed the problem and the solution:

> The problem is how to accomplish all this without letting the reader feel that there is any jockeying for position. When a character is *pushed* into the right place for the final race, the reader becomes conscious of the author's technique. As soon as he becomes conscious of that he has lost his sense of illusion. When he does that he loses the feeling of suspense.
>
> The author must determine in advance the position in which the

characters must be placed or found for that last pell-mell rush to the finish of the book, and he must let the characters move into these positions in such a manner that the reader is interested in these motions in and of themselves. The reader must be kept sufficiently interested so that he fails to realize the significance of the positions being assumed. Then the breathless rush to the dramatic climax will carry the reader right along with it.

Gardner compared his control of story pace to a baseball game:

> A pitchers' battle in a ball game is of great interest to the critics. It is rich in statistical material. However, it doesn't make for great excitement on the part of the audiences. I don't want any pitchers' battles in my story.
>
> I always try to let a man get to first base in the early part of my stories. Then I have him steal second. The umpire makes a poor guess which lets the next man on, and the fumble of a subordinate fills the bases.
>
> This is a rough illustration of a technique by which the reader can sit in on the commission of the crime without making it seem that the detective protagonist is too stupid. It gets the story off to a flying start, and it gives the reader enough to watch so the resulting story development doesn't seem like thimblerigging.

Gardner also used a baseball analogy to answer critics of the formula story. The basic plot of a baseball game is the same day after day, year in and year out, he pointed out. The conflicts are the same, yet the spectators return time after time because, as in the well-plotted formula story, they never know what combination of events is going to occur during a game. They learn the identities of players and know what to expect of them, just as readers learn about the recurring characters in books and buy more books about them in order to see them perform.

During his lifetime Gardner talked and wrote a lot about writing, mostly pep talks to beginners with titles such as "Don't Quit," "Let's Go," and "Salesmanship for Writers." For the most part he played his secrets of technique close to his chest, obviously to protect the Gardner "touch"; however, there was another side to it: "No writer can be of any help to his fellow writers if he goes into too great detail," said Gardner. "Any time a writer divulges enough of his so-called trade secrets so that every writer can grasp a ready-made formula, the element of novelty flies out of the window and a great disservice to the profession has been done."

He could cite personal experience to back up this stand. On one occasion while he was addressing a Hollywood writers' organization, a member of the group posed a problem. He had been selling a market regularly, but the editor moved on to a better-paying magazine and the new editor immediately began finding fault with stories the old editor would have bought.

Gardner knew all about this. He suggested taking human nature into account. The new editor would be looking for some place the old editor had fallen down. He dictated the gist of a letter by which he had gotten a high percentage of sales under the same conditions:

> I am enclosing a story and I am going to tell you frankly that it is one which Editor A rejected. I thought it was a good story then, and I still think it's a good story. However, Editor A didn't like it, and that was that. I'd like to have you look at it.

Gardner forgot the meeting, but the members of the organization did not.

Two months later, Gardner was in New York. He dropped in to visit a new editor of one of the Munsey magazines. Immediately the editor opened his desk, pulled out a sheaf of letters, and shoved them across at Gardner, demanding to know what was going on among writers out in Hollywood. Each letter, in essence, was a copy of the one Gardner had dictated to the writers' organization.

While working in his plotting notebooks on the development of plots from which to dictate, Gardner frequently admonished himself to follow precepts laid down in the various plotting theories and devices which he had developed. Those to which he made most frequent reference are reproduced as appendices to this volume, "Formulae for Writing a Mystery."

15
HIS LAST BOW

Erle Stanley Gardner married Natalie Frances Beatrice Talbert on April 9, 1912. She was a secretary in the law firm with which Gardner was associated in Oxnard. The following year the marriage got off to a good start with the birth of their only child, Natalie Grace; but there were problems in the long run.

Gardner was a nomad, perpetually primed and cocked for adventure by land, sea, or air. For him, a lonely span of sky was both an inspiration and a companion. He would rather sleep outdoors than in. He sandwiched desert exploration between periods of intense concentration upon his legal work and writing career. The desolate backcountry and his courtroom experiences provided the inspiration and the raw material for his writing. He never dabbled; every undertaking was all or nothing.

Nat, as his wife was called, had an active interest in dramatics. She also tried her hand at writing but found her forte in giving dramatic monologues and lectures. She joined her husband in trips around the West and found time heavy on her hands. In Algadones, Baja California, she played roulette while he prowled the desert in search of Whispering stories and huddled over his typewriter to write them. On January 4, 1930, he wrote Archie Bittner of *Argosy* from "Down in the border country with sand, stars, sunshine and silence. With a wife who insists on playing roulette and winning, and me doing the cooking and dishwashing."

While Erle and Nat were on their trip to China, Gardner's feat of turning out a novelette every third day without secretarial help must still stand as some kind of a record. A few years later, on a trip to the

South Seas, Erle and Nat sailed aboard *The City of Los Angeles,* surrounded by writing paraphernalia and secretaries: "The steamship company has consented to take all of our office equipment; and the wife, two secretaries and myself are going out and look the South Seas over. The Dictaphone people are installing our Dictaphone equipment so that we can step from one office to another without any loss of time. We'll work about two thirds of the time and have about one third to look around and play."

As many others have discovered, such tenacious devotion to a career is guaranteed to put a strain on home life. Later, Gardner would ruefully lament to his daughter that he had been "a pretty lousy father" because of his concentration upon being a lawyer and a writer. However, the Gardners worked out the problem, and the marriage survived. After more than twenty years, from 1935 on Erle and Natalie agreed to live apart. It was an amicable separation with Gardner paying her expenses and various allowances; he visited on holidays and birthdays. This arrangement continued until Natalie's death on February 26, 1968.

On August 7, 1968, Erle Stanley Gardner married Jean Bethell, his secretary since the early days of writing during the Ventura law partnership. Because of her constant presence as his executive secretary, Jean was often dubbed the real-life Della Street. However, Gardner maintained the character was a composite of his various secretaries, the earliest of whom were Jean's sisters, Peggy Downs and Ruth "Honey" Moore.

In spite of the fact that he was almost seventy-nine years old and knew that he had cancer, there was no cessation of Gardner's activities. In March, 1968, he was honored by the Mexican government, an extravaganza which he treated in his last travel book, *Host with the Big Hat.* While writing this book, he had to clean up details on a previous book, *Drifting Down the Delta;* he was also working on a new Perry Mason novel and looking forward to another escapade with Bertha Cool and Donald Lam.

Gardner's last plotting notebook contains the preliminary work on his final Perry Mason story and the last Bertha Cool–Donald Lam yarn. In spite of the pain which becomes increasingly evident in his tortured and occasionally illegible handwriting, he was as self-demanding as ever in his plot construction, and there was no deterioration in the working of his lively imagination.

In order to present a sustained example of Gardner's mind in action and to allow the interested reader to compare his plotting notes with the finished product, those portions of his plotting book which record work on his last two novels, *The Case of the Fabulous Fake* and *All Grass Isn't Green*, are included as Appendix XI, page 265.

While writing these books, Gardner was getting married, filling speaking engagements he had made earlier, attending to the usual flood of correspondence, and making more and more frequent trips to the hospital—"durance vile," as he called his stays. Medication to keep down the pain in his hip made him groggy. Nevertheless, he managed to complete *All Grass Isn't Green* and send the manuscript to Lawrence Hughes, who had taken Thayer Hobson's place at William Morrow, on July 7, 1969. Ten days later Gardner was celebrating his eightieth birthday.

There was no letup in his work schedule. He revised *Cops on the Campus and Crime in the Streets*, wrote gratuitous articles on subjects of personal interest, and handled a steady stream of correspondence pertaining to the Court of Last Resort. In January of 1970 he made his last trip to the hospital. He returned to Rancho del Paisano. Advance copies of *All Grass Isn't Green* arrived at the ranch on March 10, the day before his death. He died on March 11, 1970, with Jean Bethell Gardner at his side. Honey Moore and Peggy Downs were standing by.

Gardner's writing had prepared him. Years before he had written to solace Ted Flynn, a fellow writer, upon the death of his wife:

> In the first place death is not unwelcome to the inner self. It is the conscious mind which clings to life. Neither is death a permanent parting. I am not certain as to the retention of individuality in the hereafter, but I do feel certain the cosmic scheme of things is fitted to the best of man's needs, and that individuality is the most precious possession a person has, is developed as the result of much suffering, and is not given up for no good reason. Death is the postulate of birth. We do not regard the coming of life as evil. Therefore we should not regard the reverse phase of the same process as evil. We can't have a flood tide without also having an ebb.

And in February, 1941, Perry Mason had told a grieving widow in *The Case of the Haunted Husband*, "Life is like that. We can only see from birth to death. The rest of it is cut off from our vision."

As a result of his Chinese studies, Gardner became interested in reincarnation and frequently discussed the subject. He was fond of relating that a Chinese had once told him that he had been a Chinese in an earlier incarnation. On one occasion a guest at Rancho del Paisano pressed him to know what he would like to be in his next reincarnation.

"I think," Gardner replied, "I'd like to be a guest at the Erle Stanley Gardner ranch."

APPENDICES

Erle Stanley Gardner's "Formulae for Writing a Mystery"

Throughout his half-century career as a writer, Erle Stanley Gardner was a student of the art he practiced. He developed many plotting theories and aids for his own use. "Few writers analyze their methods of working out plots," he said. "I always do." Gardner would talk freely about his plotting techniques—up to a point; then he would say, "Yes, I do have quite a list of basic plots, but they are my secret—let the other boys figure out their own."

He kept the most important of his studies in a notebook in his study at Rancho del Paisano, handy for reference or additional study. It was labeled "Formulae for Writing a Mystery." This notebook was carefully guarded; he usually carried it with him when he traveled. Its pages show the wear of usage.

We have selected what we believe to be the most important and the most interesting of Gardner's analytical studies. They are reproduced for the general reader, the critic, or the interested writer:

    I. The Fluid or Unstatic Theory of Plots
    II. Page of Actors and Victims
    III. Character Components
    IV. The Foundation of Character Background
    V. Chart of Romantic Conflict

    VI. Conflicts of Mother Love
    VII. Departures from the Normal Theory of Story Situation
    VIII. The Plot Tide or Thrust
    IX. The Mystery Aftermath Method
    X. Perry Mason Title Analysis
    XI. The Last Plotting Notebook

Minor changes have been made in presenting these formulae. In the case of Appendix I, The Fluid or Unstatic Theory of Plots, subdivisions have been rearranged so they follow the principal divisions to which they apply and the double-numeration system has been substituted for Gardner's rather chaotic jumble of numbers and letters. This has been done to facilitate following the many choices from which Gardner applied plot elements in building the plot of a complex mystery story. Obvious errors of spelling, capitalization, and punctuation have been corrected in the interest of improving understanding. Where there was any doubt as to meaning, Gardner's version has been preserved for the reader's interpretation.

I
THE FLUID OR UNSTATIC
THEORY OF PLOTS

1. The act of primary villainy
   1. 1. Defrauds insurance company and needs body
      1. 1. 1. Stranger
      1. 1. 2. Partner
      1. 1. 3. Client
      1. 1. 4. Investor
      1. 1. 5. Bank (*see* "Page of Actors and Victims")
   1. 2. Robs, embezzles or defrauds
   1. 3. Destroys something which will hurt him
      1. 3. 1. Confession
      1. 3. 2. Will
      1. 3. 3. Note
   1. 4. Engages in smuggling
      1. 4. 1. Dope
      1. 4. 2. Diamonds
      1. 4. 3. Contraband
   1. 5. Forges
      1. 5. 1. Wills
      1. 5. 2. Letters
      1. 5. 3. Evidence
   1. 6. Murders (*see* "Page of Actors and Victims")
   1. 7. Burns insured building or evidence
   1. 8. Kills or abducts (*see* "Page of Actors and Victims")

1. 9. Runs marriage or other mail swindle racket
1.10. Steals
    1.10. 1. Gems
    1.10. 2. Bribe money
    1.10. 3. Stolen money
    1.10. 4. Formula
    1.10. 5. Letters of value—blackmail
    1.10. 6. Rare paintings
    1.10. 7. Embezzled cash
    1.10. 8. Hoarded gold
    1.10. 9. Buried cash
    1.10.10. Bullion
    1.10.11. Evidence
    1.10.12. Stamps
    1.10.13. Stolen gems—fence
    1.10.14. Ransom money
    1.10.15. Blackmail money
    1.10.16. Incriminating documents
    1.10.17. Smuggled stones
    1.10.18. Idols or curios
1.11. Gets insurance company to insure fake gems or fakes theft
    1.11. 1. Man insures valuable gems, fakes theft after getting insurance detective to guard them, then lets the "crooks" deliver them to insurance company for reward. . . .
    1.11. 2. . . . Substitution after appraisal and insurance. Made by guy, himself.
2. Motivation for act of villainy:* Villain resorts to crime because of desire for
  2. 1. Gain motivation
    2. 1. 1. To collect insurance
    2. 1. 2. To remove person in way of inheritance
    2. 1. 3. To inherit property
    2. 1. 4. To keep person from changing will
    2. 1. 5. To keep person from marrying
    2. 1. 6. To keep person from revoking authority

*Note difference between a static and cumulative motivation. Better wherever possible to start with a departure from a cumulative murder motivation—gradually, inexorably, forced to the murder motivation. [—E.S.G.]

2. 1. 7. To secure chart [map], stolen or embezzled or other secret funds—hoarded, concealed, etc. hidden from judgment creditors

2. 1. 8. To secure freedom from marriage or other bond

2. 1. 9. To secure valuable evidence

2. 1.10. To secure property deemed valueless but which is valuable (minerals, etc.)

2. 2. Revenge

2. 3. Justice

2. 4. Silence lips

    2. 4. 1. Preventing auditor or partner securing evidence of embezzlement

    2. 4. 2. Preventing victim investigating facts which will lead to discovery of

        2. 4. 2. 1. Prior crime

        2. 4. 2. 2. Forgery of will, checks, etc.

        2. 4. 2. 3. Knowledge of real identity

    2. 4. 3. Kills a witness to what at time seems merely a trivial matter

    2. 4. 4. To prevent

        2. 4. 4. 1. Past being revealed

        2. 4. 4. 2. Telling loved one something disgraceful

        2. 4. 4. 3. Confession of other partner—joint crime

        2. 4. 4. 4. Sell-out by accomplice

        2. 4. 4. 5. Report of stool pigeon

        2. 4. 4. 6. Disclosure of loot

        2. 4. 4. 7. Disclosure of some plot to commit crime

    2. 4. 5. Destroy evidence

    2. 4. 6. Conceal proof of other crime

    2. 4. 7. Prevent discovery of other crime

    2. 4. 8. Frame some other person to

        2. 4. 8. 1. Conceal own connection

        2. 4. 8. 2. Remove object of hatred

    2. 4. 9. Leave way clear for love affair

    2. 4.10. Protect loved one from

        2. 4.10. 1. Self

2. 4.10. 2. Other crime

2. 4.10. 3. Own folly

2. 4.11. Prevent discovery that counterfeit article has been substituted for original

2. 4.11. 1. Collector's item

2. 4.11. 2. Forged will etc.

2. 4.12. Love—force a woman to marry by power over loved one etc.

2. 4.12. 1. Father

2. 4.12. 2. Brother

2. 4.13. Prevent disclosure of location of one kidnapped

2. 4.14. Witness knows some fact which will prove innocence of some person—and this innocence, once established, will inconvenience villain by

2. 4.14. 1. Proving him guilty of crime

2. 4.14. 2. Preventing his inheriting money

2. 4.14. 3. Keeping him from winning woman

2. 5. Kidnapping motivation

2. 5. 1. To get reward from others, ransom

2. 5. 2. To furnish good explanation for murdering victim

2. 5. 3. To keep victim absent from business while stocks manipulated, rumors floated, checks cashed, contracts made through subordinate

2. 5. 4. To keep victim from doing something

2. 5. 4. 1. Testifying

2. 5. 4. 2. Signing

2. 5. 4. 3. Being available for interview

2. 5. 5. To have doctor or other skilled man use knowledge

2. 5. 6. To plant some bit of evidence through absence

2. 5. 7. To have victim unable to give alibi for period of absence

3. Having committed the act of villainy, the villain tries to conceal it or escape consequences, or to help carry out motive by

3. 1. Making murder appear to be suicide

3. 2. Killing witness

3. 3. Discrediting witness

3. 3. 1. Insanity

3. 3. 2. Making him seem guilty of other crime

3. 4. Building fake alibi

3. 4. 1. Tampering with clocks—setting ahead or behind, smashing
3. 4. 2. Bribing or confusing witness
3. 4. 3. Speeding from place to place
3. 4. 4. Pretending to be
    3. 4. 4. 1. In locked room
    3. 4. 4. 2. Sick
    3. 4. 4. 3. Drugged
    3. 4. 4. 4. Asleep
    3. 4. 4. 5. Unconscious
3. 4. 5. Securing double
3. 4. 6. Switching dates—juggling calendars
3. 5. Ditching pursuit
    3. 5. 1. Nails for tires
    3. 5. 2. Tampering with other cars, bridges, etc.
3. 6. Abducting some witness
3. 7. Tries to secure possession of some seemingly trivial and insignificant item—clue
3. 8. Forges
    3. 8. 1. Paper
    3. 8. 2. Will
    3. 8. 3. Note
    3. 8. 4. Letter
3. 9. Places incriminating things in place of concealment
    3. 9. 1. Gun
    3. 9. 2. Mask
    3. 9. 3. Plunder
3.10. Frames a fall guy by planting evidence
3.11. Fakes his own death—suicide or otherwise
3.12. Concealing corpus delicti
3.13. Confusing identity of corpse to conceal real motivation etc.
3.14. Deliberately plants false or misleading facts for others to follow
3.15. Assuming the identity of the victim
3.16. Getting a double for himself
3.17. In trying to escape, murderer must
    3.17. 1. Leave premises unseen
        3.17. 1. 1. Steals car—perhaps afraid to have own car seen in neighborhood. Therefore

may leave his own car near stolen car location or may steal car of person to be framed

3.17. 1. 2. Calls taxi from nearby store (hero surveys to find nearest telephone at night)

3.17. 1. 3. Surprised on premises: knocks on wrong door or philanders some surprised woman

3.17. 1. 4. Masquerades as milkman, servant, clerk, janitor, waiter, messenger

3.17. 1. 5. Walks and has unexpected adventure
    3.17.1.5.1. Held up
    3.17.1.5.2. Witness to crime or car smash, detained, gives phoney name, caught
    3.17.1.5.3. Accosted by girl in distress
    3.17.1.5.4. Injured by accident

3.17. 1. 6. Leaves room and pounds on door, or slips over roof or fire escape, gets car, drives to front door and rings

3.17. 1. 7. Exit through back yard or alley
    3.17.1 7.1. Recognized by friend en route

3.17. 2. Hides on premises—to reappear later

3.17. 2. 1. Starts fire or explosion, removes clothes, gets in bed and is "rescued"

3.17. 2. 2. Sticks around—comes in as reporter, photographer etc.

3.17. 2. 3. Hides nearby: joins crowd which gathers
    3.17.2.3.1. If car stops with four people, there will then be five spectators
    3.17.2.3.2. Is seen to join spectators from wrong direction
    3.17.2.3.3. Leaves spectators too soon, first to leave

3.17. 2. 4. Sticks around shooting at mythical assailant

3.17. 2. 5. Sticks around shooting innocent man and claiming assailant

3.17. 2. 6. Sticks around after luring known crook into vicinity and killing or wounding

3.17. 3. Remove fingerprints or objects holding prints

3.17. 4. Dispose of weapon

3.17. 5. Wash off bloodstains

3.17. 6. Dispose of bloodstained clothes

3.17. 7. Account for his absence

3.17. 8. Dispose of plunder, any object taken from room or body

3.18. Plans to confuse police on

3.18. 1. Place where murder was committed

3.18. 2. Time when murder was committed

3.18. 3. Identity of person murdered

3.18. 4. Motive for committing murder: kills one or two people against whom he has no motive to prepare way for killing victim really wanted

3.18. 5. Weapon by which murder was committed

3.19. Commits a series of crimes to confuse police as to real motivation: Wishing to murder C for gain where motivation would be so obvious as to point suspicion at him, the murderer finds A and B who have nothing in common with C and kills them first, thereby making police believe motivation deals with what they have in common

3.20. While crime is under investigation, suspect attempts to divert suspicion by "discovering" and communicating to detective some key bit of evidence which tends finally to incriminate suspect and which he would naturally have concealed had he known in advance what it was

4. In trying 3 * or afterward, villain is confronted by complications incurred through

4. 1. Detective seeking on other matter

---

*This reference is to Step No. 3. The villain's cover-up (see page 215).

4. 1. 1. Villain has been violating parking law and detective wants him on that

4. 1. 2. Trying to serve him with civil summons over some trivial lawsuit

4. 2. Stray cat getting in or out through window

4. 3. Frightened, crooked, jealous or incompetent accomplices

4. 3. 1. He starts taking the girl of his accomplice

4. 3. 2. Accomplice is afraid of cats, mice, or has hay fever and allergic to certain pollen

4. 3. 3. Accomplice terribly superstitious, has omens, mascots

4. 3. 4. Accomplice has weakness for redheads or blondes or just women

4. 3. 5. Accomplice is henpecked by wife who wears the pants of the family and of whom he is more afraid than of leader or of imprisonment

4. 3. 6. Accomplice is inveterate gambler, always shaking dice or playing with marked cards and can't resist temptation to stop whatever he is doing and play

4. 4. Failure of plans by fortuitous accident (little girl has dog who barks; villain kicks dog into street—in front of truck—girl jumps out and is hurt)

4. 5. Mistaken assumption in original premise

4. 5. 1. Thinks day is Thursday the 12th whereas it is Friday the 13th which, when discovered, makes him jittery. He takes too elaborate precautions which in turn betray him

4. 5. 2. Thinks some minor person is an arrant coward. This character actually has been a cringing coward over minor matters but to protect his (a) girl, (b) property, (c) job becomes a veritable wildcat

4. 5. 3. Gets the 3-hour time differential between N.Y. and San Francisco mixed up

4. 5. 4. Thinks July south of equator is hot

4. 6. Minor witnesses to secondary facts

4. 7. Accidental leaving behind of telltale evidence

4. 8. Escape of intended secondary victim (Person intended as second victim and who is to be at a certain place at a certain

time—in which event he would have been murdered—has gone out on some errand of mercy, or to buy present for his wife with whom he had quarreled. This saves his life and complicates crime for villain)

4. 9. Accomplice unconsciously may betray woman accomplice in love with enemy, becoming jealous or filled with remorse

4.10. Suffering some accident in person or to car, plane etc. used in escape

4.11. Someone in whom he trusts is a spy

4.12. He happens to see auto accident and is subpoenaed as a witness

5. The hero contacts *an* but not necessarily *the* act of villainy either by chance or by deliberation

  5. 1. Contact by chance

    5. 1. 1. Auto accident

    5. 1. 2. Resemblance to one of actors or victim

    5. 1. 3. Coming to rescue of witness or victim

    5. 1. 4. Being selected as the fall guy

    5. 1. 5. Having specialized knowledge when villain needs

      5. 1. 5. 1. Doctor

      5. 1. 5. 2. Lawyer

      5. 1. 5. 3. Chemist

    5. 1. 6. Wrong number on telephone call incoming or outgoing

    5. 1. 7. Encountering stranded

      5. 1. 7. 1. Witness

      5. 1. 7. 2. Victim

      5. 1. 7. 3. Accomplice

    5. 1. 8. Becoming interested in some secondary phenomena because of specialized knowledge—either by actual contact or newspaper reading

    5. 1. 9. Being an unwitting obstacle in villain's plan

      5. 1. 9. 1. Wrong parking place

      5. 1. 9. 2. Theater ticket, etc.

    5. 1.10. Being by chance in some particular location needed by villain

      5. 1.10. 1. House

      5. 1.10. 2. Bed

      5. 1.10. 3. Room

5. 1.10. 4. Parking station
5. 1.10. 5. Reserved seat
5. 1.10. 6. Hotel room
5. 1.10. 7. Pullman section etc.

5. 1.11. Having same name as
5. 1.11. 1. Accomplice
5. 1.11. 2. Victim
5. 1.11. 3. Messenger
5. 1.11. 4. Lawyer
5. 1.11. 5. Detective
5. 1.11. 6. Doctor
5. 1.11. 7. Fence

5. 1.12. Noticing by chance secondary phenomena
5. 1.12. 1. Papers piled on stoop
5. 1.12. 2. Milk bottles
5. 1.12. 3. Crying dog, etc.

5. 2. Deliberate contact
5. 2. 1. Hero is lawyer

5. 2. 1. 1. Defending	Witness
5. 2. 1. 2. Prosecuting	Friend
5. 2. 1. 3. Advising	Victim
	Heir

5. 2. 2. Hero is relative of victim seeking vengeance
5. 2. 3. Hero is friend of fall guy seeking justice
5. 2. 4. Hero is detective employed by
5. 2. 4. 1. Witness
5. 2. 4. 2. Fall guy
5. 2. 4. 3. Relative
5. 2. 4. 4. Scheming crook
5. 2. 4. 5. Rival villain
5. 2. 4. 6. Insurance company
5. 2. 4. 7. Lawyer
5. 2. 4. 8. Friend of some actor

5. 2. 5. Hero is private citizen interested in clearing up crimes because he is
5. 2. 5. 1. Crusading politician, grand juror, preacher, newspaperman
5. 2. 5. 2. Hobby rider
5. 2. 5. 3. Excitement craver

5. 2. 5. 4. On a bet

5. 2. 5. 5. From sense of justice

5. 2. 6. Hero is newspaperman

    5. 2. 6. 1. Columnist looking for sob sister angle

    5. 2. 6. 2. Checking on other story

    5. 2. 6. 3. Protecting paper in libel

    5. 2. 6. 4. Getting political dirt

    5. 2. 6. 5. Checking up on incidental crime

    5. 2. 6. 6. After the story

5. 2. 7. Hero is law enforcement agent

    5. 2. 7. 1. G-man, district attorney, grand juror

    5. 2. 7. 2. Detective, cop or sheriff—hick constable

    5. 2. 7. 3. Radio cop

5. 2. 8. Hero is handwriting expert

5. 2. 9. Hero is judge who heard evidence and dissatisfied

5. 2.10. Hero is clerk or steno who heard evidence and dissatisfied

5. 2.11. Hero is clerk, assistant or steno working for judge, lawyer, detective etc. satisfied boss on a limb and trying to solve on own

5. 2.12. Hero is priest who hears story of misfortune from victim or fall guy or friend

5. 2.13. Hero is some philosopher—either millionaire or laborer—who hears story of misfortune from victim or fall guy or friend

5. 2.14. Hero is friend of D.A. or other law enforcement officer

5. 2.15. Hero is crook who robs crooks

5. 2.16. Hero is student of crime, psychology, newspapers

5. 2.17. Hero is person sympathizing with incidental misfortune: dog, cat, etc.

5. 2.18. Hero is confidence man preying on dough-heavy crooks

5. 2.19. Hero is reward hunter

5. 2.20. Hero is "want-ad man" interested in building up results from want ads

5. 2.21. Hero is reader of "personals" who likes to investigate

      5. 2.22. Hero is talkative crime hound, nuts on detective stories
6. When conflict has been joined and hero comes in contact with villainy there are certain complicating circumstances which make for character conflicts and story
    6. 1. Zeal of honest incompetent (hick cop) upsets hero's plans
    6. 2. Rival of hero tries to discredit him
    6. 3. Some character is an imposter
    6. 4. A witness is
        6. 4. 1. Mistaken
        6. 4. 2. Lying
        6. 4. 3. Killed
        6. 4. 4. Abducted
        6. 4. 5. Bribed
        6. 4. 6. Intimidated
    6. 5. Heroine's mind poisoned against hero
    6. 6. Hero violates law to gain ends and is sought
    6. 7. Witness mistakes hero for villain
    6. 8. Hero arrested for incidental crime (speeding)
    6. 9. Detective takes hero into custody as witness or mistakes for villain
    6.10. Parents of heroine hostile to hero
    6.11. Hero out of funds: robbed, broke, because of assumed identity can't cash check, loses clothes and cash
    6.12. Heroine's maid is a spy
    6.13. Hero is watched
    6.14. Hero is captured by villain
    6.15. Assistant of hero fails to keep appointment
        6.15. 1. Abducted
        6.15. 2. Arrested
        6.15. 3. Bribed
        6.15. 4. Drunk
    6.16. Assistant of hero mistakes someone else for person he is to protect
    6.17. Assistant of hero deceived by forged, false, or misunderstood instructions
    6.18. Man who is to prove something or help insured arrested, detained, killed or sick and taken to hospital, gets drunk
    6.19. Witness injured, unconscious, amnesia

6.20. Check accepted and cashed by hero is forgery

6.21. Hero finds evidence indicating heroine or her relatives implicated with villain

6.22. Unforeseen accident—breakdown car

6.23. Unexpected visitor

6.24. Unexpected encounter with watchdog

6.25. Overlooks something vital in haste or panic

6.26. Coincidence intervenes

6.27. Inaccurate watch, clock, recollection of witness

6.28. Assistant also falls in love with heroine

6.29. Anonymous note enters case

6.30. Technicalities of law obstruct plans

6.31. Misguided friend seeks to help (Happy Hooligan type)

6.32. Mistaken identity of subordinate character *

6.33. Hero follows blind trails because

    6.33. 1. Witness or client lies

    6.33. 2. Fake clues planted

    6.33. 3. Heroine tries protect loved one

    6.33. 4. Effect of evidence misconstrued

7. The complications become involved with the suspense element

  7. 1. Hero does something reader knows is a mistake

  7. 2. Hero walks into trap

    7. 2. 1. Blindly

    7. 2. 2. Deliberately

  7. 3. Hero trusts someone reader knows to be spy

  7. 4. Hero passes by some key clue or witness

  7. 5. Heroine has some independent secret she is trying to cover up and reader knows this

  7. 6. Heroine or assistant to hero violates instructions carelessly or because thinks hero wrong

  7. 7. Hero is balked by some legal technicality and in circumventing it

    7. 7. 1. Suppresses evidence

    7. 7. 2. Breaks into house to secure evidence

---

* A sends B to contact C, and instructs C he has done so. C doesn't know B personally. D contacts C, says he is B and then, later on, B is found murdered. All the time it is supposed he contacted C at a certain time and, therefore, the murder was after that hour. But the hero shows it was before and that D, having murdered B, took his credentials and met C.

---

7. 7. 3. Steals car or other movable property as evidence

7. 7. 4. Tries to get in contact with a witness by telling a false story

7. 7. 5. Knowing witness he wants is a con man, he poses as a sucker

8. Villain feeling net closing about him tries to escape by some further act which points to a more exciting dramatic climax when carried through

8. 1. Kills or abducts witness

8. 2. Steals or tries to steal evidence

8. 3. Seeks to substitute evidence—duplicate guns, etc.

8. 4. Seeks to or does dispose of accomplice

8. 5. Tries to escape

8. 6. Tries to frame or trap hero

8. 7. Seeks to plant further confusing clues

8. 8. Seeks to remove and hide undiscovered clue by second trip to scene of crime

8. 9. Tries to direct attention to evidence indicating his innocence

8.10. Tries intimidation directly or indirectly

8.11. Tries to rectify former actual or believed mistake

9. Hero sets solution factors in motion or traps villain

9. 1. Fakes confession of accomplice, although identity actually unknown

9. 2. Gets villain to try to hide additional valuables or incriminating thing in same place as used for others

9. 3. Leads villain to think hiding place looted and so sends him running to survey loss

9. 4. Lets villain believe loot or incriminating evidence he has concealed in danger

9.2-3-4. 1. Betraying hiding place, villain led to believe

9.2-3-4.1. 1. Must travel

9.2-3-4.1. 2. Fire or flood

9.2-3-4.1. 3. Given new valuable loot will put in same place

9.2-3-4.1. 4. Thinks building will be torn down

9.2-3-4.1. 5. Some scientific method will discover

9.2-3-4.1. 6. Thinks a lie detector, anesthetic or hypnotism has caused to reveal information which can be used to work out, so will run to hide. Talking in sleep

9.2-3-4.1. 7. Thinks some witness or accomplice has seen

9.2-3-4.1. 8. Has chance to sell for fancy price, or to duplicate unique stone (imitation of one stolen)

9.2-3-4.1. 9. Wants girl to wear or to show

9.2-3-4.1.10. Made to believe stolen counterfeit

9.2-3-4.1.11. Reward offered, but must submit photograph

9.2-3-4.1.12. Wants to remove something he fears is telltale

9.2-3-4.1.13. Given a newer, safer hiding place

9.2-3-4.1.14. Place being taken to pieces—will remove to place already searched if given chance

9.2-3-4.1.15. Villain who has taken peculiar type of loot is given to believe has been robbed or betrayed and sees other wearing what he believes are stolen things—or woman, seeing other woman wear, believes male accomplice has given

9. 5. Duplicates some object villain has hidden or destroyed

9. 6. Plants fake evidence

9. 7. Injects hatred, jealousy, suspicion into villain's accomplices or associates—or in mind of villain; makes accomplice think villain is about to make him fall guy

9. 8. Tricks him into displaying knowledge only villain could have

9. 9. Leaving others to solve main act of villainy which is too tough, hero concentrates on secondary act and gets solution

9.10. Traps villain into secret preparations for flight

9.11. Hero bluffs villain into believing he has key evidence he does not appreciate but which villain knows others will, thereby causing villain
    9.11. 1. To try to kill
    9.11. 2. To discount it
    9.11. 3. To flee

9.12. Hero gives each of four suspects false information and then traces back those who acted, those who didn't
    9.12. 1. No one can tell false
    9.12. 2. Villain knows false

9.13. Deliberately starts frame-up on accomplice or loved one of villain, forcing confession or action from villain

9.14. Plants evidence framing accomplice and making accomplice think done by villain to frame

II
PAGE OF ACTORS AND VICTIMS

VILLAIN:	ACT:	VICTIM:
Banker	Murders	Unwitting witness
Guardian	Robs	Ward
Hypocrite	Abducts	Beneficiary of trust
Gambler	Frames	Blackmailer
Debtor	Swindles	Gambler
Victim	Deceives	Creditor
act of villainy	Blackmails	Beneficiary under will
A lover (actuated by	Bribes	Rival
love for other per-		Husband
son in jam)		Insurance company
Relative of villain		Life
Attractive swindler		Theft
Adventuress		Accident
		Detective
		Friend of hero
		Wife of loved one or
		other victim or
		witness to hold
		against surrender of
		evidence

THE VICTIM:

1. Holds fate of some subordinate character in his hands and reader led to speculate on how the victim will use that power.

2. Is, therefore, engaged in doing something important to the story at the time of the murder.

3. Is surrounded by natural rather than artificial clues—such as pants in drawer (D.A. *Calls It Murder*).

Note: For plot ideas, characters are typed in a story resulting from that plot idea. The characters must be untyped. Your adventuress becomes a very human woman with problems of her own which are common to millions of women. She has solved those problems by becoming an adventuress and in showing that, show women readers what happens. Then and next, the good and bad sides of that solution. Bring characters home to the reader.

III
CHARACTER COMPONENTS

Every character in a story can and should have:
1. Point of strength
2. Likeable or humorous weakness
3. Prejudices
4. Common characteristics
   a. Talking too much
   b. Driving while drunk
   c. Gambling
   d. Superstitious playing hunches
   e. Cheating
5. Father, mother, other relatives dependent or wealthy.
6. Emotions—Love, hate, dislike etc. for other characters.
7. Problems—And this is where you sell the character to the reader. Life isn't static. The villain is still bothered with relatives, in-laws, taxes, a wife who may be cheating. But mostly he has problem such as the reader has and he decides to solve such a problem in a certain manner which makes the story, and attracts the reader. A villain committing a crime for money should be shown needing that money to identify him with the readers—money—needing. Yet readers sometimes get tired of the money-needing problem and in reading for escape want to read of characters who are free from this problem. Emotional problems are different except that marriage emotion problems are more nearly like money-needing problems.

IV
THE FOUNDATION OF
CHARACTER BACKGROUND

Each character has
1. Persons whom he loves
                        hates
                        disdains or fears
                        of whom he is jealous
2. Backgrounds of emotion
   caused by
brother	who has emotion	for the principal
sister	hate	character or person
mother-in-law	love	close to him or some
husband	fear	other person in the
wife	affection	story
sweetheart	jealousy	
relatives		
ex-spouse		

for instance ex-spouse hates and fears principal character or his brother, sister, mother etc. or loves (and is affected by the results of that love—as mistress, unrequited love etc.) the character or his relatives.

Each of the characters has

worries	clothes
triumphs	vacation plans
things to conceal	play life
debts	reading tastes
desires	sport likes and
hobbies	dislikes
	a job and likes,
	fears, hates or
	loves the boss

Hatred can be caused by or from
1. A past wrong
2. A complete misunderstanding
3. A conflict of interests
   business
   emotional
   sport

Fear

That person will do or say something to spouse
                                      detective
                                      boss
                                      mother-in-law
                                      officers
                                      partner

    which will
        accuse person of infidelity
                theft or embezzlement
                murder
                deception
        disclose secret agreement
            some past transgression
            social
            sport
            legal
        prevent the person who fears from
                marriage

inheriting property
being received in society
making business deal
living happily with spouse

V
CHART OF ROMANTIC CONFLICT

Parties prevented from marriage:
1. Husband or wife dead but not declared dead for seven-year period when body not found
2. A clause in a will
3. Parental opposition coupled with financial control
4. Other husband or wife living and impossible to get a divorce

Obstacle to love:
1. Childless marriage
2. Husband or wife in love with someone else and other spouse wants to regain affection
3. Suppressed deceit which will ruin marriage if known
   a. Some crime
   b. Some marital deceit
      (1) Past affair
      (2) Adopted child (thought genuine)
      (3) Illegitimate child
      (4) Relative convicted of crime
      (5) Nationality
      (6) Extramarital activity
      (7) Double life
      (8) Family feud
      (9) Financial status
          poverty
          riches
          inheritance
          earnings

> royalties
>
> wages
>
> acting

4. Husband or wife has child by prior marriage which new spouse resents, or child resents new spouse
5. Previous alimony being used as club: for instance, woman who could work claims to be suffering chronic ailment, thereby keeping alimony alive
6. One spouse has some bad habit
   a. Gambling
   b. Drinking
   c. Drugs
   d. Nagging
7. Family relatives, mother-in-law, sick sister etc.
8. Relatives who visit and borrow money
   a. Ne'er-do-well brother
   b. Sister who will shock friends
   c. Slick promoter relative
9. Friends who hate one spouse and are making trouble
10. Someone given to gossip of malicious sort, poisoning mind of one spouse
11. Pets kept by one spouse, hated by other

VI
CONFLICTS OF MOTHER LOVE

1. Fight for the care and custody of the children
   a. Divorce action pending and mother claimed unfit
      (1) Gambling
      (2) Drinking
      (3) Cheating
      (4) Dishonesty
      (5) Something in her past
      (6) Contagious disease such as leprosy
      (7) Disloyalty
   b. Mother trying to get evidence that will prevent father from having custody of children
2. Child about to do something mother feels will make unhappy
   a. Daughter thinking of running away with married man
   b. Son about to get tangled up with married woman
   c. Daughter about to marry man mother suspects of being
      (1) Criminal
      (2) Enemy agent
      (3) Married and undivorced
      (4) Dope fiend
      (5) Gambler
      (6) Murderer
      (7) Defrauder
      (8) Bluebeard
   d. Daughter sticking with husband when she should leave him
   e. Daughter adopting child that
      (1) may be illegitimate child of hers or husband's

     (2) may have hereditary taints, moral

  f. Daughter making mistakes in marriage relationship

     (1) Nagging

     (2) Giving husband too much or not enough freedom

     (3) Playing into the hands of the "other woman" etc.

3. Mother discovers son is a criminal and tries to hide his crime

  a. Son has murdered previous wife to marry again

  b. Son has victimized someone to get money in the distant past and the crime may be discovered

4. Son is in bad company and exposed to temptation

5. Something in the past of the parents may be uncovered to cause children shame, embarrassment

VII
DEPARTURES FROM NORMAL
THEORY OF STORY SITUATION

1. Woman leaves husband
   a. takes daughter or son—or leaves
   b. takes bank account, car etc.
2. Man has amnesia, marries, recovers—and can't remember marriage. Man has amnesia, can't recall witnessed facts in crime. Man has amnesia, can't tell whether he is guilty of crime
3. Man leads double life successfully and dies
4. Person disappears
   a. love motivation
   b. pride
   c. escape
   d. concealment to avoid subpoena, testifying against loved one— or under mistaken idea of guilt
5. A man wrongs a woman
   a. discharges her unjustly
   b. marries and runs away
   c. leads double life
   d. accuses wrongfully
   e. disparages
   f. harms—or seeks to harm child
6. A mother's love and sense of protection is aroused because
   a. married daughter being led to abandon husband and child
   b. daughter being seduced
   c. daughter taught to have vices
   d. daughter betrayed into trap

7. Woman has illegitimate child and
   a. conceals
   b. adopts (husband deceived)
   c. loses—finds later
   d. abandons for adoption (thinks every child that age may be hers)
8. Woman through deception or adoption has child of another
9. Man serves term in pen, escapes, pardoned, discharged
10. Man has hit-and-run charge
11. Man is great gambler and can't control
12. Forges check or some document and tries to regain
13. Has daughter who has disgraced him
14. Goes on chronic drinking sprees
15. Is afraid—either phobia or cowardice
16. Has embezzled money—tries to restore, conceal, escape
17. Attempt to influence life of another by force, fraud, chicanery
    a. get party to secure divorce—or prevent
    b. get party to marry or prevent
    c. get party to accept or reject bribe
    d. secure undue influence on judge, witness, etc.
    e. make party leave country
    f. buy or sell property—invest in mine etc.
18. A man tries to accomplish some beneficial object by unconventional means:
    a. protect the good name of a girl or a friend
    b. live down some scandal in his own past
19. A man's relative has been sent to the pen and the man must do something about his release
20. The wife of a man's best friend is having an affair and the friend is trying to get her back to her senses
21. Man deserts wife and then
    a. secretly remarries
    b. mixes in politics
    c. becomes prosperous
    d. wife has child after separation and he wants to adopt
    e. his child gets movie contract

VIII
THE PLOT TIDE OR THRUST

1. The first phase of the story
   a. characters
   b. minor complications or adventures
   these develop into
2. The major complications
   a. murder
   b. someone whom the reader cares for affected as
      (1) suspect
      (2) in love with suspect
      (3) whole course of life changed
      (4) happiness jeopardized
3. At this point comes the *Counter Thrust*
   The hero ceases to pick up the cards as dealt him by fate and starts a plot of his own. The main thing is to have the hero take *action* and not follow along a cold trail. The best bet is to combine
   (a) chase

   > speed
   > doubling back
   > tricks to throw off pursuit

   and
   (b) Counter Thrust: Hero makes plans of his own; these are virtually a counterplot
      (1) suppresses clue
      (2) plants false clues
      (3) sets traps and watches

(4) starts one character playing against another

(5) puts himself in position to become second victim of the murderer

(6) starts putting some logical victim for second killing in exposed place

IX
THE MYSTERY AFTERMATH
METHOD

Original mystery can be caused by
    a. disappearance
    b. concealed background
    c. past crime
    d. entangling alliance in past
    e. strange object which ties in with activities
results in
    a. attempt at concealment
    b. false explanations
    c. payment of blackmail
    d. murder
Disappearance—
                Husband or wife
                  runs away with other person
                  taken for dead
                  lapse memory
                              Reactions of surviving spouse
                                  love continues
                                  marries again
                                  hatred
                                  fear

X
PERRY MASON TITLE ANALYSIS

Adjective of mystery
 The Case of the Mystified Model
      Sullen Bridegroom
      Sleepy Bridegroom
      Mystified Witness
      Uncertain Witness
      Mortified Witness
Adjective of action
 The Case of the Deadly Dilemma
      Pointing Weapon
      Spinning
      Running
      Whirling
      Shooting
      Walking
      Circling Secretary
      Kidnapped Witness
      Evasive Witness
      Vanishing Victim
        Witness
        Accomplice

Noun meaning feminine
 Seamstress
 Model
 Actress
Feminine occupations
 Actress
 Nurse
 Actress
Contrast
 Smiling Corpse
 Good-natured Hangman
Mystery
 Terrified Actress
 Unwilling Accomplice
Continuing action
 Sullen Secretary
 Mischievous Daughter
 Running Target
 Running Victim
 Zigzagging Target
 Running Defendant

Title Words

Adjective	Noun
Venturesome	Governess
Smiling	Nurse
Light-Hearted	Cashier
Carefree	Chaperone
Contraband	Sister
Willing	Girl
Terrified	Widow
Horrified	Witness
Vanishing	
Talkative	
Uncertain	
Screaming	

The Case of the Hesitant Widow
Talkative Chaperone
Negligent Chaperone
Screaming Girl   Witness   Companion
The Case of the Glancing Bullet
Colorblind Corpse
Startled Siren
Mortified Siren
The Case of the Vanishing Bridesmaid
The Case of the Bountiful Bridesmaid

XI
THE LAST PLOTTING NOTEBOOK

Erle Stanley Gardner's last plotting notebook records preliminary plot construction on *The Case of the Fabulous Fake* and *All Grass Isn't Green*, as well as occasional notes concerning other projects in which he was engaged during the final two years of his life. Those portions pertaining to his last two works of fiction are reproduced here to give a sustained example of how he used his notebooks to develop the plots from which he dictated the finished products.

He began work in this notebook on January 22, 1968, searching his mind for a Perry Mason plot. His first few tries were unsuccessful. He came back at intervals, but it was several months before the story began to jell. As usual, along the way Gardner was annoyed at himself:

Tues. Jan. 22, 1968—Temecula:
   Mason gimmick—Man, rich in the hands of unscrupulous sister—Medical inspection—incompetent—favorite nurse—wants to make will but completely dominated by the conservator—Old will leaves all to the sister—only living relative: Man guarded all the time—Mason gets into wooded area and has him get lost—desert area—has helicopter pick him up—flies to Las Vegas—marries nurse—brings him back to desert where he is "found" by a prospector who collects reward.
   Dunphy vs. Dunphy 161C. 87   118 Pac. 945—Vitale vs. Vitale 147 C.N. 2nd 665   305 Pac 2nd 690.

Fri. Feb. 16, 1968—Temecula:
   Woman—a wife or a mistress who decides to get rid of the man and get even with him so she "disappears" under such circumstances every

one feels that he murdered her—His loss of friends and prestige etc.

Sun. Feb. 18, 1968—Palm Springs:
   A girl who was thrown out when she became pregnant, grows up and wants to have her child received into the home of her parents, only to find an imposter has usurped the position. Perhaps the folks are dead, dying after usurper got in and the gal may have let the kid out for adoption and has no idea where it may be now, but it had a birthmark and she is playing with the idea of advertising—This gives a problem background for Mason, but I don't think it compares with a case where someone has power which is being used in such a way as to bring about an injustice. The despotic trustee, the crooked guardian—Perhaps we approach this same problem from another angle. The daughter had vanished, perhaps dead or supposed to be dead, and an old family servant is with the somewhat doddering old grandparent. A man shows up as the "father" of the child which he claims he brought up. He had photos and stuff of that sort to support his claim and the child is accepted. Actually the mother isn't dead but has taken another name and can't disclose her true identity without breaking the heart of loving foster parent. There should be someone in the position of power—

   Gardner broke off his train of thought and picked up a black pen, to contrast with the blue ink which he was using. He printed a warning note in the center of the page: "The above might make a better plot for an A. A. Fair story than for Mason." In the margin he printed a reminder, "Explore for Donald Lam." He went on in blue:

   How about an elderly man who has made a will, or says he has in favor of his favorite grandchild—and the cousins with whom he is living, or the nephew and his wife are moving in and are going to destroy the will—in that event it must be a closer relative—the girl, then, is not a grandchild, or perhaps not a relative at all. Mason could have the guy go for a ride: During this ride he makes a will. Della has a portable typewriter and they get two witnesses. Am afraid this is too similar to the book I wrote about the niece or granddaughter coming back from Honolulu. I need a person or persons in a position of power about to make unjust use of that power. A man, or a woman, with something in the past that has been heard from. Not a standard blackmail approach, but perhaps a case where this man has to testify and the blackmailer is going to the opposing attorney and have him ask the impeaching question as to whether the guy has ever been convicted of a felony. Then Mason gets around the blackmail by seeing that the case is solved before it ever gets into court. This can be worked out. An elderly man murdered. The real villian* inherits the money, or stands to inherit it. He is very anxious to show that a nurse or housekeeper committed the crime. Mason's client knows facts that indicate, but do not prove, her innocence— He has a past which the villian knows about and warns the guy not to get on the stand. Mason can't take the girl's case without betraying his client so his hands are tied. The man can be killed, apparently by having the house burn as the result of a gas explosion, but actually this is a dodge to cover up a bullet. The bullet can have gone through a window and lodged in a tree. The villian has an iron clad alibi which Mason breaks down by showing that the man who is giving him the alibi wasn't where he said he was. Whereupon the "truth" comes out that the villian was leading a double life and is married to another woman, who may be the real wife so that he can't inherit through the family connections. Mason is therefore placed in a position to do blackmail of his own to counter the other's threat—but, of course, Mason goes farther and proves the gal innocent by showing the villian is guilty of the crime—digging out the bullet and identifying the gun which fired it. The man is a cripple who lives in a wheel chair. He gets along with the aid of a housekeeper but after she goes home, has the gal come and read to him after he gets into bed. On the night of his death the girl came a little early, entered the house, and was seen unlocking the front door, then remembered she was supposed to bring some soap from the supermarket down the street and, since she was early, went back to get the toilet articles. Had gone only halfway when she heard the gas explosion—thought she smelled gas when she went in. A neighbor swears he saw her go in and then come out just as the explosion took place, making a liar out of her—she could have been in the supermarket when she heard the explosion and ran out to see what it was, at which time she saw the flames coming out of the windows. The firemen believe there was gasoline spread around. The old man has made a will leaving the villian a hundred thousand and the remainder of his estate to the girl—make it two hundred thousand out of an estate worth well over a million.—If the gal is convicted of murder she can't inherit and the villian gets it all. The solution is gas and an electric clock set to go off at a certain time and the gal coming to work from a bus always reaches there at a certain time, except on this occasion when "someone" phoned and asked her to come early—the bus is out. The driver would

* Despite the hundreds of villains about whom he wrote, through his entire life Gardner misspelled the word, particularly when writing hurriedly. Occasionally he would catch himself as he went and correct with an interlineation, but more often than not it came out *villian* and he left it to a secretary to make the correction in typescript.

know her— Or leave it in and have only the one driver who knows her because she is with him every night. He has to admit she wasn't on his bus that night. The room can be soaked with gasoline and a spark generated when the clock reaches a certain minute or when a door is opened—an inner door. The gal went in twice and the first time didn't open the inner door. The neighbor saw the girl go in the first time, carrying a gasoline can which she admits. Only the witness saw her go in the second time. She was carrying gasoline at the request of the old man—perhaps a cleaning fluid. In any event the witness can give her an alibi—or corroborate her story. He is a relative or employee of the villian in the piece. He says she set the can of gas at the foot of the stairs. There is an explosion and fire.

It would be more than two months before Gardner got back to Perry Mason. During the interim he went to Mexico for the filming of a documentary in which he was the central figure. The trip entailed a strenuous circle tour from Tijuana to Mexicali, Chihuahua, the Barranca country, Mexico City, Guadalajara, Mazatlán, La Paz, and back to Tijuana. Along the way Gardner gathered experiences, people, and pictures for his last travel book.

Sun. Apr. 28, 1968—Temecula:
Back to Mason story.
This young gal is the favorite of a very wealthy and very old man. She is on her way to pay off a blackmailer. The old man is furnishing the money without the blackmail victim knowing anything about what's being done. The girl comes to L.A. to pay the money and get the evidence. The old man is to cover for her, but has a heart attack which she doesn't know about and the cash is short. She puts an ad in the paper "I am here and have what you want" and signs it "36-24-36" Gertie who reads all the personals spots it. The gal goes to make the pay off— The man in the case is either married or just getting married. He has an old scandal—a son while in high school—turns out it wasn't his son at all, but the girl picked him as being the best potential father— Mason gets Drake to shadow his client getting her address from the newspaper ad. She goes to pay off the blackmailer and he is murdered. She eludes Drake's men and skips out and can be elected for the murder unless corrective steps are taken at once.

Gardner had started dictating the story, but he was not at all satisfied with the results, which now had *The Case of the Restless Corpse* as a working title. It needed to be "ripped to pieces."

Sun. July 7, 1968—Temecula:

Mason story. I am trying to nail down an impossible plot, which means I am dragging my heels on the story. To begin with the idea of the son paying off the father's blackmail by using a girl is unreal. Let's get back to fundamentals. The man will have to be 32 or 33 at the youngest, the girl around 27 to 29. She is his devoted secretary. She overhears the telephone conversation when she gets back from lunch early or doesn't go. The amount is 5,000 or 10,000. The man draws it out and puts it in his locked desk. She has a key. He also has a gun in the desk. The man is gone, the gun is gone. The cash is there. The girl decides he is going to kill the blackmailer. She wants to prevent this. How about having her employer tell her he has to go to Denver and if he isn't back she is to take the money and pay off. Then he forgets to put in the voucher. The son must *never* know— This son—too young— prefer a straight laced younger brother—a junior partner in the firm.

Mon. July 8, 1968—Temecula:

Mason. This whole plot is cock-eyed. There has to be a reason for the girl wanting to duck out and be incognito. It can be because of a brother she loves who is paying blackmail and the gal can be an heiress— Or she can be trying to get a friend out of trouble. The blackmail angle is more for a Fair yarn.— But this business organization is the pure bunk. I need another background, another motivation from page 50.

Thurs. July 18, 1968, On board River Queen—Delta:

The start of the story is so theatrical it overshadows any sequence which is not equally dramatic and trying to make such a sequence gives the whole story a weird, theatrical turn. The first thing to get clearly fixed is who this gal is and what her objective is. The sum of money should be decreased a lot. Have it 2500 or some such amount that a working girl could save and keep in the form of cash without making a splurge over withdrawal. Then the gal could be in love with a guy who actually does have a shortage— He could be a weak willed brother— The guy tries to put the bite on her for 2500 and she won't go for it. He dips into the till, slips out and is hurt in a car crash— She visits him in the hospital and finds he is unconscious with 2500 in cash and a note signed 36-24-36 in his wallet stating this is the final demand etc. etc. So she takes over and someone actually removes the money after she replaces it. The brother may not be paying blackmail but may be receiving it in return for letting phony Certificates of Origin pass through their regular commercial channels. He has this money in cash. He is the one who put the ad in the paper and got the money. She thinks he embezzled the money and is the victim.

This girl has a brother. They are both working for the same company. They had an uncle die and left each of them ten grand. The boy played the horses and lost his money or most of it. The girl worked and made money. Then she felt the brother was being blackmailed. He is in an automobile accident and is unconscious. They notify her and she goes there finds he has 5 grand and the blackmail note. She assumes he has taken the money from the company. She says nothing about it but takes 5 grand of her own money and goes to settle the case.

Fri. July 19, 1968—On boat in Delta:
    Continuation of Mason plot. The brother is unconscious and suddenly takes a turn for the worse and is not expected to live— Is it possible the girl could have been a passenger in the car and the money, the blackmail letter etc. could have been in a brief case which she took with her intending to leave at the hospital? The brother was representing the V.P. of the importing firm a s.o.b. who is in hock for 5 grand and he eased this out intending to repay, but when the brother had his accident he boldly embezzled another 5 grand leaving a shortage of ten thousand dollars, and then framed it on the sister who he can prove took the brief case. The firm can keep relatively large sums of cash on hand for certain purchases which are better not covered by ordinary vouchers. The Company has a president who is absent, a voluptuous bookkeeper who is shacked up with the V.P. from time to time and she may be the real blackmailer using as a stooge a L.A. pimp who can be the murder victim.

On the last day of July, Gardner wrote Larry Hughes at William Morrow that he was having more trouble with this story than he had ever had with a Mason story. "I would like to have each succeeding book sufficiently ingenious so the trade can't say I am riding on my reputation." By that time he was on his third revision and had decided to wait a month or so before going on.

There were other things to do: his marriage to Jean Bethell and a honeymoon to Mexico as well as some chores on *Host with the Big Hat*. When he got back to Perry Mason he made another complete revision, now calling it *The Case of the Falsified Client*, "a brand new plot so that the thing isn't quite as pedestrian as it was." He used his plotting notebook to make brief notes for guidance in revision and then to plot the final five chapters in preparation for dictation:

Sun. Oct. 20, 1968—Palm Springs:
    Need more central characters in S.F. [San Francisco] Get typist—

secy—mail and file and income tax man. Have much of action over week end.

Sun. Nov. 17, 1968—Palm Springs:

Mason. Mason arrives in San Francisco goes hotel phones 767— No word from Diana— No message. Next morning arrives 10.30 Diana breezes in—missed plane—delay in traffic— Can't stand questioning. Mason goes to office with her. Spent night hospital. Homer Gage there
  Stewart Garland Income tax there.
  Franklin Gage absent three or four days on business trip.
  This is Friday. There is an office meeting to see if anyone can reach Franklin Gage.
  Milton Chester Gen office mgr. there.

Mon. Nov. 18, 1968—Palm Springs:

Mason tells Gage of Edgar's death, gets a note from one of the girls— phones ------, tells him the news—to lead Stella on for a while to see if Cassel will be back before he hears about Edgar and then returns to L.A. On Monday a.m. Della brings him the news. Diana is now wanted for murder—or Mason can go up there to the hotel just as the cops come.

Sun. Dec. 8, 1968—Palm Springs:

Mason—from Record 18—Mason instructs Drake to get the lowdown on Moray Cassel—the guy is psychologically a pimp. Put everything on him. *Find* the woman. Drake finds several women— Ostensibly Cassel is an importer of Mexican curios—Drake runs down the woman—can't ring a bell. One mysterious woman who slapped hell out of him and walked out with a swollen eye— Cassel carries a gun. Police say nothing about the gun. "What the hell, Perry, you can't prove self defense." Cassel's gun in place in its holster—bullet fired from the front. No connection with Edgar but some with Escobar Import & Export Co. Income tax people quietly nosing around—won't talk but intimate a deal. The police find the gun 6″ barrel 22— Getting out of purse a job and spilled credit card. Diana's fingerprint on gun. Expert shows how it could be carried in purse. Mason shows as harder to get it in than to take it out. Solution—Franklin Gage married, has child by secy—very quiet. Cassel finds out, locates. He blackmails the gal and tries to find out who the father is. Now who killed Cassel—Franklin? No—too obvious and out of character. He gave Edgar 5000 for taking the rap of being the father and making the pay-off. Homer Gage more the murdering type. Franklin had to lay low while Edgar unconscious—Mason frames the crime on Edgar but afterwards lets it out it could have been the girl but in his opinion they could never have convicted the mother and he isn't doing the police work on a defense attorney's fee— Or Mrs. Franklin Gage could have been protecting her social standing— Mysterious money flows into Mason's office to finance the defense.—Can't blame it on Edgar because I need Cassel alive to confront Mason in L.A.— Slowly, remorselessly Mason has to build his case on cross examination of the police— What they found and what they didn't find— Records missing from safe? Then murderer must have known combination— Cassel's notebook found where it had been thrown away— Combination of safe written in a sort of code.

Thurs. Feb. 13, 1968—Palm Springs:
Wind up of Mason. Mason has to get Franklin Gage to Los Angeles— Gets him to bring one of the secretaries down: This is a decoy action. An overcoat in Cassel's closet which doesn't fit. Murderer used it to conceal gun. Franklin could have had child by one of the secretaries and Cassel found out about it. Then Franklin got Edgar to take the rap, but the accident caused a change in Homer. Homer is a more likely murderer. Can Mason get them both down there for the trial? He wants the audit—shows ten thousand short. Mason has to identify the overcoat. The murderer used it to conceal the gun, entered the room, left the gun and the coat. Took an extra five grand.

The following day Gardner wrote Larry Hughes that the story was finally all dictated and transcribed—but it still needed revision. It would be another three weeks before he could get it to him. This was a far cry from the week it took to plot and dictate *The Case of the Velvet Claws* thirty-seven years earlier. The story was published in November as *The Case of the Fabulous Fake*.

Before starting his last Bertha Cool–Donald Lam book, he did most of the work on *Cops on Campus and Crime in the Streets*, a police book he had wanted to write for some time. Once he got underway, the "A. A. Fair story," as he still called the Cool-Lam yarns, went much easier than the Mason novel, but Gardner always had a preference for writing in the first person.

Fri. Apr. 11, 1969—Palm Springs:
A. A. Fair story.
Start with guy in Bertha's office very doubtful about whether the agency can do the job etc. Wants a blonde sweetheart located—a gal who walked out on him and vanished. Donald pointed out the guy is a

liar after he leaves. Gets storage Co. and finds address of gal—Gen. Del. in Tucson.

Wed. Apr. 23, 1969—Temecula:

Donald takes dummy box to the storage co. "This should have been in the shipment left with you yesterday."

Thurs. May 1, 1969—Palm Springs:

I need a basic plot for all this. The man, of course, does not want the gal found because of a love affair, but because of some ulterior motive. The question is whether Donald can be a part of that scene, or whether he should repudiate the employment and if so how it can be done. It would have to be at the instance of the client who could think he could find a better agency— This is not quite cricket. Suppose two men are trying to locate the gal. If this is so why are they trying to beat each other to the solution, and will Donald be able to satisfy the reader unless he starts protecting the girl. If the man gave a check and stopped payment it would put Donald somewhat in the clear— Or the man might tell Donald, "I am called away on a matter of great urgency. When you find this girl protect her." "From what?" Donald asks. "From everything and Everybody" the man says. Donald hands it to him straight, "From Everybody?" "Yes." "That," Donald says "would include you." The man laughs and says "Okay, let's leave it at that."

Later How about changing the whole story and having the quarry a man who is supposed to be a writer? Donald locates the man through a gal friend who has also vanished— The man can be located and mixed up in a racket. He gets tough. Donald protects the gal. In any event there should be two men and some of the element of a race in order to build suspense, mystery and conflict.

Fri. May 2, 1969—Palm Springs:

Trouble with this story is right at the start. Donald shouldn't be hired to find a woman, but a man, and he searches for the man's girl friend and finds her and becomes interested in her and through her finds the man—or finds the man is trying to kill the girl, or to get her involved in a racket, or that he already has involved her and she wants out.

Sat. May 3, 1969—Palm Springs:

It isn't necessary to have a General Delivery address. She could have left directions that she would forward an address, or she could have left a specific address. If general delivery, it should have been a place like Mexicali or Calexico and Donald can spot her via calling the motels. Then the boy friend could be there or across the line. This can bring in local color, but almost necessitates marijuana. Dope is getting too common place. Would rather have the border used in some other way.

Wed. June 11, 1969—Temecula:
Fair story from page 31

Now Nanncie can't be with the bad guys because Donald has to help her. Hale should be one of the good guys who was abducted by the bad guys. We need a victim and some bad guys in this story. The corpse might well be Donald's client, since he can't be a bad guy—because we can't have the agency working for bad guys and Donald can't double cross a client which he would be doing if the client is a bad guy and Donald took up with Nanncie. Therefore Donald has to find Nanncie in Calexico and take up with her and in the long run try to help her. She may or may not have one of the bad guys keeping tabs on her and giving Donald a rough time.

Mon. June 16, 1969—Temecula:
Fair story—Donald reports to Bertha from Mexicali. She tells him the client, Calhoun, wants a report at any hour as to progress. He wants to know what we are finding and what we are doing. No matter what time, he wants a report. Donald finishes his dinner, and returns to Calexico, finds the gal about to take off—raining and can't get a cab. Donald gives her a ride and takes her back to Mexicali where the guy is waiting for her. Or Donald finds she has been followed. The main idea is that Hale is a writer who located a source of information on marijuana smuggling and by telephone arranged to sell it to a national magazine, but his informant let the cat out of the bag and Hale knew he was a marked man, so he took off voluntarily or else was kidnapped— Better have this source of information phone, or send a messenger that they both are in danger. So the two of them take off with the understanding they are to meet in Mexicali— But why south of the border? There has to be some logical reason. Perhaps to get a reward from intercepting a big shipment, or, perhaps a hi-jacking. The girl is pretty well tied up with Hale, but Calhoun doesn't really care about Hale. His interest is in the girl and he feels she is in great danger. So Calhoun comes by car to Mexicali or Calexico as soon as Donald communicates with him. Then there has to be a murder in Calexico. This can be the murder of a dope runner who has just crossed the border with a big shipment of marijuana. The girl can have made a rendezvous with him. She has but little money and Calhoun can have followed the girl to the early morning rendezvous. The driver can have been murdered. Calhoun is a likely suspect. Time of driving—1½ hours L.A. to Palm Springs—Indio—Miles 52 to Riverside 24 to

Beaumont 51 to Coachella 83 to Brawle‧ ‧bout 25 to border. Los Angeles to El Centro 211 m. about 5 hou‧ ‧riving time.

Tues. June 17, 1969—Temecula:

Fair Calhoun shows up, also Sellers—Hale working on big dope story. Calhoun really interested in Nanncie—so he says. Nanncie has taken a powder. Sellers has a body of a guy who trails a pontoon houseboat back and forth from San Felipe— The pontoons are filled with marijuana on each return trip. Calhoun married. Rich. Can't afford to have his name appear in any way in connection with Nanncie's. Divorce proceeding and property settlement about to be negotiated. Donald has to get him off the hook. Sellers takes them to Police Headquarters— The boat trailer is there. Sellers takes off a cap on one of the pontoons. Donald makes a grandstand telling of the missing companion.

Wed. June 18, 1969—Temecula:

A. A. Fair from record #8—about page 86 or so.

Now Donald must either find Hale through Nanncie or vice versa. Nanncie left the motel at an early hour in the morning. Did she go with someone or in a taxi?—A taxi and Donald trails. Calhoun had given her the gun for her own protection. She had given it to Hale and they had discovered Hale and taken the gun from him. "Puggy" had been the second man in the automobile.

Thurs. June 19, 1969—Temecula:

Fair story Find Hale who says he was following the dope shipment, was detected by Puggy, overpowered and tied up. Puggy got the gun Nanncie had got from Calhoun and given it to him.

Fri. June 20, 1969—Temecula:

Revisions— Have Donald find the gun and try to duck it, but a sharp eyed gamin sees he has discovered something and moves over to him. Donald calls police.

Have Hale tied with fish line and at the proper moment Donald proves where he purchased it at about six o'clock in the morning.

Have the preliminary hearing at El Centro—the defense lawyer cross-examines Donald and quite evidently tries to cast Donald in the role of being the murderer.

Sun. June 22, 1969—Temecula:

Fair story from Record 16—about p 172. Roberts puts a gal on the stand who is a friend of Nanncie's. She testifies during this [hearing] gun in the possession of Nanncie at the time she gave it to Hale. Then a witness in adjoining unit tells of Calhoun's early visit to see Nanncie— This lets the cat out of the bag. Police bring Hale into court. I bring Pedro Gonzales from my car— Hale bought the cords with which he was tied. Get Newberry to ask for a recess by him to put on a case. He refuses. I get Calhoun to fire his lawyer and put on his own case. Hale under cross-examination goes to pieces when challenged to take off his shirt.

As was frequently the case by the time Gardner got to the last plotting session on a book, he had so thoroughly immersed himself in the character that he was using the first person in his notebook. He mailed the final draft of the manuscript to his publisher on July 7.

BIBLIOGRAPHY

BIBLIOGRAPHY

The bulk of Erle Stanley Gardner's commentaries on writing techniques and literature is contained in unpublished sources in the Gardner Papers at the Humanities Research Center at The University of Texas, Austin, Texas. It includes correspondence with editors and other writers, interoffice communications, copies of unpublished speeches and manuscripts, and personal notebooks and papers which he generated during the development and practice of his craft. Following is a bibliography of published materials by Gardner:

"And I Mean You" (pamphlet), Research Institute of America, Inc., August, 1957.

"Armed Forces Destined to Have Permanent Effect on Style of Mystery Story," *Chicago Daily News*, special Christmas book issue, December, 1944.

"An Author Looks at Agents," *American Fiction Guild Bulletin*, February 15, 1935.

"The Case of the Early Beginning," *The Art of the Mystery Story*, Howard Haycraft, ed. New York: Simon and Schuster, 1946.

"Come Right In, Mr. Doyle," *The Atlantic Monthly*, September, 1947.

"The Coming Fiction Trend," *Writer's Digest*, September, 1936.

"Dip Your Pen in Fire," *Author & Journalist*, March–April, 1968.

"Doing It the Hard Way," *Writer's 1937 Year Book*. Cincinnati: Writer's Digest, 1937.

"Don't Quit," *Author & Journalist*, July, 1946.

"Erle Stanley Gardner Claims Mystery Readers Best Detectives," *The Pocket Bookseller*, September, 1944.

"Gardner on Book Contests," *Author & Journalist*, October, 1943.

"Getting Away with Murder," *The Atlantic Monthly*, January, 1965.

"The Greatest Detectives I Know," *McClurg Book News*, January–February, 1944.

"Greener Grass," *Authors' League Bulletin*, November, 1945.

"How I Came to Create Perry Mason," *The Listener*, April 12, 1948 (Wellington, New Zealand).

"How to know you're transparent when you'd like to be opaque" ("by Perry Mason as told to Erle Stanley Gardner"), *Vogue*, July, 1956.

"Introduction," *The Graduate Fictioneer*, by H. Bedford-Jones. Denver: The Author & Journalist Publishing Co., 1932.

"Let's Go," *Author & Journalist*, October, 1932.

[Letter to the editor], *Author & Journalist*, January–February, 1967.

"Literature of Relaxation," *Cleveland News*, Christmas book supplement, December, 1942.

"Local Color," *Writer's Digest*, January, 1932.

"The Many Meanings an 'Escape' Novel Holds for Its Many Readers," *New York Herald-Tribune*, January 18, 1959.

"Memorandum from: Erle Stanley Gardner," [advice to beginning writers], mimeographed handout, n.d.

"A Method To Mystery" (under pseud. A. A. Fair), *The Writer*, August, 1944.

"My Stories of the Wild West," *The Atlantic Monthly*, July, 1966. Reprinted, *Literary Cavalcade*, January, 1967.

"The Nation's Greatest Educational Factor," *TV Guide Roundup*, by the editors of *TV Guide*. New York: Holt, Rinehart and Winston, 1960.

"A Note from Erle Stanley Gardner," foreword to *The Case of the Lucky Legs*. New York: Pocket Books, May, 1941.

"The Pleasures of Photography," *Popular Photography*, June, 1961.

"Salesmanship for Writers," *Author & Journalist*, May, 1938.

"A Ship and a Poem: Two Incidents That Shaped a Man," *San Francisco Examiner*, March 16, 1958.

"Speed Dash," *The Atlantic Monthly*, June, 1965.

"They Wanted 'Horror'," *Writer's Digest*, August, 1939.

"What Chance Has the New Writer?" *Writer's Digest*, January, 1931.

"What's Holding Us Back?" *The Writer*, February, 1939. Reprinted, *The Writer's Handbook*, A. S. Burack, ed. Boston: The Writer, Inc., 1941.

"Who Is Perry Mason?" *Chicago Daily News*, October 2, 1965.

"Within Quotes," *Writer's Digest*, August, 1938.

"The Writer's View," *Author & Journalist*, June, 1943.

INDEX